IMAGINING AFRICA

**Recent Titles in
Contributions to the Study of World Literature**

Ulysses, Capitalism, and Colonialism
M. Keith Booker

Imperial Knowledge: Russian Literature and Colonialism
Ewa M. Thompson

Demythologizing the Romance of Conquest
Jeanne Armstrong

Camelot in the Nineteenth Century: Arthurian Characters in the Poems of Tennyson, Arnold, Morris, and Swinburne
Laura Cooner Lambdin and Robert Thomas Lambdin

Writing the Body in D.H. Lawrence: Essays on Language, Representation, and Sexuality
Paul Poplawski, editor

Postcolonial and Queer Theories: Intersections and Essays
John C. Hawley, editor

The Novels of Samuel Selvon: A Critical Study
Roydon Salick

Essays on the Fiction of A.S. Byatt: Imagining the Real
Alexa Alfer and Michael J. Noble, editors

Victorian Writers and the Image of Empire: The Rose-Colored Vision
Laurence Kitzan

Immigrant Narratives in Contemporary France
Susan Ireland and Patrice J. Proulx, editors

Aristocracies of Fiction: The Idea of Aristocracy in Late-Nineteenth-Century and Early Twentieth-Century Literary Culture
Len Platt

Salman Rushdie's Postcolonial Metaphors: Migration, Translation, Hybridity, Blasphemy, and Globalization
Jaina C. Sanga

IMAGINING AFRICA

Landscape in H. Rider Haggard's African Romances

Lindy Stiebel

Contributions to the Study of World Literature, No. 105

GREENWOOD PRESS
Westport, Connecticut • London

Library of Congress Cataloging-in-Publication Data

Stiebel, Lindy.
    Imagining Africa : landscape in H. Rider Haggard's African romances / Lindy Stiebel.
       p.   cm.—(Contributions to the study of world literature, ISSN 0738-9345 ; no. 105)
    Includes bibliographical references and index.
    ISBN 0-313-31803-4 (alk. paper)
    1. Haggard, H. Rider (Henry Rider), 1856–1925—Knowledge—Africa. 2. English fiction—African influences. 3. Landscape in literature. 4. Africa—In literature.
    I. Title. II. Series.
    PR4732.S75   2001
    823'.8—dc21   00-049070

British Library Cataloguing in Publication Data is available.

Copyright © 2001 by Lindy Stiebel

All rights reserved. No portion of this book may be reproduced, by any process or technique, without the express written consent of the publisher.

Library of Congress Catalog Card Number: 00-049070
ISBN: 0-313-31803-4
ISSN: 0738-9345

First published in 2001

Greenwood Press, 88 Post Road West, Westport, CT 06881
An imprint of Greenwood Publishing Group, Inc.
www.greenwood.com

Printed in the United States of America

The paper used in this book complies with the
Permanent Paper Standard issued by the National
Information Standards Organization (Z39.48–1984).

10 9 8 7 6 5 4 3 2 1

Copyright Acknowledgments

The author and publisher gratefully acknowledge permission to reprint the following materials:

Parts of Chapter 3 were previously published in *Alternation* 5, no. 2 (1998): 91–102, and *Being/s in Transit*, ASNEL Papers 5, Ed. Liselotte Glage. Amsterdam: Rodopi Press, 2000: 125–140. Permission to reprint is gratefully acknowledged.

Parts of Chapter 4 appeared under the title "As Europe Is to Africa, So Is Man to Woman: Gendering Landscape in Rider Haggard's *Nada the Lily*," in *Current Writing* 12, no. 1 (2000). Permission to reprint is gratefully acknowledged.

Parts of Chapter 5 appeared under the title "The Return of the Lost City: The Hybrid Legacy of Rider Haggard's African Romances," in *Alternation* 4, no. 2 (1997): 221–237, and in *Multiculturalism and Hybridity in African Literatures*, Annual Selected Papers of the African Literature Association No. 7, Eds. Hal Wylie and Bernth Lindfors. Trenton, N.J. and Asmara, Eritrea: Africa World Press, 2000: 279–296. Permission to reprint is gratefully acknowledged.

Extracts from Lilias Haggard, *The Cloak That I Left* (London: Hodder and Stoughton, 1951). Copyright held by Commander Mark Cheyne. Permission to reprint is gratefully acknowledged.

CONTENTS

Preface   ix

Introduction   xi

Chapter 1: Towards a Discourse of "Africanism"   1

Chapter 2: Imagining Africa   11

Chapter 3: Rider Haggard—"King Romance"   37

Chapter 4: Haggard's African Topography   53

Chapter 5: The Haggard Legacy   103

Chapter 6: Conclusion   131

Bibliography   137

Index   151

PREFACE

This project is the result of several years' research in South Africa, England and the United States, and thus thanks for financial assistance is due to the South African National Research Foundation and to the University of Durban-Westville Research Committee, whose research grants enabled me to travel to far-off archives and libraries.

My sincere thanks are extended to the following people: Professor Margaret Lenta of the Department of English, University of Natal (Durban) and Professor Norman Etherington of the Department of History, University of Western Australia, for their incisive comments on earlier drafts of this book, Glenda Robson for administrative assistance, Judith Shier for compiling the index, and, of course, my family for their constant support. Thanks are also due to Commander and Mrs. Mark Cheyne (Sir Rider Haggard's descendants); Roger Allen, founder and editor of the Rider Haggard Society, England; and especially Stephen Coan, assistant editor at *The Natal Witness*, for their willingness to answer my queries.

I would like to thank the following librarians and archivists who have helped expedite my research: Diana Madden at the Brenthurst Library; Paulette Coetzee at the National English Literature Museum; Bobby Eldridge at the Killie Campbell Africana Library; Seema Maharaj at Inter-Library Loan, University of Natal; Jean Kennedy, county archivist at the Norfolk Record Office; and Cliff Farrington at the Harry Ransom Humanities Research Center, University of Texas at Austin. Drafts of various chapters were presented at a number of conferences over the past few years, including the African Literature Association's annual meetings at Guadeloupe and Austin, Texas; at the Association for New English Literatures meeting at the University of Hannover; at a South African literature colloquium at Palacky University, Czech Republic; and at the Association of English Teachers of Southern Africa annual meeting at the University of the North and at the University of South Africa. For all the constructive criticism and helpful comments from these conference participants, I am deeply grateful.

INTRODUCTION

> What is the function of landscape or cityscape descriptions in novels and poems? What is the function of topographical terms in philosophical or critical thinking? The answers seem obvious. Landscape or cityscape gives verisimilitude to novels and poems. Topographical setting connects literary works to a specific historical and geographical time.... Sooner or later, [however] in a different way in each case, the effort of mapping is interrupted by an encounter with the unmappable. The topography and the toponymy . . . hide an unplaceable place.
> —J. Hillis Miller, *Topographies* 6-7

This book is concerned with the function of landscape in Rider Haggard's African romances of providing, in the ways that Hillis Miller describes above, both an historical and geographical context and also a mapping space for the wishes, desires and anxieties of the writer. More than any other writer of his age, Haggard used the African landscape of his early manhood years in South Africa to create both for himself and his many readers "a country of the mind" (Hillis Miller 1995: 19). He created a generic "African topography" in his romances set in Africa which, because it became formulaic, became instantly recognisable to his reading public both in the late nineteenth century and twentieth centuries. Onto this topography, this "produced" space (Lefebvre 1991), Haggard projected his contradictory imperialist impulses, his intense and fearful sexual desires, his misgivings on some of the central issues of his age, such as civilisation and barbarism, and cultural relativity. Evidently, these ambivalent positions were not idiosyncratic to Haggard, for his enormous popular success, especially with his earlier romances, speaks of a sympathetic response from a wide range of Victorian readers. That certain of Haggard's African romances have never been out of print argues the case for a continuing nostalgic appreciation of the stylised landscape and the far-fetched adventures that unfold within its frame. From the critical reader's point of view, the study of Haggard's African romances through the lens of landscape construction and spatial ordering yields insights not only into Haggard's complex personality, but also the *Zeitgeist* of the late Victorian imperialist age, through the medium of the fiction that that public chose to read in such quantities. Chrisman holds that "Haggard's example leads us to conclude that fiction is a particularly potent medium for the contradictory articulation of imperialist identity" (1992: 303); my contention is that, in Haggard's case, the prism of landscape is a particularly useful one through which to focus in order to see such "contradictory articulation" literally mapped out.

Early Haggard scholarship, for example Cohen (1960, 1965), comprised largely biographical information which later scholars such as Ellis (1978), Higgins (1980, 1981) and T. Pocock (1993) built on. Commentary on Haggard's use of African landscape, especially in its sexualised aspect, really began with Bunn (1988) who wrote an article on *King Solomon's Mines* and *She*. Stott (1989) and Gilbert and Gubar (1989) also wrote on Africa as female body, again using the well-known *King Solomon's Mines* and *She* as examples. A number of scholars, starting with Pierce (1975) and among whom are listed Rice (1981), Rich (1984), Chrisman (1990, 1992) and Etherington (in the annotated edition of *She*, 1991), discussed aspects such as Haggard's use of "bird's-eye view" positioning, African "ruins," and Africa as lost Eden. The present study, however, is the first sustained piece of work on Haggard's treatment of landscape in his African romances, and, while it draws on the work of the scholars mentioned above, it widens the focus considerably to include previously little known or little researched Haggard novels and nonfictional writing. As such, this book ventures into uncharted territory as well as noting the few well-travelled routes. No other lengthy work on Haggard has argued for landscape to be given such a central place in Haggard's writing.

My book begins with a chapter drawing on post-colonial theory, which looks at the importance of literature as a way of understanding the age of imperialism and at the centrality of landscape as an imaginative arena in which the contradictory imperialist impulses and desires are played out. The possibility of a discourse of "Africanism" along some of the same lines as Said's "Orientalism" paradigm (1978) is suggested, as is the centrality of land to Haggard's novels and public service career. Chapter 2 traces the ways in which an image of Africa, especially as regards its land, came to take shape in Europe, particularly in the eighteenth and nineteenth centuries, and what use Haggard made of this image. His various visits to South Africa as a public servant in the service of Empire are discussed, especially in terms of their contribution to his efforts to construct in writing a space which he could understand and interpret, and yet which defied his attempts by remaining at a deep level "unmappable" and "unplaceable," as Hillis Miller's quotation observes. Chapter 3 considers Haggard's choice of the romance form for his African adventures as particularly appropriate given his idealistic, romantic nature, together with the fact that the romance form was also particularly well suited, with its dreams of wish fulfilment and yet also of dark menace, to the late nineteenth-century British mood. The African interior I argue in particular, as the last unknown space on the map to be colonised, provided both Haggard and his readers with a suitable site for romantic dreaming, far away from a home nation undergoing considerable domestic changes. Chapter 4 charts what I call Haggard's generic "African topography" as he repeated it through his African romances, particularly those prior to 1892 when his mapmaking vision seems most sustained and intense, but not excluding reference to some written after that date.

What I do not aim for is any systematic reading of successive Haggard romances. I try instead to draw out characteristic features of his "topography" from his work in order to advance particular arguments. Thus I describe aspects of the Haggard "map" such as Africa as vast Eden, as wilderness, as dream underworld, as sexualised bodyscape and finally as home to ancient white civilisations. These are aspects of many of his African romances which, because frequently formulaic, repeat these abovenamed features compulsively and, at times, anxiously. Finally, Chapter 5 traces what might be called the "Haggard legacy" in twentieth-century South African literature, especially as regards use of landscape, with those romance writers most directly connected to him being placed in the foreground. The lineage of this nostalgic tradition contains such different writers as John Buchan, Sol Plaatje, Stuart Cloete and Wilbur Smith, together with its reincarnation in various forms of popular culture such as film and theme parks.

In conclusion, I look at the most enduring element of Haggard's—at times contradictory—love affair with the African land and its peoples; his fresh romanticising of the landscape which in the works of others has often been debased. In the contemporary "green" nostalgia of the late twentieth century, this impulse has been adopted and to some extent transformed as witnessed in contemporary efforts to preserve parts of "Nature" in (ironically) enclosed wilderness areas, in an effort to protect "nature [from] becoming lost to thought" (Lefebvre 1991: 31). The irony, of course, lies in the fact that, as Carter points out, "Without the unenclosed horizons of South Africa, Rider Haggard would have had no basis for his romances" (Carter 1996: 28). Ironies aside, however, the fact that Haggard's African romances—and particularly their symptomatic landscapes—can still resonate a century after the publication of his first major success speaks for the need to take Haggard seriously as mapper of his age's anxieties and desires.

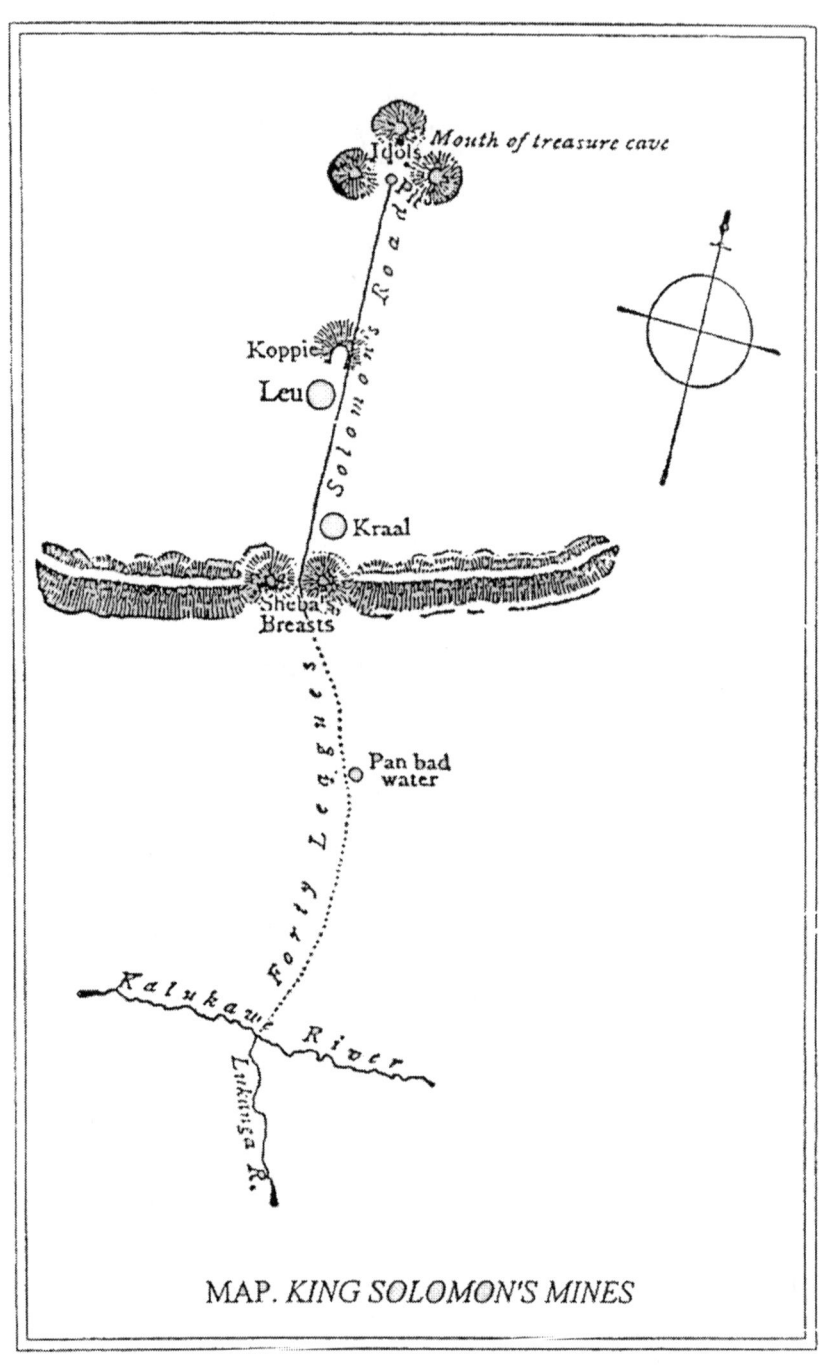

Map 1: Treasure Map, *King Solomon's Mines* (1885)

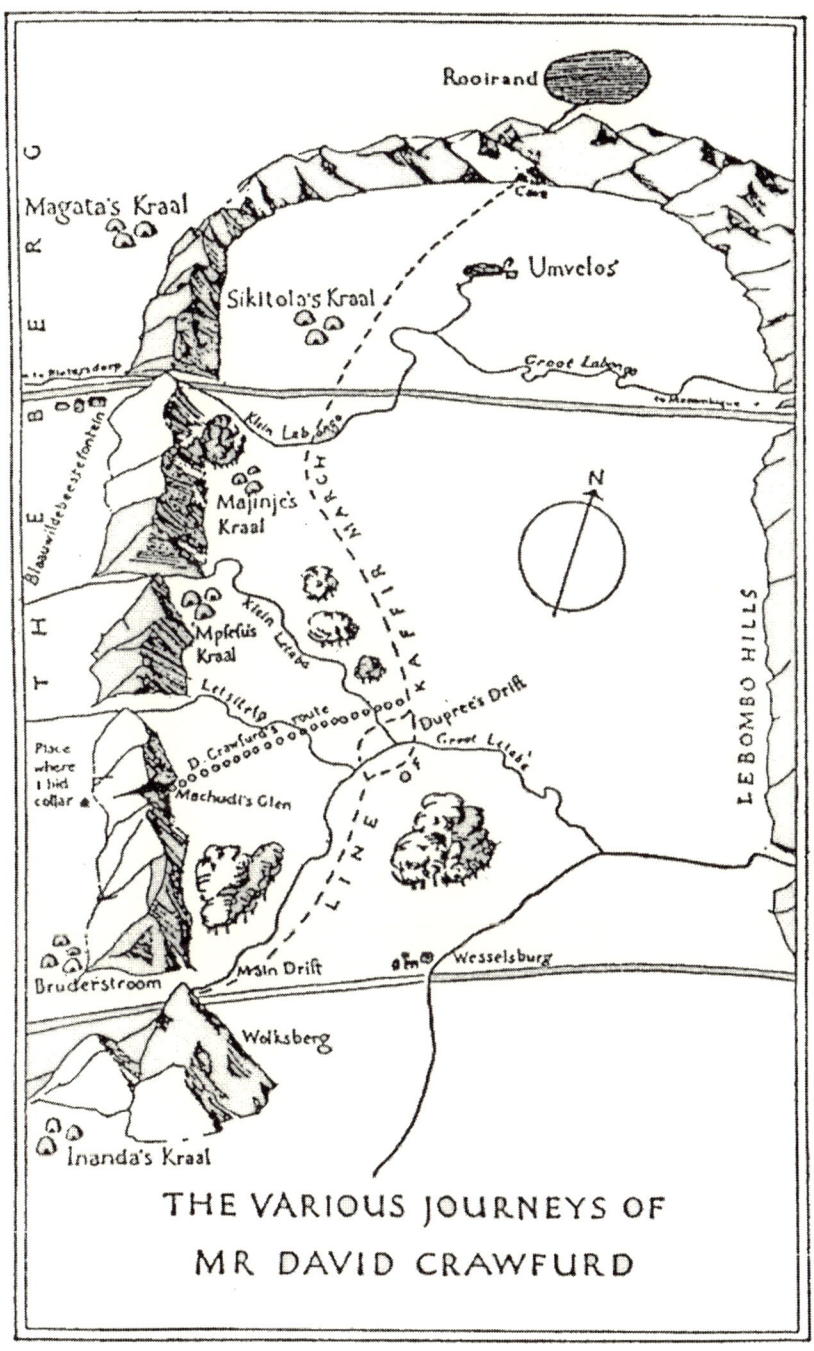

Map 2: Map, *Prester John* (1910)

CHAPTER 1: TOWARDS A DISCOURSE OF "AFRICANISM"

> To a criticism concerned with mapping the exclusions and affirmations of an imperialist culture whose legacy has still not been spent, these same texts can be made to reveal both imperialism's grandiloquent self-presentation and those inadmissible desires, misgivings, and perceptions concealed in its discourses.
> —Benita Parry, *Space and Place*, 238

> The heart of Africa is in Haggard's romances just what Conrad said it was in *Heart of Darkness*—a special psychological terrain in which European man confronts and nearly succumbs to his deepest fears.
> —Norman Etherington, *Victorian Studies*, 77

To understand how a culture imagines its world, both "home" and "away," one looks to its literature. In late nineteenth-century Britain, at the height of Empire, with a third of the world's lands under its domination, literature was for many Britons one of the few possible ways to visualise the heat and dust of India, the snows and icebergs of Canada, and the game-filled plains of Africa. Together with other post-colonial critics, Said has commented on the interconnectedness of nineteenth-century British culture and the policies of imperialism, and since the novel was the dominant literary form of the time, it became central to an understanding of both. He writes "The novel, as a cultural artefact of bourgeois society, and imperialism are unthinkable without each other . . . imperialism and the novel fortified each other to such a degree that it is impossible, I would argue, to read one without in some way dealing with the other" (Said 1994: 84). What is interesting for the post-colonial critic in making a study of a writer of Empire and how s/he imagines his or her world, both familiar and foreign, is to study the subtext, the slippages and cracks that underlie the superficially seamless surface of imperialist discourse: "What criticism can recover, through dismantling the plural discourses and reconstructing the displacements and erasures, is the effaced historical contest and unrehearsed enunciations of the anxieties in the conquering imagination, both necessarily repressed by the exigencies of ideological representation" (Parry 1993: 224). It is in the revealed "anxieties" that the dynamics of power can be traced: in the repeated need to reconfirm dominance over the Other in narratives of the time, to proclaim success over foreign peoples and lands, to achieve one's goals—material or psychological—and to return home.

The lands of Empire, the "rival geographies" (1994: xxii-xxiii) as Said names them, act as screens on which to project the anxieties and desires that underlie the dominant discourse of Empire. If the novel is central to nineteenth-century English culture, so is land—both physical and imaginary—to imperialism. At a fundamental level, imperialism is about the invasion, conquering and securing of land previously belonging to or settled by others: "Imperialism after all is an act of geographic violence through which virtually every space in the world is explored, charted, and finally brought under control" (Said 1994: 271). Land, arguably even more than indigenous inhabitants, acts as the imaginative arena within which the imperial drama is played out. For those at "home" in England in the nineteenth century, novel writers had above all to represent a localised landscape that helped their readers move from a vague sense of remote space to its contextualisation in a recognisable place on the map of their imagination: "From an initial apprehension of the space of the new land, various practices are developed which produce places. These places exist by virtue of their ability to be integrated into the social structure and administrative apparatus of Empire" (Noyes 1993: 122).

The facilitators of such a process were the explorers and amateur scientists who were the first Europeans to gaze upon these foreign lands in the years prior to their assimilation within Empire. In the late nineteenth century, however, it was popular novelists such as Henry Rider Haggard who crystallised the representations or "word pictures" of the imperial landscape for the domestic market. Their task was to bring the "ideological geography" of these distant lands "into the boundary of the known and the British" (Hofmeyr 1980: 200). Haggard, son of Empire and popularly thought of as the "Kipling of Africa," captured in his romances more than any other writer of his time the quintessential British image of Africa's lands, which I shall discuss in detail in a later chapter. In his centrality in this regard lies his interest, for beneath the seemingly dominant, masterful tones sound the notes of anxiety and desire, what Bhabha calls "the signs of a discontinuous history, an estrangement of the English book." He says further: "[these signs] mark the disturbance of its authoritative representations by the uncanny forces of race, sexuality, violence, cultural and even climatic differences which emerge in the colonial discourse as the mixed and split texts of hybridity" (Bhabha 1994: 113).

In an effort to understand these signs and their sources, the contradictions and ambivalences within a writer such as Haggard and the translation of these into his African landscapes, it is useful to start at Said's seminal work, *Orientalism* (1978), with its thesis on the representation of other cultures. In this work Said argues persuasively that over a period of time and through a complex set of representations, the West constructed "the Orient" as a discrete idea in opposition to what might be called "the Occident." All branches of knowledge and endeavour were complicit in the gradual appreciation of what "the Orient" came to mean.

> [Orientalism] is . . . a *distribution* of geopolitical awareness into aesthetic, scholarly, economic, sociological, historical, and philological texts; it is an elaboration not only of a basic geographical distinction . . . but also of a whole series of "interests" which, by such means as scholarly discovery, philological reconstruction, psychological analysis, landscape and social description, it not only creates but also maintains; it *is*, rather than expresses, a certain *will* or *intention* to understand, in some cases to control, manipulate, even to incorporate, what is a manifestly different (or alternative and novel) world. (Said 1995: 12)

"The Orient" then, as it was understood in nineteenth-century Europe, was a construct, bearing only a tenuous relationship to any actual reality, and, in fact, saying more about the culture that produced it than the object of study. Central to such a discourse is some factual information on "the Orient"—its lands, peoples, customs, languages—for with information comes the illusion of knowledge, power and confidence in one's own knowledgeability: "Knowledge of the Orient, because generated out of strength, in a sense *creates* the Orient, the Oriental and his world" (40). Such knowledge, though empowering for the West, nonetheless acts as a constraint upon alternative modes of thought. What knowledge of the Orient does is to "acquire" the Orient, through diverse channels—exploration, scholarly study, travel—then "domesticate" or process it through laws, codes, treatises and books for consumption by the West (166). Said notes a change in this codifying of knowledge of the Orient in the late nineteenth century—from such knowledge being "textual and contemplative into being administrative, economic and even military" (210); in other words from being mostly of an intellectual nature into finding practical application in the colonies. Of particular interest to me, since my focus is on the representation of land, is the fundamental shift Said notes in perceptions of geography and space: " The *geographical space* of the Orient was penetrated, worked over, taken hold of. The cumulative effect of decades of so sovereign a Western handling turned the Orient from alien into colonial space" (211). For novel writers this could mean that over a period of time, by repeatedly generating similar depictions of a foreign landscape, they had managed to tame the "Otherness" of what they saw or imagined and render it somehow "ours" and under control. I argue that such is the power of imagined foreign landscapes that anxieties that underlie the imperial and later colonial project would be likely to surface, in a writer such as Haggard, in these repeated, almost fetishistic representations of perceivedly exotic, foreign landscapes, even in those supposedly domesticated.

An underplayed passage in *Orientalism* (though later amplified by Bhabha in 1994) provides an entry to understanding why this could be so. Said draws a distinction between what he terms latent Orientalism—"an almost unconscious (and certainly an untouchable) positivity"—and manifest Orientalism—"the various stated views about Oriental society, languages, literatures, history, society, and so forth" (206). Manifest Orientalism relates to quantifiable and verifiable information about the Orient. Change is possible here as further discoveries are made and information is gathered, collated and amended. Latent Orientalism is, however, unchanging, for it contains a permanent, "quintessential" (221) perception of the Orient; the popular stereotypes, the dreams, desires and anxieties which the Orient engenders in the West. In the following passage, Bhabha points out Said's rather uneasy recourse to psychoanalytic terminology, which summarises Bhabha's sense of the "ambivalence of Orientalism" (Bhabha 1994: 71).

[Orientalism] is, on the one hand, a topic of learning, discovery, practice; on the other, it is the site of dreams, images, fantasies, myths, obsessions and requirements. It is a static system of "synchronic essentialism," a knowledge of "signifiers of stability" such as the lexicographic and the encyclopaedic. However, this site is continually under threat from diachronic forms of history and narrative, signs of instability. And, finally, this line of thinking is given a shape analogical to the dreamwork, when Said refers explicitly to a distinction between "an unconscious positivity" which he terms *latent* Orientalism, and the stated knowledges and views about the Orient which he calls *manifest* Orientalism. (Bhabha 1994: 71)

If the foundation of manifest Orientalism is scholarly texts, intellectual information, "evidence," then the foundation of latent Orientalism is identified by Said as "geography": "Geography was essentially the material underpinning the knowledge about the Orient. All the latent and unchanging characteristics of the Orient stood upon, were rooted in, its geography" (Said 1995: 216). Land forms the literal bedrock of the enduring fantasies, desires and anxieties of the West imagining the "Othered" Orient. The "signs of instability" Bhabha refers to threaten to undermine the unitary entity "Orientalism" that Said constructs. Though Said points out this ambivalence in colonial discourse between latent and manifest Orientalism, he attempts to resolve it by arguing that both strands were united by a common intention. Bhabha, rather more fruitfully, seeks to tease out the implications of this inner dissonance at the heart of Orientalism; seeks to explore the implications of ambivalence in the coloniser towards "Otherness," "that 'Otherness' which is at once an object of desire and derision" (Bhabha 1994: 73). Robert Young succinctly summarises Bhabha's position: "Colonial discourse does not merely represent the other, therefore, so much as simultaneously project and disavow its difference, a contradictory structure articulated according to fetishism's irreconcilable logic. Its mastery is always asserted, but is also always slipping, ceaselessly displaced, never complete" (Young 1990: 143).

This anxiety, which lies at the heart of colonialist discourse, results in the need for constant repetition and reiteration of mastery, but in the inevitable, subtle undermining of that tenuous mastery. As I will later show, in the case of Haggard's depiction of landscape there is frequent fetishistic repetition of setting, of attempted assertion of dominance, and always simultaneously an undermining of the project, a vacillation between desire and fear typical of the late nineteenth-century British relationship to Africa.

With the word "desire" one is in the realm of psychoanalysis, a realm into which Said rather tentatively and Bhabha more forcefully ventures. And it is here one perceives a gap in their respective analyses, for neither gives a clear sense of a gendered colonial subject nor of the powerful influence sexuality plays in representations of the Other whether in the form of peoples or geography. Said raises the question only to dismiss it; he remarks on the frequent association between the Orient and sex: "Why the Orient seems still to suggest not only fecundity but sexual promise (and threat), untiring sensuality, unlimited desire, deep generative energies, is something on which one could speculate: it is not the province of my analysis here, alas, despite its frequently noted appearance" (Said 1995: 188).

Robert Young remarks *à propos* of Bhabha's theories on colonial discourse:

Bhabha's model nowhere broaches the question of a gendered colonial subject, but rather seems to regard the troubled structures of sexuality as themselves a metaphor for colonial ambivalence . . . his generalized discussion of the desire of the subject in psychoanalytic terms without any consideration of sexuality as such prompts many questions. . . . In short, how can you talk about structures of desire in psychoanalytic terms outside the structures of sexuality? (Young 1995: 153)

Neither does another influential post-colonialist critic, JanMohamed, with his model of the manichean allegory as summarising the colonial mindset, give due weight to desire and sexuality as powerful motivators within colonialist discourse. He defines the manichean allegory as

a field of diverse yet interchangeable oppositions between white and black, good and evil, superiority and inferiority, civilisation and savagery, intelligence and emotion, rationality and sensuality, self and Other, subject and object. The power relations underlying this model set in motion such strong currents that even a writer who is reluctant to acknowledge it and who may indeed be highly critical of imperialist exploitation is drawn into its vortex. (JanMohamed 1985: 63)

In the field of literature, JanMohamed singles out the adventure story, especially the "racial romance," as being "the most significant formal manifestation of the manichean allegory" and comes close to suggesting the centrality of sexuality to his project in the following:

A number of subgenres . . . are always based on the manichean allegory: the adventure story—such as those of G.A. Henty that are specifically designed for young boys or those of Edgar Wallace and H. Rider Haggard that are also geared to adults—about Europeans battling dark, evil forces; the story utilizing Africa as an alluring, destructive woman—from Haggard's *She* and *Nanda* [sic] *the Lily* to Marguerite Steen's *Sun is My*

Undoing—that recalls Kurtz's fixation on the dark, satanic woman; and the story presenting Africa as a dark labyrinth. (JanMohamed 1985: 71)

Despite his awareness of the gendering of Africa as woman, and the colonial subject and creator of such texts as generally male and always patriarchal, JanMohamed is not primarily interested in pursuing the analysis further in this regard. This seems unfortunate, for as Robert Young observes, "Colonialism, in short, was not only a machine of war and administration, it was also a desiring machine. This desiring machine with its unlimited appetite for territorial expansion, for endless growth and self-reproduction, for making connections and disjunctions, continuously forced disparate territories, histories and people to be thrust together like foreign bodies in the night" (Young 1995: 98).

He makes explicit what JanMohamed hinted at in his description of the "racial romances" quoted above: "The many colonial novels in English betray themselves as driven by desire for the cultural other, for forsaking their own culture: the novels and travel-writings of Burton, Haggard, Stevenson, Kipling, Allen or Buchan are all concerned with forms of cross-cultural contact, interaction, an active desire, frequently sexual, for the other" (Young 1995: 3).

In short, it seems that to gain a fuller understanding of Said's "manifest" and "latent" Orientalisms, Bhabha's "ambivalence," JanMohamed's "manichean allegory" (which he delineates in "imaginary" and "symbolic" discourses), and Benita Parry's "inadmissible desires" (which "interrupt" the imperialist narrative with which this chapter started), greater cognisance must be taken of the *gendered* colonial subject and specifically sexual desire as key elements. These points will be explored in greater depth in later chapters.

Some of the passages quoted above have referred to Africa as opposed to the Orient, which was the focus of Said's study. However, the broad precepts of Said's thesis on Orientalism and Bhabha's elaboration on the ambivalence of Orientalism can have wider application than to the Orient alone. Europe's imaginative construction of Africa, one could argue, has been similarly weighed down by a wealth of manifest "Africanism" in the form of scientific information, classification systems, maps, and so on, and by a web of latent "Africanism" with its popularly believed notions of what the "essential" Africa might be like. Said, in the new afterword to the 1995 edition of *Orientalism,* noted that he was encouraged that his book had "made a difference to the invigorated study of Africanist and Indological discourses" (340). In his work *Culture and Imperialism* he stressed again the important interconnection between the novel, particularly, and imperial attitudes in the nineteenth century: "To most Europeans, reading a text like *Heart of Darkness* was often as close as they come to Africa, and in that limited sense it was part of the European effort to hold on to, think about, plan for Africa. To represent Africa is to enter the battle over Africa, inevitably connected to later resistance, decolonization, and so forth" (Said 1994: 80).

In other words, in the same way as the Orient was constructed by the West and cast in the role of subjugated (yet desirable) Other, the West in a comparable display of power and through a similarly complex web of representations constructed a discourse of "Africanism."[1] Such a discourse also had more to reveal about Europe in the late nineteenth century than about any actual Africa: "The myth of the Dark Continent was largely a Victorian invention. As part of the larger discourse about empire, it was shaped by political and economic pressures, and also by a psychology of blaming the victim through which Europeans projected onto Africans their own darkest impulses" (Brantlinger 1988: 95).

Again, as Said suggested with regard to Orientalism, the bedrock of a discourse of Africanism—in the sense in which I use the term—is its geography, the land; a land that is physicalised and sexualised by the novel writers in nineteenth-century England who used Africa as their setting. How this myth of the Dark Continent, particularly in relation to representations of land, came to enjoy the power it did (and, to some extent, still does) will be explored in the next chapter.

Specifically, the representation of African landscapes and African settings in Haggard's romances reveals the tension between desire and fear that the theorists mentioned earlier find running as a common thread in imperialist and colonialist discourse. At this point it will be useful to raise two aspects of Haggard's career and writing in a preliminary way while dealing with a discourse of Africanism in a general sense: the centrality of land to his novels and his public service career, and his popularity.

In 1912 Haggard wrote in a letter to Theodore Roosevelt, with whom he had established a friendship, on the matter of "the problem of every civilized country on Earth. The glutted, foul, menacing cities, the gorgeous few, the countless miserables! And beyond, the empty Land, which could feed them all and give them health and happiness." (Haggard 1926 vol. 2: 188) Though Haggard is remembered for his African romances, he himself valued his numerous writings on the land, on agriculture, on projects to resettle the urban poor and to encourage returning soldiers to settle on the land, far more. During his 1905 visit to the United States as government commissioner to investigate the feasibility of the Salvation Army's "Labour Colonies" as a model for the British colonies, he lamented: "It is a hard thing, in the first place, to live down the reputation of being a writer of fiction. . . . Still, humbly, imperfectly, I did attempt it. I have not done much. Yet I have done something" (1926 vol. 2: 265).

From his first work specifically on the land, *A Farmer's Year* in 1899, to *A Gardener's Year* in 1905 and his numerous, meticulously researched reports on the state of rural England—mostly funded from his own pocket—runs a concern with the primacy of the land in developing a people's character and, therefore, how an exodus from the land bleeds away the nation's vitality. Born into the landed gentry, he personally maintained his attachment to the land by being a gentleman farmer most of his adult life. It would not be surprising then, given his "almost mystical feeling for the land" (Pocock 1993: 147), that during his years in South Africa as a member of Sir Henry Bulwer's staff, the African landscape would engage him so deeply. For while the English landscape with which he was so familiar as a boy and young man growing up on the family estate was "domestic," and tame, here was land which was "wild," untamed, and Other. Given as well his situation during that first African visit —his youth, unattached "young blade" status, the relief he was likely to feel at escaping a tyrannical father, his pride at being part of Empire's work—it would be fair to speculate on the immense effect on him of the exotic terrain. Indeed, this powerful effect is confirmed in the repeated treatment of African landscapes in his romances.

It is at this point that Said's notion of Orientalism and the representation of the Other becomes useful, with its delineation of "manifest" and "latent" levels, together with Bhabha's amplification of the "ambivalence" that resonates between the two levels. For Haggard, inevitably a product of his age, would have come to Africa with some ideas of what he would find there given the increasing British interest in South Africa of the time, and indeed given the long history of British involvement in Africa generally, through its explorers, scientists and missionaries. In other words, he would have been influenced by the discourse of Africanism of his day, which had been constructed over a period of time by Europe for Europe, as Said argued. Compounding the "inner dissonance," the "interruptions" of colonialist discourse that are manifestations of the ambivalence at the heart of representations of the Other, is Haggard's own contradictory nature. Henry Miller has described it thus:

There is a duality in Rider Haggard which intrigues me enormously. An *earthbound* [italics added] individual, conventional in his ways, orthodox in his beliefs ... reveals through his "romances" a hidden nature, a hidden being, a hidden love which is amazing. His method of writing these romances—at full speed, hardly stopping to think, so to speak—enabled him to tap his unconscious with freedom and depth. (Miller 1952: 93)

I would like to argue that Haggard's "duality" (which will be more fully explored) together with the inevitable "ambivalence" contained within representations of another culture, place/space, finds its expression particularly clearly in his African romances, and that the *locus operandi* in particular of this phenomenon is his African landscape. Miller's emphasis on Haggard's "unconscious" recalls Said's "latent" strand of Orientalism in which the subject's dreams and fantasies of the Other reside. These are projected in his quest romances on to a sexually charged terrain: "For the imperialist romancers, the earth is the eternal feminine—the body to be conquered, penetration followed by possession. Haggard is no exception" (Patteson 1978: 121). The unconscious subtext of sexuality in Haggard's romances was part of the reason for his enormous popularity at the time; he had tapped into the collective unconscious of his age: "Mr. E.M. Forster once spoke of the novelist sending down a bucket into the unconscious; the author of *She* installed a suction pump. He drained the whole reservoir of the public's secret desires" (Pocock 1993: 245). A contemporary of Freud, Haggard wrote romances that "were immensely popular because they fed the imagination of a vast reading public that had already accepted the premises, but not the conclusions, of the looming Viennese psychology ... [Haggard] knew that sexual passion lies at root of all things human. Though he did not know to what extent he had written these notions into his novels, a Freud or Jung could see them at once" (Etherington 1978: 84). Both Freud's and Jung's interest in Haggard's almost automatic writing of his first romances, together with their dream-like content, will be discussed in later chapters.

The continuing popularity of Haggard's African romances (some, like, *King Solomon's Mines*, have never been out of print) attests to the enduring power of, in part, his African landscapes, and perhaps in the late twentieth century a sort of nostalgia in this age of urban cityscapes for the imperialist myth of the "empty land." The following chapter traces the antecedents of this myth of the Dark Continent in so far as they illuminate Haggard's particular representation of Africa and his own positioning within a discourse of Africanism.

NOTE

1. Mazlish, in an article entitled "A Triptych: Freud's *The Interpretation of Dreams*, Rider Haggard's *She*, and Bulwer-Lytton's *The Coming Race*," also asks this question: "Is there also an Africanism which is a 'representation' of Africa that reflects its European observers rather than the peoples and lands of that continent itself?" (1993: 727). He notes that there would be at least one major difference between Orientalism and Africanism, and that is the theme of hunting, which is fundamental to the latter as a "means of symbolic dominance" (727) of the environment, and yet not significantly present in the former discourse.

While it may be tempting to use the term "Africanist" discourse in the same sense in which Said talks of an "Orientalist" discourse, I am well aware that since at least the 1960s, the term "Africanist" refers specifically to a discourse generated by black Africans about Africa—Afrocentric—that is the very opposite of what I am trying to describe by the term "Africanism."

CHAPTER 2: IMAGINING AFRICA

> The lure of Africa is its mystery—once geographical, now psychological. The map of Africa itself carries enchantment. It is never merely a geographical chart; the writers project upon it personal imagery expressing mystery and threat, and their fascination with both.
> —Dorothy Hammond and Alta Jablow, *The Africa That Never Was*, 135

> How has travel and exploration writing produced "the rest of the world" for European readerships at particular points in Europe's expansionist trajectory? How has it produced Europe's differentiated conceptions of itself in relation to something it became possible to call "the rest of the world"? How do such signifying practices encode and legitimate the aspirations of economic expansion and empire? How do they betray them?
> — Mary Louise Pratt, *Imperial Eyes*, 5

The purpose of this chapter is to trace how an image of Africa, especially as regards its land, came to take shape in Europe, particularly in the eighteenth and nineteenth centuries, and what use Haggard made of this image. Before this time, Europe had had limited contact with Africa, as is witnessed by Pliny's famous dictum, "*ex Africa semper aliquid novi*" (appropriately enough also the motto for *Allan Quatermain*). From the outset Africa was thought of as exotic, strange, and Other, as we may surmise from Pliny's use of *novi*. For my purposes, however, the eighteenth and nineteenth centuries are more interesting for it is during this period, the age of exploration and discovery in Africa, that the European picture of Africa fills out and sets in the popular imagination.

One of the primary stepping stones on the explorer's route from a perception of space "out there" to a perception of place, is the act of naming:[1] "By the act of place-naming, space is transformed symbolically into a place, that is, a space with a history. And, by the same token, the namer inscribes his passage permanently on the world, making a metaphorical word-place which others may one day inhabit and by which, in the meantime, he asserts his own place in history" (Carter 1987: xxiv).

The irony involved in naming after "discovering" notable geographical features is that such features usually already have a "native" name by which they are known to the indigenous people. The French missionaries Arbousset and Daumas in the first half of the nineteenth century illustrate this point in the account of their "discovery" of principal river sources in South Africa: "We have satisfied ourselves that the rivers of which we are about to speak . . . take their rise in a mountain which the natives call Pofung. . .but which we have designated in our map by the name of 'Mont aux Sources'" (Arbousset 1852: 113-114).

The renaming of geographical features seems part of the process of setting up Said's "rival geographies" (1994: xxii-xxiii)—though the rivalry seems a little lopsided as the European explorers clearly had faith in their own authority in possessing the master discourse as far as naming was concerned. Said acknowledges this: "In your narratives, travel tales, and explorations your [European/Western] consciousness was represented as the principal authority, an active point of energy that made sense not just of colonising activities but of exotic geographies and people" (1994: xxiii-xxiv).

Haggard, given his deep interest in indigenous South African culture, is generally tactful on this score, frequently including the "native" name for geographical features, as in: "On the twentieth day . . . we came to the banks of a largish river, the Gonooroo it was called. This I crossed, and then struck inland towards a great range of mountains, the blue crests of which we could see lying on the distant heavens like a shadow, a continuation, as I believe, of the Drakensberg range that skirts the coast of Natal" (Haggard [1887] 1965: 20). This extract summarises Haggard's approach to the question of naming: he is at pains to make his protagonist, Allan Quatermain, adopt the "native" name for the river while also accepting "Natal," named thus by a Portuguese explorer, and "Drakensberg," a word of Dutch derivation.[2] This tension between indigenous and European names encapsulates in microcosm the attitudes of the benevolent colonist that Haggard wished to be. Indeed, in one of his romances (*The Ghost Kings*, 1908) Haggard allows the black wizard, Zikali, to criticise Quatermain's English linguistic limitations by saying: "Although you think that you speak Zulu like a native, [you] have never really learned it properly because to do that you must think in it and not in your own stupid tongue, that has no words for many things" (1908a: 43). Zikali's last few words are interesting, for balanced against the desire to name is the fear of not being able to name the foreign terrain, of not having the right words. Boehmer notes in such instances in colonialist texts that "description admits defeat, submitting to the horror of the inarticulate. The native or colonized land is evoked as the quintessence of mystery, as inarticulateness itself" (1995: 95). Quite frequently Haggard, through Quatermain, confesses before scenes both of wonder and horror: "I only wish I had the power to do justice [to the scene before him]. But I cannot, so it is useless talking more about it" (Haggard 1995: 169). Nearly every one of his African romances has such a line in it attesting to Quatermain's muteness in the face of the unknown, but it is soon lost in the welter of naming and description that he *is* able to accomplish.

One of the most important tools for ordering these exotic geographies and ultimately laying the foundations for the confidence of the late eighteenth- and nineteenth-century explorers in Africa, was the Swedish naturalist Carl Linneaus's system of plant classification, *The System of Nature* (1753). His classification system was designed to enable the natural historian to make order out of chaos, to assign a place in a hierarchy and a Latin name to every living plant. Parallel systems were also proposed for animals, minerals and eventually humans, with "genetic" characteristics included: "One by one the plant's life forms were to be drawn out of the tangled threads of their life surroundings and rewoven into European based patterns of global unity and order. The (lettered, male, European) eye that held the system could familiarize ('naturalize') new sites/sights immediately upon contact, by incorporating them into the language of the system" (Pratt 1992: 31). Supposedly scientific and therefore objective, the African human "type" suffered immeasurably in Linnaeus's description in comparison to the European "type." After a listing of African physical characteristics comes the damning "Governed by caprice" as opposed to the rational European "Governed by laws" (quoted in Pratt 1992: 32).

Both naming and classifying were part of the growing manifest discourse of "Africanism" of the time, as was the related practice of mapping. A map is a source of power through knowledge; it is the imposition of order on the unknown but suspected disorder of the blank page. It is never a neutral activity, for the mapper brings a subjective gaze to bear upon the space and selects that which is important to be mapped according to previously established subjective criteria: "Maps are a kind of language, or social product which act as mediators between an inner mental world and an outer physical world. But they are, perhaps first and foremost, guides to the mind-set which produced them. They are, in this sense, less a representation of part of the earth's surface than a representation of the system of cognitive mapping which produced them" (Penn 1993: 23).

The political potential of mapping is obvious. New territories can be delineated by drawing lines upon paper, important potential resources can be emphasised and disadvantages such as resistant indigenous peoples, animals and difficult terrain can be demonised. For example, Harley points out how, in nineteenth-century British maps of Africa,

the decoration on maps... disseminated the image of the Dark Continent.... In [some] cases the symbols of "otherness" assumed the form of bizarre racism. Natives are shown riding an ostrich or a crocodile, engaged in cannibal practices, located in captions as "wild men." ... Female sexuality in depictions of African women ... is often explicit for the benefit of male-dominated European societies. (Harley in Cosgrove and Daniels 1988: 299)

In the nineteenth century, as British advances in Africa proceeded, maps assumed a pointedly political function, combining both a manifest or informational function with a latent sense of desire or wish-fulfilment: "As much as guns and warships, maps have been the weapon of imperialism. Insofar as maps were used in colonial promotion, and lands claimed on paper before they were effectively occupied, maps anticipated empire" (Harley in Cosgrove and Daniels 1988: 282).

Haggard's use of a treasure map in *King Solomon's Mines* is worth mentioning briefly here as it encapsulates many of the ideas just mentioned (see map 1). It is a map drawn by a dying Portuguese trader en route to the diamond mines of King Solomon in Kukuanaland. As a staple ingredient of the adventure story, Haggard's map was widely admired as in Andrew Lang's comment to Haggard: "Many thanks for *King Solomon's Mines*. How grand the map is" (Haggard 1926 vol. 1: 223). However, from a twentieth-century post-colonial perspective, an analysis of this treasure map reveals far more:

Haggard's map assembles in miniature the three narrative themes which govern his novel: map-making as a form of military appropriation, the transmission of white male power through control of the black female, and the plundering of the land's riches. What sets Haggard's map apart from the scores of treasure maps that emblazon colonial adventure narratives is that his is explicitly sexualised. (McClintock 1990: 113-114)

Furthermore, in Haggard's treasure map, as in many maps of eighteenth- and nineteenth-century explorers, the myth of the "empty" landscape is perpetuated. Though it has been argued that Haggard's map is a "bodyscape" of Africa as woman (as I shall later discuss), the map is in effect empty of people, the way to the treasure unimpeded by any other claimants to the Promised Land. This is because "Maps as an impersonal type of knowledge tend to 'desocialize' the territory they represent. They foster the notion of a socially empty space. The abstract quality of the map . . . lessens the burden of conscience about people in the landscape" (Harley in Cosgrove and Daniels, 1988: 303). This myth of the "empty" landscape was pivotal to explorers seeking new lands to settle or exploit materially, for "[o]nly empty spaces can be settled, so the space had to be made empty by ignoring or dehumanizing the inhabitants" (Tiffin and Lawson 1994: 5). The blank spaces on the map call out to be peopled or, in the common term of the day with its unconscious sexual connotation, "penetrated," but not by those currently (though to the European, invisibly) there. The imperialist's aim is what J.M. Coetzee calls "an ideal community" (1988: 9). "Ideal" in eighteenth- and nineteenth-century terms one would imagine to mean a utopian community, if anything, more akin to European ways and discourse rather than to African culture.

Again, in this regard, Haggard exhibits the tensions and contradictions of his age, for at times he supports the "empty land" myth by his lyrical descriptions of vast, seemingly uninhabited, lands. Yet, because of his genuine interest in and respect for the Zulu people particularly, they are in a sense ever present in his fiction, to the extent of his having one romance, *Nada the Lily*— which is narrated by a black man—dedicated to the telling of their history. Indeed, Haggard frequently displays his adherence to a kind of social Darwinist cultural relativity in his comparison of European and African cultures, to the former's detriment

> By what exact right do we call people like the Zulus savage? Setting aside the habit of polygamy . . . they have a system not unlike our own. They have, or had, their king, their nobles and their commons. They have an ancient and elaborate law and a system of morality *in some ways* [italics added] as high as our own and certainly more generally obeyed; they have their priests and their doctors; they are strictly upright and observe the rites of hospitality.
>
> Where they differ from us mainly is that they do not get drunk until the white man teaches them to do so, they wear less clothing, the climate being more congenial, their towns at night are not disgraced by the sights that distinguish ours, they cherish and are never cruel to their children, although they may occasionally put a deformed infant or a twin out of the way. . . .
>
> Now let him who is highly cultured take up a stone to throw at the *poor, untaught* [italics added] Zulu . . . generally because he covets his land, his labour or whatever else may be his. (Haggard [1913]1952: 73-74)[3]

In this instance, apart from the obviously patronising phrases that I have stressed, Haggard— far from erasing the Zulu people's presence— is forcefully making their presence felt.

The fourth element in the formation of the image of Africa, together with naming, classifying and mapping, is the frequent practice of explorers and travellers in the eighteenth and nineteenth centuries of painting the landscape they saw. Such paintings, executed in European artistic techniques and conventions, literally gave colour to the European image of Africa: "The alien landscape is tamed by being rendered in familiar terminology, not only for the artist's comfort, but also for his (European) viewer to whom the country has to be opened up" (Van der Watt 1993: 29).

Visually, the emerging elements of both the manifest and latent strands of a discourse of Africanism were portrayed in the landscape paintings of artists such as Thomas Baines. Baines is a particularly interesting figure as far as Haggard is concerned as he died in Durban a few months before Haggard, as a member of Sir Henry Bulwer's staff, arrived there in 1875. Baines was a friend of Sir Theophilus Shepstone, Haggard's mentor on matters African, and it seems likely that the young, impressionable Haggard would have seen some of Baines's paintings while in Durban. If so, his imagination might have received this kind of influence:

Many of Baines's landscapes depict what was hitherto unknown or little known to the British public or colonists—spaces interrupted by mountains and rivers which, when crossed, permit further territorial expansion. The viewer (and by allusion the explorer/ colonizer) is invited to enter and travel through pictorial space, and—through the gaze—to take possession of a real spatial situation. (Carruthers and Arnold 1995: 92)

Haggard's African landscapes frequently depict similar vistas of vast expanses of untamed wilderness, seen from an imaginary aerial perspective. Carruthers and Arnold analyse Baines's painting, "Bird's eye view of the Victoria Falls from the West" (1874)—which shows a herd of elephants in the foreground with the Zambezi river and Victoria falls, laid out map-like, in the background—using words that could with some qualification be used for Haggard's African landscapes as well: "He structures a statement that is literally and metaphorically dependent on a point of view. By adapting a 'bird's-eye view,' a commanding magisterial gaze, the artist surveys miles of African terrain as detail subsumed by distance. His gaze is also the imperial gaze, for here is Edenic Africa awaiting civilization and uninhabited except by elephants" (1995:99).

More will be made of Haggard's extended use of the bird's-eye view of landscape in chapter 4. Etherington points out that Haggard would have used Baines's "Map of the Gold Fields of South Eastern Africa" (1873) while working on Shepstone's staff in the Transvaal. Furthermore, he suggests that the three treasure seekers in *King Solomon's Mines* might have paralleled the following gold seekers in Mashonaland around 1869: "Sir John Swinburne, Captain A.L. Levert and the old South African artist and explorer Thomas Baines engaged in extensive negotiations with Lobengula at the time of a succession crisis" (Etherington 1977b:437). Indeed, Haggard himself mentioned Baines and his potential influence primarily as an explorer:

When I was a lad in Africa I met many men, the pioneers of settlement and exploration—those who had first become acquainted with some of the great savage races of the interior, or who had helped to shape history when they and the white man came face to face. Although I think Mr Baines, one of the first wanderers in much of the country which is now Rhodesia, died shortly after I reached Natal [Baines died 8 May 1875; Haggard arrived August 1875], I knew his family and heard something of the country from them and others. (Haggard, L. 1951: 122)

Further, in Haggard's preface to Wilmot's *Monomotapa* (1896), he refers to "Baines, and other travellers now dead, [who] reported on the existence of great ruins in the territories known as Matabele and Mashona Lands" (Wilmot 1896: xiii). It is certain then that Haggard knew of Baines, his journeys of exploration and, more than likely, his Gold Fields map and landscape paintings.

In summary then, the various elements discussed above—naming, classifying, mapping and painting—were the cornerstones of a composite image of Africa and corresponding discourse of Africanism of Haggard's time. This image of Africa emerged primarily in explorers' and other travellers' accounts of their discoveries and adventures. Their accounts were eagerly received by a European reading public, with the pinnacle of popularity achieved in England by David Livingstone's account of his time in Africa. In the first few months after its publication in 1857 Livingstone's *Missionary Travels* sold 70,000 copies; by the end of his last African journey in 1872 he had become "a national saint" (Brantlinger 1988: 180). The power of such portrayals of Africa cannot be overestimated.[4] What they described in their travels constituted an ongoing "cliffhanger" to a public eager for entertainment and instruction.

> The great explorers' writings are nonfictional quest romances in which the hero-authors struggle through enchanted, bedeviled lands towards an ostensible goal: the discovery of the Nile's sources, the conversion of the cannibals. But that goal is also sheer survival and return home to the regions of light. The humble but heroic authors move from adventure to adventure against a dark, infernal backdrop where there are no other characters of equal stature, only bewitched or demonic savages. (Brantlinger 1988: 180-181)

This description of exploration as quest adventure is particularly appropriate given Haggard's use of the romance form in his African tales. Martin Green calls adventure tales "the energising myth of English imperialism. They were, collectively, the story England told itself as it went to sleep at night; and, in the form of its dreams, they charged England's will with the energy to go out into the world and explore, conquer, and rule" (1979: 3). Haggard, as I shall show in chapter 3, uses the quest romance form in the positive, energising sense Green suggests, but also unwittingly explores the reverse side of the Victorian dream metaphor: its nightmares.

Although Haggard was an infant when Livingstone's *Missionary Travels* was first published, he could not have failed to be aware of Livingstone's travel accounts and indeed of the other major African explorers of his time and earlier: Mungo Park's *Travels in the Interior Districts of Africa* (1799), the first edition of which sold out in a month; Richard Burton's *Lake Regions of Central Africa* (1860) "which ... achieved considerable renown in that prolific and highly competitive era of travel writing" (Pratt 1992: 201); and John Speke's *Journal of the Discovery of the Source of the Nile* (1863), written amidst a bitter public quarrel with his colleague Burton. I referred earlier to a Victorian public eager for entertainment and instruction. This, I will argue, has correspondence with Said's manifest and latent strands of Orientalist discourse, and, for this work's purpose, the discourse of Africanism. For what these accounts offered, in varying degrees, was a discourse on Africa, a way of imag[in]ing Africa both on an informational, manifest level and on a subconscious, latent level of desire. Pratt points out the two contrasting styles of explorers' writings: the scientific and the sentimental (1992:75). The scientific accounts, such as those of the Swede Anders Sparrman (*Voyage to the Cape of Good Hope* [1783]), the Englishmen William Paterson (*Narrative of Four Voyages in the Land of the Hottentots and the Kaffirs* [1789]) and John Barrow (*Travels into the Interior of Southern Africa in the Years 1797 and*

1798 [1801]) strive to achieve order through naming, mapping, classifying and sketching in as precise and scientifically "objective" a manner as possible. The "sentimental" accounts draw on an older tradition of survival literature and allow experience, engagement and reciprocity in their dealings with the land and its peoples. The best examples of such writing which Pratt forwards are from Mungo Park's *Travels in the Interior Districts of Africa* (1799) and Francois le Vaillant's *Voyages dans l'interieur de l'Afrique* (1790). The first, scientific mode offers a wealth of facts, "knowledge" of Africa with vested imperialist interests obviously or tacitly apparent; the second, sentimental mode is complicated by a desire for ambiguous engagement with the Other, whether its lands or people: "If . . . the landscanning, self effacing producer of information is associated with the panoptic apparatuses of the bureaucratic state, then this sentimental, experiential subject inhabits that self-defined 'other' sector of the bourgeois world, the private sphere—home of desire, sex, spirituality and the Individual" (Pratt 1992: 78). My reading of Haggard's African romances, books which Raby defines as "clearly related to the journals of the explorers and scientific travellers" (1997: 232), finds Haggard occasionally adopting the scientific mode of relaying information as in the detailed accounts he gives of Zulu customs, dress and habits (see for example, Haggard [1885] 1992: 127-128), but more often caught in the strong undercurrent of the sentimental mode, especially as regards his landscape depictions, which will be further explored in the next chapter.

Earlier, I suggested the importance of having a clear sense of a gendered colonial subject in all analyses of encounters between the West and its Others. It is important, therefore, to note the masculinist tone of the explorers' accounts of what they saw in Africa. Seen in this light, "Africa invites the white male explorer, it challenges him and it tempts him. The white man must explore and penetrate this foreign territory, but he must also resist it or be threatened with absorption into otherness" (Stott 1989: 77). Even when the explorer was a woman, such as Mary Kingsley (*Travels in West Africa* [1897], *West Africa Studies* [1899], and *The Story of West Africa* [1900]) the tone the reader hears is still predominantly masculinist and patriarchal, though a few critics have pointed out the contradictory nature of her position.[5] As a woman writing within an overwhelmingly masculinist genre, Kingsley's texts reveal "contradictory voices . . . since Kingsley's text [*Travels in West Africa*] is certainly not wholly liberated from the positioning of the narrator as culturally or racially superior. . . . And despite containing a strong critique of the exploitative nature of the colonial relation, . . . this critique is merely aimed at improving rather than dismantling colonialism" (Mills 1993: 153,155). These "contradictory voices" could perhaps also be understood as emanating from Kingsley's attempts to weld the manifest, "scientific" and also latent, experiential, "sentimental" discourses into a seamless whole. Particularly interesting is the way in which one critic sees this dilemma revealed in Kingsley's treatment of landscape: "Kingsley's contradictory subject position is particularly evident in her landscape descriptions. Her subjective identification with places as well as people coexisted with attempts to emulate more masculine, imperial strategies of objectifying vision" (Blunt 1994: 161).

In Kingsley's descriptions of the West African landscape she passes through, her ambivalence is evident. Equally ambivalent is her contradictory position on the question of imperialism, which she publicly supported while simultaneously voicing her concern for the African people, who were to suffer the effects of the imperial project. Landscape descriptions also serve for Haggard, a contemporary of Kingsley, as a canvas on which contradictions are depicted, contradictions both peculiar to Haggard and symptomatic of the late Victorian age generally. His "contradictory voices" did not stem from an ambiguous author-subject positionality (as a white upper-class male, he was secure in this respect) but from tensions related to imperial enterprises and to a repressed sexuality, as I shall later show.

While the manifest strand of the discourse of Africanism noted, measured, quantified and categorised the land and indigenous inhabitants, the latent strand conjured up the myth of the Dark Continent, supported frequently by the "facts" of the former strand. In its more positive aspect of wish-fulfilment, Africa in the nineteenth century was portrayed as paradisal, its wide, open spaces teeming with game. In particular, the South Africa of the early nineteenth century contrasted favourably with the "White Man's Grave" of West Africa:

The Africa of this image is beautiful, open, sun-drenched—a golden land. . . . The nineteenth-century writers on South Africa laid the groundwork of the image in their depiction of the southern veldt as a region where the British could enjoy the active, outdoor life so dear to their hearts and so increasingly difficult to obtain at home. . . . It may have initiated in real geography, but its true province is in the British imagination. (Hammond and Jablow 1970: 157)

Haggard has frequent recourse to this paradisal, restorative image of Africa—among many such examples one could quote is the following description of an African dawn:

At first one would see nothing but a vast field of white mist suffused towards the east by a tremendous golden glow, through which the tops of stony koppies stood up like gigantic beacons. . . . Presently this great curtain would grow thinner, then it would melt, as the smoke from a pipe melts into the air, and for miles on miles the wide rolling country interspersed with bush opened to the view . . . as far as the eye could reach it would be literally black with game. . . . Ah, how beautiful is nature before man comes to spoil it! (1951: 34-35)

Such a view of Africa stressed a positive primeval aspect; an unspoiled place where the European male could make a fresh start, test himself against physical (and unspoken psychological) challenges, and emerge victorious. By the 1884-1885 Berlin Conference, identified as the culmination of the "Scramble for Africa," a parallel, contradictory, pessimistic image of Africa as a place of darkness was firming in the public imagination. A combination of explorers' accounts, widespread interest in Darwin's evolutionary theories in *The Origin of the Species* (1859), which was popularly, if misleadingly, believed to lend scientific status to racist beliefs in higher and lower races, and a constant linking of ongoing, inhuman slave-trading practices to Africa after the Emancipation Act of 1833, contributed to the darkening of Africa. Not only was this darkening projected onto Africans but onto Africa herself. I use the word "herself" deliberately, for Africa as land found its most demonised yet desirable form in the metaphor of the sexual lover/mother/murderess. The latent strand of the discourse of Africanism is deeply invested in sexual desire and, when projected onto land, "The landscape that emerges from the explorer's pen is not a physical object: it is an object of desire, a figure of speech outlining the writer's exploratory impulse" (Carter 1987: 81).

It is no wonder that Victorian England, locked into a straitjacket of middle-class sexual repressiveness and decorum, found the apparent sexual licence and supposed sexual opportunity of some of its colonies both attractive yet fearful: "Animated by man's desire, it [the land] takes on the seeming attributes of woman, whether described as passive landscape or an alien force; a place of exile or belonging; a landscape of promise or of threat. . . . It presents the fantastic possibilities of a spiritual quest and vision and also the nightmare fears of madness and death" (Schaffer 1990: 61). Though Schaffer's work is on Australian landscape, this comment is equally applicable to Africa. Africa, with its well-documented heat, reputed fecundity and "savage customs," was ripe to be cast as the Other woman. One particularly inflamed description of Africa-as-woman in Winwood Reade's *Savage Africa* (1864 vol. 1: 383) marks an extreme version of this myth—in it, Africa is a black mother confused with a subliminal lover figure, and finally a killer:

There is a woman whose features, in expression, are sad and noble, but which have been degraded, distorted, and rendered repulsive by disease . . . whose lap is filled with gold, but beneath lies a black snake, watchful and concealed; from whose breasts stream milk and honey, mingled with poison and with blood; whose head lies dead and cold, and yet is alive; in her horrible womb heave strange and monstrous embryos. . . . Look at the map of Africa. Does it not resemble a woman with a huge burden on the back? (quoted in Hammond and Jablow 1970: 71-72)

This was published when Haggard was nine years old and extreme though it is, it is indicative of the kind of discourse on Africa within which Haggard grew up. Though he was never to write anything as crass as this, his landscapes, as I shall show in chapter 4, are distinctly sexualised. Though this point has been previously made in relation to one or two of Haggard's works, such as *King Solomon's Mines* and *She*—see, for example, Bunn (1988) and McClintock (1990)—my analysis, by looking at hitherto little-researched Haggard romances, proves this statement far more comprehensively. Ironically, the link between African landscape and black female sexuality in popular opinion was confirmed, unwittingly perhaps, by Freud in his 1926 "Essay on Lay

Analysis" in which he described his age's lack of knowledge of adult female sexuality, an area of study which he significantly named the "dark continent" of psychology (Gilman 1985: 238).

HAGGARD IN SOUTH AFRICA

These, then, were some of the features of an image of Africa current in the discourse of Africanism in Haggard's day. Haggard's African romances inevitably drew in part from such a discourse and also added a contemporary perspective: "Haggard's texts fed into and were sustained by a cultural map of epics, travel narratives, exploration and the 'boy's adventure,' set within a contemporary history of new imperialism abroad and a growing pedagogic militarism in public schools at home" (Carter, Donald and Squires 1993: 191).

Haggard had also had first-hand experience of South Africa on three occasions, most notably his first and lengthiest stay. He arrived in Durban in 1875, aged nineteen, as a member of Sir Henry Bulwer's staff in Natal. The youngest son of a Norfolk squire, he had not had the public school education of his older brothers but had nevertheless grown up in an atmosphere in which the public school ethos prevailed. Sandison stresses the British public schools' importance in the "codification of the imperial ideology" (1967:13) and an earlier scholar, Elwin, confirms this:

The British Empire was built in the country houses of England's squirearchy. Generation after generation, the sons of squires, equipped with constitutions hardened by an open-air, country life, with a sufficient smattering of scholarship, and with training in the tradition of what was understood by the term "gentleman," ventured into the distant corners of the world, to create and uphold the prestige which came everywhere to be associated with the name of an Englishman and England. (1939: 223)

The Bulwer family were also from Norfolk and Haggard's father, rather unsure of what to do with his youngest, unpromising son must have been pleased to give him an opportunity to make something of himself in far-off Africa. Haggard remarks of himself, arriving in South Africa:

I was a tall, young fellow, quite six feet, and slight, blue-eyed, brown-haired, fresh-complexioned, and not at all bad-looking. . . . Mentally I was impressionable, quick to observe and learn whatever interested me, and could hold my own in conversation. I was however, subject to fits of depression and liable to take views of things too serious and gloomy for my age—failings, I may add, that I have never been able to shake off. (Higgins 1981: 18)

The seeds of Haggard's complex personality are immediately apparent—the man of enthusiasm and energy sapped by doubts and pessimism.

When Haggard arrived in Natal, the British metropolitan government's plan was to maintain the uneasy peace between the minority group of white settlers and the black tribes, and push for a confederation of South African states comparable to that achieved in Canada. Haggard took as his mentor Theophilus Shepstone, Natal's experienced Secretary for Native Affairs, as he admired

Shepstone's system of indirect rule over Zulu chiefs and his tolerance of Zulu customs. The figure of the Englishman who rules wisely over a savage people was thereafter recurrent in Haggard's African romances. Despite Britain's apparent reluctance to extend its Empire, expansion continued in Southern Africa given its strategic and commercial importance.[6] As proof of this, Shepstone and his party, including Haggard, travelled up to the Transvaal in 1877. Ostensibly, Shepstone's aim was to protect the Boers from Zulu attack, but the real purpose was to annex the territory as a further step in Carnarvon's plan to confederate the states of South Africa, thus safeguarding British settler interests, mining developers and mining capital. Haggard, in fact, raised the flag in Pretoria in May 1877 to signal the annexation and was filled with imperialist optimism for this wealthy territory: "If the Transvaal at all realises what is expected of it, it will before long, with its natural wealth and splendid climate, be one of the most splendid foreign possessions of the British crown and if, as is probable, gold is discovered in large quantities it may take a sudden rush forward and then one will be borne up with it" (Haggard 1926 vol. 1: 27).

Despite his pessimism and his increasing belief in popularly held social Darwinist theories of process and flux, which were held to signal the ultimate end of all civilisations, Haggard maintained a public belief in the imperial project. By way of contrast, his African romances, in which he invested his latent desires, seldom contain explicit mention of imperialism—Pierce points out that only *Allan Quatermain* extols imperialism directly: "All our magnificent muster roll of colonies, each of which will in time become a great nation, testify to the extraordinary value of the spirit of adventure which at first sight looks like a mild form of lunacy" (Haggard [1887] 1995: 101, quoted in Pierce 1975: 114). Sandison maintains that Haggard's belief in the imperial idea was tempered by his response to Darwinist evolutionary ideas, that it was his "awareness of flux and change which gave Haggard his humanity and humility" and denied him consolation from orthodox belief in a higher, benevolent Divinity (Sandison 1967: 30).

All his life, Haggard, the son of a Norfolk farmer and subsequently a farmer himself, placed his faith in the land, and it was the land in South Africa that left an indelible mark on the impressionable youth. Higgins writes on this point: "The scenery so impressed him that he always believed Natal was the most beautiful country [*sic*] in the world" (1981: 19), though in his autobiography Haggard described the allure for him of Africa's landscapes more accurately: "There is little of what we admire in views in England, but Nature in her wild and rugged grandeur" (1926 vol. 1: 59). It was the wildness of African terrain as opposed to the domesticity of English farmland that captured him. He elaborated on this contrast through his alter ego, Allan Quatermain:

I longed once more to throw myself into the arms of Nature. Not the Nature which you know, the Nature that waves in well-kept woods and smiles out in corn-fields, but Nature as she was in the age when creation was complete, undefiled as yet by any human sinks of sweltering humanity. I would go again where the wild game was, back to the land, whereof none know the history, back to the savages, whom I love. ([1887] 1995: 12-13)

Haggard's first-hand experience of African landscape was of the sort to encourage such exhilaration: he went riding, hunting and accompanied Sir Henry Bulwer on his official tours of Natal. The thirty-five day trek from Pietermaritzburg to Pretoria before the annexation of the Transvaal occasioned many nights around the campfire. Haggard vividly remembered "the moonlit nights of surpassing brilliancy which we watched from besides the fires of our camp. These camps were very pleasant, and in them, as we smoked and drank our 'square-face' after the day's trek, I heard many a story of savage Africa from Sir Theophilus himself, from Osborn and from Fynney" (Higgins 1981: 22).

These stories of "savage Africa" would have been made up of personal anecdotes and hearsay, confirmation for the white man of "what Africa is really like." Haggard was able, after a while, to add his own anecdotes to the saga; he had several "adventures" including seeing a war-dance outside Chief Pagate's kraal, avoiding ambush one moonlit night after leaving the Basuto chief Sekhukhune's kraal in May 1877 and, in a later incident, being saved after falling concussed from his horse in the veldt. He kept copious notes of all he saw, including details of Zulu customs and language, for he was deeply impressed by the Zulu people whom he found to be dignified and hospitable, "the Romans of Africa," led by Cetshwayo whose "manners, as is common among Zulus of high rank, are those of a gentleman" (Haggard (1882) in Pocock 1993: 21). Haggard's belief that all people are some part savage, with "civilisation" acting as a more or less successful veneer, helped him escape the worst excesses of racism: "Succumbing to and identifying with the savage are vital ingredients in the reiterated formula of his exotic tales. It may be that Haggard's own need for self revelation led him to take this approach. . . . The European characters of Haggard's romances do what he could not do. They dive deeply into African darkness and emerge shaken but refreshed" (Etherington 1984: 55).

Haggard's admiration for the Zulus and love of African land are all of a piece for he saw the former in terms of the latter. Thus, when the Transvaal was handed back to the Boers after the shock British defeat by the Zulus at Isandlwana in 1879, and when growing Boer restlessness influenced Gladstone to undo Shepstone's careful planning, Haggard wrote bitterly: "The natives are the real heirs to the soil and surely should have protection and consideration . . . we have handed them over without a word to the tender mercies of one, where natives are concerned, of the cruellest white races in the world" (Haggard [1882] in Pocock 1993: 51-52).

In 1879 Haggard left Shepstone's administration, having risen to the position of Master and Registrar of the High Court, to go ostrich farming with a friend, Arthur Cochrane. His thoughts at this time turned increasingly to marriage. In 1877 he had wished to return to England to propose to a young lady, Lilly Jackson, whom he had met in England two years before, but his father forbade him to interrupt his career. In 1878, being in a better financial position, he wrote to Lilly asking for her hand only to learn to his bitter, and it seems everlasting, regret that she had given up the long wait and married another. The theme of thwarted, eternal love was repeated in Haggard's fiction, bearing testimony to his frustrated and idealised love. Various critics of Haggard's work suggest that after this news and until he left for a break in England in 1879, he embarked on his first sexual relationship. It has also been conjectured that this relationship was with a black woman,[7] thus fixing in reality the strong sexual element in latent Africanism. The wider range of sexual opportunity that the colonies offered, away from the formal social constraints of England, made for tempting possibilities: "In 1880, going overseas to work as an official almost invariably meant an enlargement of sexual experience. . . . Nor were literary figures, from Byron to Flaubert to Rider Haggard and E.M. Forster, immune from the temptation to explore the sexual opportunities of the overseas world in a way they could not or would not have done at home" (Hyam 1992: 5, 212). Haggard himself corroborates this *laissez-faire* situation in the colonies in a reference to the early days of British settlement in Durban when he has Quatermain remark that "such white men as dwelt there had for the most part native followings, and, I may add, native wives" ([1912] 1959: 100).

As Higgins asserts, the frequency in Haggard's African romances of a relationship of mutual sexual attraction between a white adventurer and a black maiden seems to support the possibility that Haggard might have had an affair with a black woman (Higgins 1981: 35-36). For a person of Haggard's class and moral upbringing, there would have been inevitable guilt attached to the relationship and if, as I have conjectured, Haggard saw the black people in terms of their land[8] then it is possible that, at an unconscious level, such complex and contradictory feelings could be attached to the African landscapes of his romances. This, however, remains at the level of conjecture for there is nothing written to support such a hypothesis in Haggard's surviving letters or diaries. What has been documented is an affair he had while in Pretoria with a Mrs. Ford ("the Gay Missus") who bore his child, named Ethel Rider Ford. Arthur Cochrane sent a telegram to Haggard then in England with the sad, but relieving, news of "the sudden death of my young God child and of your—? Yes, the poor little thing is dead and perhaps it is a good thing for all concerned" (Manthorpe 1996: 89-92).

During his 1879 break in England, he met and married Louisa ("Louie") Margitson, heiress to a modest Norfolk estate. Plucky, forthright and a loyal wife to Haggard for forty-five years, she lacked passion and was never anything like the sensual, physical, romantic heroines Haggard so powerfully created:

Thus her common sense temperament lacked, almost entirely, imagination in the sense that Rider possessed it. . . . She was not interested in literature and had no understanding of what her husband was writing or, even more important, thinking. It is also apparent that, after the birth of Dorothy in March 1884, Haggard and his wife ceased to have a sexual relationship. Clearly this led not just to repression, but also to disappointment, for Haggard, a child of his class and environment, longed for a large family. (Higgins 1981: 90)

Although Higgins must be incorrect in dating the end of Haggard's sexual relationship with Louie as 1884—their third daughter, Lilias, was born in 1892—there seems no doubt from Lilias's unusually frank testimony and that of other family members, that theirs was not a close physical or intellectual union, certainly not after 1892 when Haggard was only thirty-six. Lilias Haggard, in her biography of her father's life, confirms the shortcomings of her parents' marriage, speculating however that these spurred her father on to compensatory literary endeavour: "Had he found the perfect mate, whose general characteristics may be gathered from the collective heroines of his romances, would his spirit have been so free to roam? His marriage went as far with him as it needed to go, and for the rest of the time he was with his own thoughts. He was thrown in upon himself, and his novels were his principal outlet" (1951: 20).

In a letter to his brother William in December 1879, Haggard described his future wife as "a brick of a girl" (1926 vol. 1: 166) and in the various letters he wrote to his wife over the years that is the dominant impression one derives of Louisa—solid, dependable and unimaginative. The later letters betray a note of wistful longing for his wife from whom he is frequently absent on his travels, or she from him while she visits relatives. Increasingly, as an older man, Haggard would, as did many other Victorian men, seek out the homosocial world of gentlemen's clubs.

The young couple left for South Africa in November 1880 to farm ostriches near Newcastle. The farmhouse, Hilldrop, was Haggard's first domestic, familial place in the wider, untamed African space.

It lay on a green apron of grass between two rocky knees of the flat-topped hill, overlooking a sweep of open country. Orange trees stood around it and the verandah of the stone-walled, thatched house was entwined with vines and moonflowers. Inside, a large drawing-room made them feel, once it was filled with their furniture from England, as much at home as they could ever feel in this vast and violent continent. (Pocock 1993: 43)

Two things interest me about Pocock's description: his use of latent Africanism as in the comparison of the ordered, English centre ("drawing-room") and the disordered, African periphery ("vast and violent continent"); and his unconscious sexual physicalisation of the land into a seated woman ("apron of grass") between whose "knees" the masculine, stone house stamps its authority. The sexualisation, specifically feminisation, of African landscape is apparent as an ongoing discourse in the late twentieth century, it seems.

Though the ostrich farming was not financially successful, Haggard and his partner Cochrane worked very hard at earning a modest living through brick making and selling hay. Haggard's beloved only son was born on the farm, but the family decided to leave South Africa after the British defeat by the Boers at Majuba in 1881, only a few miles away from their farm. Though this departure marked the end of Haggard's longest and most formative experience of Africa, the impressions gained were to last him a lifetime of romance writing,

> It is impossible to overestimate the effect of South Africa on Haggard and his writing. Witnessing the confrontation between British colonialism and the Zulu people caused him to reappraise and define his thinking about the fundamental issues of sex, politics, and religion with which he would struggle in his future novels. The physical environment supplied the raw material for a thousand varied landscapes of the imagination. (Etherington 1984: 2)

Lilias Haggard said of her father: "For Africa he was always homesick" (1951:172), which is a telling phrase for it implies that, in a psychological or spiritual sense, Haggard desired a rootedness in African soil, where he lived for only about six years out of a lifetime based in England, his physical, hereditary home. Haggard found it hard to articulate Africa's appeal, linked as it was to the land and the Zulus, and his uncharacteristic loss for words lends credence to its roots in the latent, desire-laden strand of the discourse of Africanism: "There is a great charm about this country; what it is I cannot say" (Haggard, L. 1951: 85).

In England, he studied law by day and wrote by night. His first book was a nonfictional work, *Cetewayo and His White Neighbours* (1882), which was a carefully researched and argued defence of Shepstone's policies in South Africa. In it, he argued against Gladstone's division of Zululand in 1880 into thirteen small chieftaincies instead of annexation to the British crown and a system of benevolent, "indirect" rule favoured by Shepstone. His thoughts focused on the fundamental issue of land: "On only one condition, if at all, have we the right to take the black man's land; and that is, that we provide them with an equal and a just Government, and allow no maltreatment of them, either as individuals or tribes, but, on the contrary, do our best to elevate them, and wean them from savage customs. Otherwise, the practice is surely indefensible" (Haggard 1888: 267-270).

Here Haggard displays his rather naive public optimism in the "civilising mission" of imperialism, though the seeds of his growing private pessimism at some of the more cynical and materialistic aspects of British imperialism are also evident. *Cetewayo and his White Neighbours* (first edition 1882, *Cetewayo*, second edition 1888, *Cetywayo*) did not sell very well and it was only with his third novel, *King Solomon's Mines* (1885), that he struck gold. The novel, written in response to a wager with one of Haggard's brothers that he could not better Stevenson's *Treasure Island* (1883), captured the public imagination eager for African adventures: "His imagination soared free across the great landscapes he conjured up. . . . It was not just the 'rattling good yarn' . . . but was intensely visual. Until now Africa had seemed a distant, hot country of desert and jungle, but now Rider Haggard had brought the 'Dark Continent' into vibrant colour" (Pocock 1993: 62). Pocock again draws on the discourse of Africanism, still current over a hundred years after the publication of *King Solomon's Mines*, but he usefully highlights the visual quality of Haggard's African landscapes, which in some senses are reminiscent of Baines's African paintings previously discussed. Published in September 1885, *King Solomon's Mines* was reprinted four times by December. In its first year it sold 31,000 copies, which made it one of the biggest sellers of that year, and it has never been out of print since (Ellis 1978: 100-101; Cohen 1960: 95). Similar spectacular sales figures were run up by his next few novels: *Allan Quatermain*, written in the summer of 1885, *Jess*, written in the autumn of the same year, and *She*, written between January and March 1886. Unlike the anti-Boer "novel" *Jess*, the other two were African "romances" drawing heavily on Haggard's experiences in South Africa. The difference between the two forms is considered in the next chapter. Haggard's continuing fame as a writer rests on these African romances, together with those written up to 1892 when *Nada the Lily* appeared (*Maiwa's Revenge* 1888; *Allan's Wife* 1889). Thereafter, it seems as if Haggard's spell of almost compulsive writing is broken. Although he wrote at least ten more African romances, besides his novels and romances set in other parts of the world, none has the power of those written before 1892. Etherington claims that "[his] interests shifted to politics and agricultural reform" (1977a: 189); whereas Pocock proposes that "since the deaths of his mother and Jock [Haggard's beloved only son, of measles in 1891], he no longer wrote with relish. It was as if he had perfected no more than a money-making formula" (1993: 92).

The sales figures of the early African romances indicate that Haggard had struck a deep chord in the late-Victorian reading public. Filled as they are with repressed desire, these romances are quintessential examples of the latent strand of Africanism. Late Victorian fears and desires, both sexual and imperial, found expression in their pages, particularly when projected onto the landscapes: "Therein lay the secret of Haggard's enormous popular success and the reason for his African settings. In Africa . . . the beasts which Victorians feared to encounter in themselves could be contemplated at a safe remove" (Etherington 1977a: 196).

From 1892 Haggard divided his energies between writing about African landscapes, the state of British farmlands and on agricultural matters generally. During the period of his success in romance writing, Haggard suffered at the same time a number of disappointments. He stood unsuccessfully as a Conservative candidate for a Norfolk constituency (motto "Prosperity to the Plough") in the general election of 1895, his involvement in a new journal called *African Review* was embarrassingly short-lived, and on a personal level, he was very depressed by Jock's death. Lilias Haggard, born in 1892 to "replace" Jock, was later of the opinion that thereafter her mother broke off all sexual relations with her father to avoid having any more children (Etherington

1984: 14). Pierce conjectures in similar vein, "It seems that Jock's death caused or contributed to a measure of estrangement between Haggard and his wife. There were no more children [after Lilias] and they seldom travelled together again" (1975: 50). Haggard threw himself into a punishing round of work, writing on average one work of fiction a year, as well as undertaking public service work on various commissions looking into the state of British land. Perhaps Hyam is not far wrong when he writes, "The rulers of empire as a group display a high degree of emotional deprivation. Without resorting to vague assertions about sublimation, it is possible to see a basic truth in the contention that 'love's loss was empire's gain'" (1992: 49).

Haggard's yearning for the unattainable Lilly Jackson ended with her death in 1909 of syphilis contracted from her profligate husband. As proof of his attachment to her, Haggard supported her in her last years and continued in his novels to use the theme of the eternal passions of star-crossed lovers.

Haggard's second visit to South Africa was made to serve on the Dominions Royal Commission after his knighthood in 1912. The Commission's task was to report on the state of various parts of the Empire including India, Ceylon, Australia, New Zealand, South Africa and Canada. It was February 1914 by the time the Commission reached South Africa and Haggard fell into "that strange mood which lasted all the months he was in Africa; a feeling as if he had come back from another life. Everything was so changed, towns unrecognizable, transport revolutionized by trains and motors. . . . Then on a sudden, he would find some place unaltered, untouched by the years, smiling in the sunshine as it smiled in those high-hearted days of his youth" (Haggard, L.1951: 220).

Besides his work on the Commission, it was a nostalgic trip for Haggard, his wife Louie, and daughter Lilias. They visited their farmhouse Hilldrop near Newcastle, and a few days later in Pietermaritzburg Haggard met up with his old Zulu servant, Mazooku, who greeted him with "'Chief of old! Father! Here am I returned to serve you'" (Higgins 1981: 216). This was a moment straight out of an African romance and Haggard was suitably touched, maintaining Mazooku as part of his entourage during his trip and rewarding him with money to build a home "away from the White man" (Haggard, L. 1951: 179) on his departure. He visited the battlefield at Majuba, the house he and Cochrane had lived in while in Pretoria, and then continued up to Rhodesia where he visited the Zimbabwe ruins. There he discovered to his amusement and chagrin that the local guide book claimed he had used these ruins as the setting for ancient Kôr in *She*. He denied the specific connection, saying:

These and similar legends I have heard and read elsewhere, are quite apocryphal. When I wrote *She* and the other romances referred to, I had only heard in the vaguest way of the Zimbabwe Ruins, and not at all of the famous caves in East Africa, which are also reported to have been her residence. These works were in the main dictated by my own imagination, stimulated only in the case of *K. S. Mines* by faint rumours I had heard when during my residence in South Africa. (Haggard [1914a] 2000: 157)

Haggard's (probably more than vague) knowledge of the existence of the Zimbabwe Ruins could have come from Thomas Baines's "Map of the Gold Fields of South Eastern Africa" (1873), which, as a member of Shepstone's staff in the Transvaal, he would have used, as I have mentioned. This map shows "Simbaby, ruined cities C. Mauch, Sept. 1871" and "Supposed Realm of Queen of Sheba." J.R. Jeppe's "Map of the South African Republic" (1877), also used by British administrators of the time, shows the route of Mauch (the "discoverer" of the Zimbabwe Ruins in 1870) and features a "view of the ruins" (Etherington 1977b: 437).

By attributing the ruins and stone carvings in *King Solomon's Mines* and the ancient city of Kôr to the work of ancient white civilisations, probably of Phoenician origin, Haggard contributed to a powerful part of the myth about Africa in the nineteenth century. This myth was linked to race theories of the nineteenth century which held that African cultures were inevitably less sophisticated than European ones. The discovery of ancient stone-walled sites and gold mines in Africa posed a problem since these were unknown in comparable European Iron Age sites. Hence the theory that other, European, races must have built them in some far distant age. Popular theory also held that the southern African region was the site of the Biblical Ophir, a belief traceable back to sixteenth-century Portuguese explorers. Thus when Mauch found Great Zimbabwe in 1870, its antiquity and singularity led him to claim it as the site of King Solomon's Ophir, built for the Queen of Sheba, with a Phoenician substratum. Though there was some scientific resistance to this idea by, for example, Hartmann who had seen Africans building in stone, "[h]is scepticism was quickly relegated into obscurity, and Mauch's views were popularised further by support from Thomas Baines [and his] rather romantic imaginings of Great Zimbabwe" (Tangri 1990: 295).

What Baines romantically imagined in paint, Haggard did in words: he specifically linked Southern Africa with Ophir in *King Solomon's Mines* (the mines reached by a route leading between Queen Sheba's Breasts) and its cultural artefacts with an ancient Phoenician civilisation. Allan Quatermain speculates, looking at three stone colossi who guard the diamond mine entrance: "Perhaps these colossi were designed by the same Phoenician official who managed the mines" (Haggard [1885] 1992: 258).

She has frequent references to ancient white civilisations and their influence in Africa—Ayesha herself is a unique remnant of that ancient period. Horace Holly remarks on coming across an ancient wharf complete with mooring ring in the swamps:

A country like Africa . . . is sure to be full of the relics of long dead and forgotten civilisations. Nobody knows the age of the Egyptian civilisation, and very likely it had offshoots. Then there were the Babylonians and the Phoenicians, and the Persians, and all manner of people, all more or less civilised. . . . It is possible that they, or any one of them, may have had colonies or trading stations about here. Remember those buried Persian cities that the consul showed us at Kilwa. (Haggard [1886] 1991: 45)

Haggard, through the narrative's framing "Editor," then gives a learned footnote on the discoveries at Kilwa, on the east coast of Africa, and mentions John Kirk, a member (like Thomas Baines) of Livingstone's expedition to the Zambezi. Etherington's footnote to this reads: "This allusion suggests that the journals of Livingstone and other members of the expedition may have been the source of some geographical and zoological details included in this chapter" (in Haggard 1991: 216). What this piece of investigative analysis suggests to me is that Haggard, like some other writers on Africa of his day, combined both the manifest "informational" and latent "wish fulfilment" strands of a discourse of Africanism in an attempt to construct an Africa that he could understand and interpret, and yet which defied his attempts. Chrisman suggests that this contradictory impulse is typical of imperialist discourse, which seeks "to find a rationality for its own operation" yet also simultaneously needs to maintain ruins such as Great Zimbabwe as "a vacant site of indeterminacy" (1990: 50); what Haggard would call a "safe and secret place" (Haggard 1894: 762), which I shall discuss in the next chapter. The popularity of Haggard's works, however, made his contribution to the myth of ancient white civilisations in Africa potentially far-reaching. Tangri speculates:

It might not be too cynical to perceive in the work of Haggard a profound influence on later white lay opinion in southern Africa, already receptive to ideas about Ophir and foreign colonists after centuries of speculation. Certainly, local apostles of the Ophir theory like Chilvers paid due homage to Haggard, and the basic ideas he perpetuated can be found in all early reports on Great Zimbabwe which advocate an exotic origin for the site. (1990: 295)

Chilvers, in his chapter on Great Zimbabwe, includes, in fact, a photograph of Rider Haggard standing in front of the ruins during his 1914 visit. The caption explicitly links his romances to that site—both the image and the caption pull together manifest and latent Africanism in a most powerful manner. Chilvers reinforces the link between Haggard and the ruins: "Behind the walls of this towering rock-pile lived Rider Haggard's vivid creation, 'She-who-must-be-obeyed'; the heroine of the romance which that master of fiction wrote in the white heat of an inspiration born of the mystery enveloping the Acropolis [of Great Zimbabwe]" (1929: 318).

Chilvers subscribes to the "white civilisation" theory of Great Zimbabwe, backed up by detailed cross-referencing to other comparable sites in Arabia, and thus to a corresponding denigration of local native skills. Interestingly enough, a 1973 South African film version of *She* was shot in the Great Zimbabwe ruins with Ayesha, the white queen, ruling over black subjects and guarding her virginity on which her immortality depends: "With this story De Villiers [the film maker] was able to cash in on the sexual anxieties of white South Africans while reinforcing the hoary and politically convenient belief that a lost white civilization rather than black men raised the walls of the spectacular buildings at Zimbabwe" (Etherington in Haggard 1991: xxxix).

From Rhodesia, Haggard travelled to Zululand after taking leave of Louie and Lilias, who were returning to England. Together with Mazooku he visited the Gqikazi homestead near which Cetshwayo died, Dingaan's kraal and Isandlwana. Much of what he learned of Zulu history he incorporated into his romance *Finished* (1917), which ends with Cetshwayo's death at the Gqikazi homestead which Haggard turns into "Jazi," meaning "finished." His tour of Zululand rekindled his affection for the Zulus and their land and thus their broken plight angered and depressed him. He wrote an impassioned letter to the Colonial Secretary, the Rt. Hon. Lewis Harcourt, arguing the Zulu cause, a plea remarkable for its time: "In the case of the Zulus, civilisation has one of its great opportunities, for certainly in them is a spirit which can be led to higher things.... If so, it seems to me, that we shall incur a heavy responsibility towards a bewildered people that we have broken and never tried to mend" (Haggard, L. 1951: 180).

As early as 1885 in *King Solomon's Mines*, Haggard was sounding a pessimistic note about the effects of British imperialism—and thereby "civilisation"—on Africans. In his farewell speech to the three white men, Ignosi says, "I will see no traders with their guns and rum. My people shall fight with the spear, and drink water, like their forefathers before them. I will have no praying-men to put fear of death into men's hearts, to stir them up against the king, and make a path for the white men . . . to run on. (Haggard 1992: 306). *Allan Quatermain* (1887) similarly ends with a warning against "the greed, drunkenness, new diseases, gunpowder, and general demoralisation which chiefly mark the progress of civilization amongst unsophisticated peoples" (Haggard 1995: 282).

There is an apparent contradiction here between Haggard, the anti-imperialist author of these statements, and Haggard, the public defender of imperialism, the close friend of Kipling who invented the term "rank jingoism" in 1898. For the public Haggard, it was "for the good of the Empire, and of the world at large, that Englishmen with English traditions, and ideas should dominate in Africa." Furthermore, "to him the English name was the most glorious in history, and the English flag the most splendid that ever flew above the peoples of the earth" (Etherington 1984: 93). His daughter, Lilias, describes her father thus: "To the spirit of Imperialism, so often abused and misunderstood, he gave freely of all he had, serving its cause whole-heartedly and often infinitely to his own disadvantage. He knew only too well the blessings of its fruit when faithfully and wisely administered; the misery and despair which followed Britain's failures to fulfil her trust" (Haggard, L. 1951: 110).

However, Haggard as romance writer did not use these confident opinions overtly in his novels, seeming to be more conscious of the "misery and despair" that imperialism brought to its subjects. Within his fictions, beneath the cover of narrative convention and fictional characters, some contradictory part of Haggard is free to show more humanity and humility, more fears and pessimism as to the outcome of the imperial project than the public, imperialist

Haggard could allow. In chapter 4 I will show how this tension is translated into his African landscapes, outwardly solid but undermined from within.

It was with some sadness that Haggard left Zululand where he was known as *"Lundanda u' dand Okalweni,* which means 'The tall one who walks on the mountain-tops', that possibly signifies, absent-mindedly, or dreaming of things above" (Haggard 1916a: 86). This title is appropriate given Haggard's constant association with the land of Africa, his search for metaphysical meaning, and his role as the dream-maker of latent Africanism. He wrote prophetically in his ship's cabin while sailing back to England in May 1914:

So to South Africa, farewell, which is the dominant word in my life. It is a fair land of which the charm still holds my heart and whose problems interest me more than ever. How will they work out their fate I wonder? When I have gone to sleep or may be to dream on elsewhere. My name will perhaps always be connected with Africa if it remains a white man's "house" and even if it does not—perhaps. (Haggard, L. 1951: 243)

The gathering momentum of the First World War cut short the work of the Royal Commission during its work in Canada, but it was not long before Haggard was proposing a land settlement plan as part of his war "offering, since I am too old to fight" (Higgins 1980: 224). This scheme can be seen as part of Haggard's long campaign to keep British people on the land and involved in agriculture as a means of ensuring national regeneration. He proposed to the British government a scheme to settle returning soldiers after the war on land in the Dominions. This would achieve two aims: to provide ex-sailors and ex-soldiers with "houses fit for heroes," a fresh rural start; and to populate the colonies with British people. In part, the old myth of the "empty land" is brought into play here—as there was so much "empty" territory in these parts, why not put the land to fruitful use?

Though the government was not interested in his ideas on this issue, Haggard managed to find support from the Royal Colonial Institute, which undertook to send him as its representative to the Dominions to sound out their governments on this issue and to seek their support. On February 1, 1916 the Institute hosted a farewell lunch for Haggard at which his health was proposed by Lord Curzon. In response, Haggard reiterated the centrality of land to his vision of the world: "You cannot live on trade alone. The land breeds people which in the end the cities eat. Without the land everything will die. Therefore the land is the most vital of all the problems with which we have to deal" (Haggard 1916b, quoted in Ellis 1978: 221).

South Africa was Haggard's first stop on this mission, and he arrived in Cape Town for this third and final visit on 28 February 1916. The South African response to his plan was quite successful: Prime Minister Louis Botha expressed the need for a greater white population, though there was the anti-British feeling on the part of the Boers to consider. The British South Africa Company promised half a million acres in Rhodesia for settler soldiers, the

Union Castle shipping line free passage and, significantly, Louis Botha promised to waive immigration restrictions for ex-servicemen and their families after the war. Haggard left South Africa on 13 March after a visit of about two weeks and proceeded on the arduous journey to Australia, New Zealand and Canada. On this trip he turned sixty, and when he met Roosevelt again in New York state, they discussed the hazards of old age and concluded that, ideally, they would choose to end their days in Africa if they could. At the trip's end, Haggard submitted his report to the Royal Colonial Institute and the House of Commons. The reception it received was disappointing, for the War claimed prior attention and the report was filed away for future reference. However, in 1917 the government, under pressure from the Royal Colonial Institute, established an Empire Settlement Committee with Haggard appointed as one of its members.[9] Further state recognition came in 1919 when Haggard was made a Knight of the British Empire for his service on the Dominions Commission and the Empire Settlement Committee.

Running parallel to his public service work was his work on various novels, including African romances. However, as he acknowledged, this latter work had become a necessary money-making activity for him, without yielding him much pleasure. Haggard revealed his own fatigue with romance writing:

My name . . . is connected in the public idea with a certain stamp of African story and especially with one famous character. Therefore Editors and Publishers clamour for that kind of story reintroducing that famous character. If I write other things I am told they are "not so good" though I well know them to be much better. . . . Oh, I grow weary of story telling and could it be managed, would devote the days that remain to me to the problems of the Land, that greatest of all Causes, and to the service of my Country. But few of us can do exactly what we wish. (letter dated June 1918, quoted in Cohen 1960: 268-269)

Sales of his fictional works declined in his latter years, for the fire that fuelled the early African romances was nearly out. This increased the tendency to depression that had always been a part of his personality, yet he took heart from the interest that his early works elicited from film makers—as many as seven versions of *She* were made in his lifetime (Ellis 1978: 278). Typically, he undervalued his influence as a romance writer, preferring to promote his "serious" empire work on land and agriculture; though he did wryly acknowledge that it was, in fact, not unpraiseworthy to have "amused millions of mankind" (Pocock 1993: 199) with his astonishing imagination.

It was this imagination that called into being one of the most powerful popular expressions of an "image of Africa" in Europe, with which this chapter began. Haggard tapped into the latent strand of the discourse of Africanism more powerfully than any other writer of his age, except perhaps Conrad. Its translation into landscape in his African romances is the subject of chapter 4. That such fictional force emanated from one so seemingly conservative as Haggard is a source of ongoing surprise.

Thus he maintained in his final years the extraordinary duality that had marked him from childhood.... To the world at large, he appeared as the bluff squire-writer, boring the pants off people with his cantankerous opinions about trade unions, Reds, the avant-garde, and the empire. In the recesses of his imagination, however, and in the company of his few intimate acquaintances,[10] he pondered endlessly the profoundest questions of morals and metaphysics. He clambered on the stony outcrops of weird landscapes after visions of other lives, lost wisdom, and immortal loves, keeping one eye always fixed on the ever-present abyss of nothingness below. (Etherington 1984: 19)

Haggard's death in May 1925 ended a career marked by hard work, both in the public and private spheres, many personal disappointments and few perceived successes, according to his exacting estimation, in the things he valued.

NOTES

1. For a fuller analysis of the processes whereby early European travellers to Southern Africa left their mark on the land, see Sienaert and Stiebel (1996:91-101).

2. Haggard frequently uses only the Zulu name, "Quathlamba," for this prominent South African mountain range. This is an interesting choice given his English-speaking readership which would have been more familiar with the European name of "Drakensberg." In *Heu Heu*, Richard Darrien, who is British, describes his mountain hideout thus: "A certain secret and almost inaccessible place in the great Quathlamba Mountains, in which people had lived whom Chaka wiped out, and there hidden themselves . . . a kind of tableland ringed around with precipices that could only be climbed through a single, narrow nek, and overshadowed by the great Quathlamba range" (Haggard [1923] 1972: 345).

3. See also Haggard's *Allan Quatermain* on the same theme:

Ah! this civilisation, what does it all come to? For forty years and more I lived among savages, and studied them and their ways; and now for several years I have lived here in England, and have in my own stupid manner done my best to learn the ways of the children of light; and what have I found? A great gulf fixed? No, only a very little one, that a plain man's thought may spring across. (1995: 10)

4. Popular interest in Africa was also fed by popular magazines such as the *London Illustrated News*, which carried frequent reports of savage African life using visual images supplied by traveller-artists. Popular exhibitions or shows portraying Africa also fed public demand for informative and entertaining accounts of African life and customs:

Imperialist powers tend to create shows out of the peoples they dominate, subjecting them to all the isolation of spectacle. There was a considerable tradition of this in the nineteenth century. The "native village" became a central part of imperialist exhibitions and, at times, a familiar sight in seaside entertainments. Colonial wars were swiftly represented on the theatrical stage or in the circus ring. (Mackenzie 1986: 11)

See also Trotter (1990: 3-20) for a description of popular spectacular shows put on in Britain—for example, "Savage South Africa" in 1899—which reinforced a particular image of Africa in the popular imagination. Haggard's diary entry for 6 April 1920 records that he was invited to open "The South Africa Week" at the Albert Hall:

Imagining Africa   35

After I had formally opened the Exhibition and spoken a few words urging the necessity for more English population in South Africa, we attended the performance of *King Solomon's Mines*. It was well given and the audience was great; so far as I could see the Albert Hall must have been about two-thirds full and after it was over the people poured out by the thousand. As the film has already been screened in various parts of London, this is remarkable and suggests that it must have considerable popularity. (Haggard 1980: 191)

It also suggested the continued public interest in South Africa, its land and peoples. Haggard's diary entry for 29 May 1923 records his attendance at the Empire Exhibition at Wembley, where he showed special interest in the Nigerian and South African exhibits.

5. See Pratt (1992: 213-216), Mills (1993: 153-174) and Blunt (1994) for discussion on this point.

6. For background on the British Empire in Africa see Bowle (1974), Penrose (1975), Hibbert (1984), and also Gallagher, J., R. Robinson and A. Denney (1961) *Africa and the Victorians: the Climax of Imperialism in the Dark Continent* (London: Macmillan). A fair amount of consensus seems possible on the following point: "Recent historians, however, following the work of John Gallagher and Ronald Robinson, have recognized that in the Victorian years down to 1880, British overseas expansion went on apace, even though the official attitude was frequently to resist that expansion" (Brantlinger 1988: 20).

7. See on this point Higgins (1981: 34-36), Etherington (1984: 5, 120), and also Pocock, T., *Rider Haggard and the Lost Empire* (1993) who speculates that Haggard may have taken an African mistress after the end of his relationship with Lily [different spellings of Lilly—I am following Higgins' spelling as he seems the most authoritative on this matter], which caused him to feel some undefined guilt. The inevitable outcome of such speculation seems that eventually conjecture becomes fact as in, for example, Mazlish's assertion: "In real life, it appears, Haggard himself had had sexual relations, his first, with a black girl and for the rest of his life felt, compulsively, that he must atone for this sin" (1993: 739). In his autobiography, Haggard comments on the shock he sustained from the news of Lilly's engagement and hints at its effect on his behaviour: "Its effects upon me also were very bad indeed, for it left me utterly reckless and unsettled. I cared not what I did or what became of me. Here I will leave this subject of which even now I feel it painful to write" (1926 vol. 1: 116).

8. Haggard's daughter, Lilias, records him as saying: "Of Allan [Quatermain] for obvious reasons I can always write, and of Zulus, *whose true inwardness I understand by the light of nature* [italics added], I can always write." (1951: 210).

9. The eventual implementation of Haggard's resettlement scheme did not prove as successful as he had hoped: "Despite free passage for British ex-servicemen to the Dominions between 1919 and 1922, emigration was less than between 1910 and 1914. ... Confounding his assumptions and those of the Empire Land Settlement Committee, there was no desire to leave Britain precipitately to settle in the Dominions. In fact during the 1930s there was a big flow of migrants back to Britain" (Pierce 1975: 130). On a personal note, ten minutes from my home town of Ballito, on the KwaZulu Natal coast, lies a sugar farming area, together with a railway station, both named Compensation. Some of the farms in this area were given to ex-servicemen after World War I in compensation for their services to Empire—it seems likely that they were recipients of Haggard's land resettlement scheme.

10. Haggard wrote in his diary, 20 March 1923: "There are three men with whom I have found myself in complete understanding during my life—Rudyard [Kipling] is

one of them and the other two were Andrew Lang and Theodore Roosevelt." One of Haggard's closest long-standing friends, then, was Rudyard Kipling, ten years younger than himself: "Each had written of new places and new things, each had grown popular with a newly shaped reading public, and to each fame had come overnight. They also shared a deep feeling for the land, the land as a symbol of England, not England the island but England the Empire, the England of Allan Quatermain and Umslopogaas, of Tommy Atkins and Kim" (Cohen 1960: 201). Their friendship was such that they could work in the same study together. They constructively criticised each others' work and even "compounded the plot of *The Ghost Kings* together, writing down our ideas in alternate sentences upon the same sheet of foolscap" (quoted in Cohen 1960: 201). Each also lost a beloved only son which inevitably drew them closer together. For an intriguing record of their voluminous correspondence, see Cohen, *Rudyard Kipling to Rider Haggard: The Record of a Friendship* (1965).

As regards Haggard's friendship with Roosevelt, this extract from a letter he wrote to Roosevelt in June 1912 outlines their shared ideas:

I take some credit to myself in that, although we have met but a few times in the flesh, I have yet been able to discern what kind of spirit is in you. I suppose the truth is that as deep calls to deep, like not only draws to but understands like. Though my powers be less, and my opportunities smaller, yet our fundamental inspiration, and the aims of our hearts are in fact the same. I too hold that the civilized world wallows in a slough worse perhaps than the primeval mud of the savage; that it is possible if not probable that it may be dragged from the slough, cleansed, and clothed in white garments. That is the bounden duty of every man, as they shall answer for it at the last, to do their honest best to bring this about, regardless of any wreaths of success, or any dust of failure, regardless of everything save the glory which, in all probability, will never crown their individual strivings. (Haggard, L. 1951: 180)

Lang's friendship with Haggard predated Haggard's relationships with Kipling and Roosevelt—Cohen points out that their friendship probably began in 1885 and ended with Lang's death in 1912 (1960: 180). Lang as classical scholar and literary critic became "a literary father figure" (Etherington in Haggard 1991: 211) to Haggard, encouraging his literary endeavours and criticising where he thought it necessary. As a mark of the high esteem in which Haggard held Lang, Haggard dedicated *She* to him, and a few years later the two co-authored *The World's Desire* (1890), an historical romance about Helen of Troy. Some years after his friend's death, Haggard wrote in his diary: "Dear, dear Andrew, how I wish you were here, how you would argue about what I have been writing and turn everything topsy turvy after your aggravating way, making out you meant something quite different to what you did, etc. But that quiet voice is still and that kind eye shines no more" (Haggard, L. 1951: 251-252).

CHAPTER 3: RIDER HAGGARD— "KING ROMANCE"

> King Romance was wounded deep
> All his knights were dead and gone
> All his court was fallen on sleep
> In the vale of Avalon!
>
> Then you came from south and north
> From Tugela, from the Tweed;
> Blazened his achievements forth,
> King Romance is come indeed!
> —Andrew Lang (1887)

> Romance is always concerned with the fulfilment of desires—and for that reason it takes many forms; the heroic, the pastoral, the exotic, the mysterious, the dream, childhood and total passionate love. It is usually fashionable, and in the exact mould of an age's sensibility. Although it draws on basic human impulses it often registers with extraordinary refinement the peculiar forms and vacillations of a period.
> —Gillian Beer, *The Romance,* 12

Before turning to the heart of Haggard's *oeuvre*, his African romances, it is important to consider the form he chose as a vehicle to convey his vision. Certainly, the romance with its grand dreams of wish fulfilment, its deeds of heroism and its binary opposite, the fear of failure, of dark menace from without, suited the late nineteenth-century British mood well. Africa, in particular, the last unknown space on the map to be colonised, provided a suitable site for romantic dreaming for a home nation undergoing quite considerable domestic changes. Northrop Frye in his seminal work on the romance articulates this moment as follows:

For if the social affinities of the romance, with its grave idealizing of heroism and purity, are with the aristocracy, then the feudalistic colonial society with its Europeans as aristocrats and its blacks as serfs, provides the ideal conditions. If the essential raw materials for romance are magic and otherness, then the "ju-ju" in Africa provides the former and the savagery and blackness of Africans provide the latter. If romance flourishes in transitional periods when society is torn, where alternatives are grasped as hostile but unrelated worlds, and when social order is in the process of being undermined and destroyed by other nascent movements, then again colonial society fulfils all these conditions. (1957: 306)

Fredric Jameson approaches the romance from a different theoretical position. Although he is critical of Frye's analysis of the romance in certain aspects, he also links the romance to society in transition in much the same words:

Romance as a form thus expresses a transitional moment . . . its contemporaries must feel their society torn between past and future in such a way that the alternatives are grasped as hostile and somehow unrelated worlds . . . the archaic nature of the categories of romance (magic, good and evil, otherness) suggests that this genre expresses a nostalgia for a social order in the process of being undermined and destroyed by nascent capitalism, yet still for the moment coexisting side by side with the latter. (1975: 158)

Frequently in his African romances, Haggard sounds this nostalgic yet contradictory note. There is nostalgia for an Africa untamed and unknown yet ripe with promise, the quintessential Africa of latent Africanism, and yet this nostalgia contradicts Haggard the imperialist who encouraged the settlement of the colonies by Englishmen, who stressed the mother country's "civilising" role in the land. To the examples of this mood already quoted from *King Solomon's Mines* and *Allan Quatermain* in chapter 2 can be added this lament taken from *Allan's Wife*'s introductory dedication to Arthur Cochrane, Haggard's friend and farming partner in South Africa:

Perhaps they [these pages] will bring back to you some of the long past romance of days that are lost to us. The country of which Allan Quatermain tells his tale is now, for the most part, as well known and explored as are the fields of Norfolk. Where we shot and trekked and galloped, scarcely seeing the face of civilised man, there the gold-seeker builds his cities. The shadow of the flag of Britain has, for a while, ceased to fall upon the Transvaal plains; the game has gone; the misty charm of the morning has become the glare of day. All is changed. (Haggard [1889]1951: v)

Published in 1889, following the discovery of gold on the Witwatersrand and also after the relinquishment of the Transvaal—including the precious goldfields—to the Boers, Haggard's tone in this book is understandably sombre. What Haggard regrets is the loss of freedom to roam the land, a pre-industrial dream now curtailed by the onset of mining capitalism.

Romance was the genre most suited to the age of empire and Haggard was judged by his contemporaries and later commentators to be the "King of Romance." The following comment links both the historical moment, the genre and the individual author neatly: "Haggard is a formative, if not *the* formative agent in the development of the genre of the imperial romance, a genre which is itself of paramount importance to the ideological articulation of imperialism as a whole" (Chrisman 1992: 15). Chrisman's reference to Haggard's writing within the imperial romance mould is useful. Given the breadth of the genre "romance," it is important to situate Haggard as writing specifically within the imperial romance sub-genre characterised by its reliance on the masculinist adventure story so popular in late-Victorian England. Imperial growth created whole new spaces and new heroic roles to be performed in these exotic places; the public schools nurtured new subjects to dream of stories set there—"quests for wisdom or treasure, struggles with demons or magicians, tests of strength against monstrous enemies" (McClure 1994: 10). These were the escapist fantasies upon which Haggard capitalised in his particular versions of the imperial romance.

The most obvious precursor to Haggard in this field is Robert Louis Stevenson, whose *Treasure Island* (1883) provided the spur to write *King Solomon's Mines*, as previously mentioned. The latter text, like its inspiration, creates a masculine mould of adventure set afar, with sexuality very much a subtext. Contemporaneous with Haggard, Ernest Glanville (1855-1925) and Bertram Mitford (1855-1914) also drew on the same romantic sub-genre, creating "a highly saleable blend of Haggard's exotically inventive romance and the Victorian public school tale of adventure" (Van Wyk Smith 1990: 24). Haggard saw himself in his early creative years as writing within a genre of the highest seriousness, despite the popular commercial success of his early works. He was at pains to draw a distinction between the Romance, as he called it (though more narrowly meaning the imperial, adventure story sub-genre), and the then dominant—and, in his view, pedestrian—genre of the realist novel, as I shall now show.

Although undoubtedly one of the foremost practitioners of the imperial romance, Haggard was far weaker as a theorist of the genre. However, his pronouncements on the subject yield useful insights into his perception of the romance form. Flushed by the great successes, both critical and financial, of *King Solomon's Mines* and *She—Blackwood's Edinburgh Magazine* hailed Haggard as "the avatar of the old story-teller," *Dial* devoted an essay to his romances, and Saintsbury praised his "return to the pure romance," all in 1887 (Cohen 1960: 116)—Haggard, just short of his thirty-first birthday, published a critical piece "About Fiction" in the *Contemporary Review* (1887: 172-180) that alienated all but his staunchest supporters in the literary world. In it, he dismissed the bulk of current British novels as "worthless," denounced the French Naturalistic school headed by Zola an "an accursed thing" and in its stead extolled "good romance writing [as] perhaps the most difficult art practised by the sons of men." In his description of the courage required to tackle this highest form of writing, the romance, he used an image of aerial elevation similar to the "bird's-eye view" position so beloved of British explorers (Pratt's "monarch-of-all-I survey" mode) and of Haggard himself in his landscape descriptions: "Here we may even—if we feel that our wings are strong enough to bear us in that thin air—cross the bounds of the known, and hanging between earth and heaven, gaze with curious eyes into the great profound beyond. There are still subjects that may be handled *there* if the man can be found bold enough to handle them" (1887: 180).

Although he tried to sound a humbler note at one point, giving himself a lower vantage point as "an ordinary conscientious labourer in the field of letters," the damage was done. Rebuttals were published in the *Pall Mall Gazette,* the *Literary World, The Spectator,* the *Whitehall Review* and the *New York Post,* accusing Haggard of indifferent writing, even plagiarism. Haggard's friends, notably Andrew Lang and Charles Longman, published letters in his defense as did his family and Haggard himself, writing from Cyprus where he was visiting Sir Henry Bulwer, then High Commissioner of Cyprus, and his erstwhile superior in South Africa. Depressed by the weight of public censure and attacks on his honour, Haggard contemplated giving up writing to which Lang responded: "If you jack up literature, I shall jack up Reading. Of *course* I know the stuff is the thing, but the ideal thing would be the perfection of style, and we don't often get that; except from Henry Fielding. . . . Probably I think more highly of your books than you do, and I was infinitely more anxious for your success than for my own, which is not an excitement to me" (Lang in Cohen 1960: 127).

In later years, Haggard acknowledged that his attack on the literary establishment was "very little short of madness" (1926 vol. 1: 264) and he made no forays into the public arena of literary criticism again. Privately he upheld the value of the romance form for himself. In a letter to his sister, Ella, in the early 1900s he wrote:

Let us for a little time think as we thought when we were young; when faith knew no fears for anything, and death had not knocked upon our doors, when you opened also to my childish eyes that gate of ivory and pearl which leads to the blessed kingdom of Romance. At least I am sure, and I believe you, my sister, will agree with me, that above and beyond its terrors and its pitfalls, imagination has few finer qualities and none perhaps more helpful to our hearts, than those which enable us for an hour to dream that men and women, their fortunes and their fate, are as we would fashion them. (Haggard, L. 1951: 179)

In similar vein, he wrote in his diary on 30 March 1917 of Kipling's work: "The truth is that he has imagination, vision and can *understand,* amongst other things that Romance may be the vehicle of much that does not appear to the casual reader" (Higgins 1980: 101). Only towards the end of his life, by then an acknowledged and established writer, knighted for his services to his country, did he venture his opinions on romance writing in public—perhaps because he knew it would be read posthumously—through the medium of his autobiography.

In chapter 16, volume 2 of Haggard's autobiography, entitled "Romance Writing," he offers some guidelines to the writing of romances (1926 vol. 2: 83-105). By way of preamble, he describes his favourite dream, which is more interesting, concerned as it is with the links between landscape and ideology, than the rather pedestrian hints on romance writing that follow it. In this dream, described in terms of the Romantic Sublime, Haggard creates what is for him a paradisal landscape of inspiration, with himself as author situated within it. The ivory gate, just referred to in his letter to Ella, reappears, opening the way to the "dreaming landscape," perhaps "the blessed kingdom of Romance" also referred to in his letter. Haggard's favourite inspirational sources are cited: the "mighty cliff," "illimitable lands," "the cataracts," a mysterious "white and wonderful city" with "domes and palaces" drawn from his characteristic discourse of Africanism; and references to ancient Egypt, as in the comparison of the "great river ... like the Nile" that fertilises the plain, all bathed in "a soft but radiant light." Within this romantic landscape "stands a strange and silent house built for me by hands that I have known. I see its central hall, where all those I loved or love in life steal in and out. I see a certain chamber, low and large, which overlooks the dreaming landscape, and more nearly, the walks of garden trees hung with bells of white and purple blossom, with unknown, golden fruits and creeping strands of vine" (Haggard 1926 vol. 2: 86-88).

This house[1] and its environs had already appeared in Haggard's life and work: it is Hilldrop, Haggard and Louie's first marital home just outside Newcastle, South Africa, and it reappears as Mooifontein in *Jess*:

It was a delightful spot. At the back of the stead was the steep boulder-strewn face of the flat-topped hill that curved around on each side, embosoming a great slope of green, in the lap of which the house was placed. ... All along its front ran a wide verandah, up the trellis-work of which green vines and blooming creepers trailed pleasantly, and beyond was the broad carriage-drive of red soil, bordered with bushy orange-trees laden with odorous flowers and green and golden fruit. (1900a: 22)

It is the colonialist's dream: an oasis of "civilisation" planted with flowers and fruit, both familiar and unknown, set on a vantage point overlooking "illimitable lands" open to the gazer's eye. The "lap" of the slope in which the farmhouse is based, and the "embosoming" hill are also characteristic of Haggard's sexualising of African landscape which will be discussed more fully in the next chapter.

Despite his great success at romance writing, Haggard shows in the dream a weariness with what had become a money-making formula for him in his later years. He is relieved to hear from his dream guide that he is not writing a romance but "the history of a world," "[f]or truly it would be a horrible fate to be doomed from aeon to countless aeons to the composition of romance" (1887: 88). Nevertheless the recurring features of Haggard's "dream landscape," the simplicity with which he describes the scene, the symbolically charged landscape, show Haggard as a romance writer despite himself: "The perennially child-like quality of romance is marked by its extraordinarily persistent nostalgia, its search for some kind of imaginary golden age in time or space" (Frye 1957: 186).

Following the "favourite dream" passage, Haggard offers various suggestions for the "difficult" art of romance writing. He suggests the vital importance of adventure, imagination and "action, action, action from the first page to the last," a dictum that he certainly followed in his own work. He urges the centrality of the story, and that the writer must be able to create a visually imaginative world for the reader. Typically, Haggard uses an example drawn from his "African" world to describe this: "He must see the characters and their surroundings; the lion springing, the Zulu regiments rushing with uplifted spears, the fire eating into the grass of the hillside, while before it the scorched snakes glide and hiss" (1926 vol. 2: 94).

Haggard's intense visualisation of a nostalgic African landscape, a painted canvas of both delight and horror as the setting for stirring action is the source of his power as a writer. C.S. Lewis, writing about stories to do with Red Indians, explains this appeal thus: "The 'Redskinnery' was what really mattered. . . . For I wanted not the momentary suspense but that whole world to which it belonged—the snow and the snow-shoes, beavers and canoes, warpaths and wigwams, and Hiawatha names (1984: 27). Similarly, one could say that this is what Haggard creates in his African romances—an "Africannery" complete with a desire-laden, latent world of heat, big game, dangerous natives, vast limitless horizons, in short the dream landscape of empire, fraught with contradictions. In his chapter on Rider Haggard's work, particularly *She*, C.S. Lewis also highlights the centrality of the story: "What keeps us reading in spite of all these defects is of course the story itself, the myth. Haggard is the text-book case of the mythopoeic gift pure and simple. . . . A great myth is relevant as long as the predicament of humanity lasts; as long as humanity lasts. Haggard will always work, on those who can receive it, the same catharsis" (1984: 130-131).

Perhaps linked to this notion of catharsis is Haggard's insistence on speed and sustained effort in romance writing: "The way to write a good romance is to sit down and write it almost without stopping" (1926 vol. 2: 93). Haggard is here referring to his early golden years of romance writing when he wrote at a scorching rate, producing his most popular and lucrative works: *King Solomon's Mines* was written in six weeks; before the end of 1885, the year it was published, he had written *Allan Quatermain* and *Jess*, then *She* during February and March 1886. Of *She* he wrote:

The fact is that it was written at white heat, almost without rest. . . . I remember that when I sat down to the task my ideas as to its development were of the vaguest. The only clear notion that I had in my head was that of an immortal woman inspired by an immortal love. All the rest shaped itself round this figure. And it came—it came faster than my poor aching hand could set it down. (Haggard 1926 vol. 1: 245-246)

To write at such speed speaks of a great deal of inner pressure, almost a kind of "automatic" writing favoured by the later French surrealists, coupled perhaps with material pressures to create a new means of livelihood for himself in preference to the law, which he disliked. Where Haggard becomes interesting is in the way he seemed to be symptomatic of his age; hence his popularity among readers who perhaps felt the same pressures in an age of increasing industrialisation. "The speed is, I think, the clue to why the adventure tale for Haggard becomes almost a confessional form, revealing the prejudices, as well as the mind of his generation" (Millman 1974: 40-41).

More particularly, Haggard came from a class under increasing pressure— the landed gentry represented in the late nineteenth century a dying agricultural tradition. England had seen a shift from an economy based largely on farming in the eighteenth century to an economy based more and more on industry— in 1760 nearly three quarters of the nation's wealth was derived from agriculture, with the manufacturing industry contributing seven percent; by 1860 agriculture had shrunk to one third of Britain's wealth, with industry now 24 percent, illustrating the impact of the Industrial Revolution on the country and the change in the role of land (Cosgrove 1984: 224). Not only did Haggard campaign for a return to the land, but he found in Britain's holdings in Africa a fresh, rich and fertile land both practically and symbolically speaking: "For those like Haggard, who faced the passing of a rural existence, the imperial landscape became more and more appealing. . . . In addition to the thrill of hazard that these foreign regions appeared to offer was the enticing freedom of an undeveloped landscape" (Katz 1987: 31). To the romance writer, it is important that the landscape be "undeveloped," for the romance, despite its formulaic nature, thrives on novelty. Haggard concludes his autobiographical chapter on "Romance-Writing" by expressing sorrow at the passing of this undeveloped quality of the landscape. He uses a rare butterfly as a metaphor with which to compare Romance: "But then their breeding-grounds in the dank tropical marshes or the lion-haunted forests were less known, and those who devoted themselves to this chase were few in number and supremely qualified for the business. Now travelling is cheap, hundreds handle the net, and all come home with something that is offered for sale under the ancient label" (1926 vol. 2: 95). Thirty-five years earlier, at the age of thirty-three, he was already nostalgic for an undeveloped Africa: "For us too . . . as for the land we loved, the mystery and promise of the morning are outworn; the midday sun burns overhead, and at times the way is weary" (1951: v). His pessimistic tone here can largely be traced to his intense disappointment at Britain's betrayal, as he saw it, of British settlers and Zulus in handing back the Transvaal to the Boers, together with his resentment at the ascendancy of mining capitalism over hunting and agriculture in this area.

Haggard's use of a hunting metaphor to compare romance writing with capturing a rare butterfly is particularly appropriate given the centrality of the quest to the romance form: "Romance is the structural core of all fiction: being directly descended from folktale, it brings us closer than any other aspect of literature to the sense of fiction, considered as a whole, as the epic of the creature, man's vision of his own life as a quest" (Frye 1976: 15). In his earlier work, *Anatomy of Criticism* (1957), Frye described the sequential adventure or quest as typically proceeding in three main stages: a preliminary perilous journey, the central crucial struggle in which the hero and his foe clash, and the final exaltation of the hero (Frye 1957: 186-187). While Frye gives his account universal application, the quest romance has specific application during the time of Empire, as previously mentioned. As an alternative form of literature to the dominant schools of realism and French naturalism, the late nineteenth-century imperial romance offered readers an escape from the humdrum and an allegorically flattering image of Empire's exploits in the colonies:

> In various ways, these stories represent a yearning for escape from a confining society, rigidly structured in terms of gender, class, and race, to a mythologized place elsewhere where men can be freed from the constraints of Victorian morality. In the caves or jungles, or mountains of this other place, the heroes of romance explore their secret selves in an anarchic space, which can be safely called the "primitive." Quest narratives all involve a penetration into the imagined center of an exotic civilization, the cave, Kor, coeur, or heart of darkness which is a blank place on the map, a realm of the unexplored and unknown. (Showalter 1991: 81)

Haggard shows in a tongue-in-cheek passage from one of his later, perhaps more cynical, romances, *The People of the Mist*, that he was fully aware of the escapist potential of the quest romance in a mercenary age. The heroine Juanna sarcastically berates the hero, Leonard Outram:

> "Oh! Mr Outram, why did you dispel my illusions? You see, I have been making up such a romantic story out of this adventure. You were the knight-errant, and I was the Christian maiden in the hands of the ogre, and when you heard of it you buckled on your armour and started to the rescue. And now you bring me down to the nineteenth century with a run. It is not Knight errantry, but a commercial transaction." (1973b: 125)

With Showalter's reference above to the known yet mysterious physical world of caves, jungles and lost lands, and to the brave hero of the romance, confident yet seeking his secret, hidden self, one returns to the two levels of Said's manifest and latent discourse, which formed the theoretical starting point for this book. On the one hand, Empire was about information gathering, laying secrets bare by mapping, naming, classifying, and yet on the other the attraction of the colonies lay in their ultimate unknowability, their secrecy. The imperial romance set in Empire's far-flung dominions depended on this duality of the knowable and therefore predictable, and yet unknowable and uncertain. Haggard realised this in his rhetorical question, "Where will the romance writers of future generations find a safe and secret place . . . in which to lay their plots?" (Haggard 1894: 762). Haggard's coupling of "safe" and "secret" highlights the romance's survival only where spaces of secrecy persist. It is a short step from references to secrecy and secret selves to Frye's statement, "Translated into dream terms, the quest-romance is the search of the libido or desiring self for a fulfilment that will deliver it from the anxieties of reality, but still will contain that reality" (1957: 193). This, in a nutshell, defines the desire of imperial romance: to show the hero triumphant over land and people but without eliminating the thrill of risk and danger, the great unknown. This is perhaps the reason for Frye's labelling Haggard's adventure tales "kidnapped romances" (1976: 57, 168), for "they represent the absorption and integration of the conventions of romance into the culture of imperialists abroad" (Low 1993: 197). To destroy the source of anxiety is to remove the impetus for the romance in which the hero has to have an Other (land, people, animals) to prove himself against: "A paradoxical tension between risk and control remains at the heart of adventure. Without risk, there can be no adventure, but since both gain and loss remain possible outcomes, excessive risk may cause the experience of excitement to give way to anxiety. Adventure in the modern sense is balanced between anxiety and desire" (Dawson 1994: 53).

Because desire and anxiety are so finely balanced in the quest romance, the happy ending often embraces a denial of fulfilment, a "happy pessimism" whereby though "man seeks a distant, passionately desired ideal: often, he is happiest when he fails to find it" (Fisher 1986: 63). Haggard frequently uses this ending as in, *inter alia*, *She* (1897) where a truly happy ending is impossible; in *Allan's Wife* (1889), which ends with a bitter-sweet vision of the dead Stella; and *The People of the Mist* (1894), which ends with what could be Haggard's motto: "To few is it allowed to be completely miserable, to none to be completely happy" (1973b: 363). A "happy pessimist" accurately describes Haggard's romantic hero, Allan Quatermain. Structurally, the imperial romance requires a masculine, virile hero to pit his strength against many odds. The masculinity of the romance is a result of the "gendering of genres" (Low 1993: 190) whereby the imperial romance became an almost exclusively male preserve: not only is Haggard's *King Solomon's Mines* dedicated to "all the big and small boys who read it" but Quatermain assures his male readers that there is "not a *petticoat*" to be found between its covers (1992: 9). Despite his masculinity however, Quatermain is not a typical romantic hero in Frye's terms. Frye associated the romantic hero with spring, dawn, order, fertility, vigour and youth (1957: 188) whereas Quatermain is an odd mixture of these. His first appearance in *King Solomon's Mines* shows him as a hunter-trader of fifty-five years of age but, if not youthful, he is vigorous as his actions prove, though modestly self-deprecating: "I am a timid man, and dislike violence, moreover I am almost sick of adventure. I wonder why I am going to write this book; it is not in my line. I am not a literary man, though very devoted to the Old Testament and also to *The Ingoldsby Legends*" (1992: 7-8).

By his next foray into fiction, however, Quatermain had recovered his zest for adventure, though now sixty-three years old and with a game leg. After his son's death he feels that "the thirst for the wilderness was on me, I could tolerate this place no more" (Haggard 1995: 9) and he gladly enters another African adventure. Hunter Quatermain dies at the end of *Allan Quatermain*, but such was readers' demand for this old, flawed African hand that Haggard revived him as a younger man recounting his earlier adventures.[2] Quatermain's mix of pragmatism and idealism, his love for the freedom of the "wide veldt and mysterious sea of bush" compared to the restriction of "this prim English country, with its trim hedgerows and cultivated fields" (Haggard 1995: 9) are close to Haggard's own sentiments. This is not surprising given Haggard's self-identification with Quatermain: "I always find it easy to write of Allan Quatermain, who, after all, is only myself set in a variety of imagined situations, thinking my thoughts and looking at life through my eyes" (1926 vol. 2: 85-86).

For Haggard, Quatermain therefore represented an unencumbered, free, adventurer spirit linking him to an African landscape in which he found his most compelling inspiration. Like Haggard too, Quatermain is shown to be scarred by experience—wife dead, only son dead, lover dead, fortunes won and lost. Sir Henry Curtis, the epitome of a British gentleman, whose judgement is thus much to be respected, pays this praise to Quatermain on his death: "[H]e was the ablest man, the truest gentleman, the firmest friend, the finest sportsman, and, I believe, the best shot in all Africa" (Haggard 1995: 280). High praise indeed!

The romantic hero moves within what Frye, suggestively for this work's interest, calls a "mental landscape" (Frye 1976: 53) arranged in a vertical perspective on four levels: at top is heaven, below that Eden or earthly paradise, then the world of earthly experience and, at the lowest level, hell or the demonic world, usually below ground. The two levels above that of earthly experience represent an "idyllic world," which is associated with happiness, peace, and sunshine; whereas the level below that of earthly experience is termed "the demonic or night world" characterised by "exciting adventures, but adventures which involve separation, loneliness, humiliation and the threat of more pain" (1976: 53). There are many features of this hierarchical landscape, with its ascents and descents between the levels, that seem to be illustrated in Haggard's African romances. I shall refer to them briefly here and will demonstrate them more fully later in the next chapter. The most useful for my purposes is the linking of mental states with physical spaces and features—the "night world," for example, is "often a dark and labyrinthine world of caves and shadows where the forest has turned subterranean, and where we are surrounded by the shapes of animals" (1976: 111). As an example of this world, Frye cites *She,* but there are night world caves in *King Solomon's Mines, Maiwa's Revenge, Allan's Wife, Nada the Lily, Heu-Heu or the Monster* and others. These caves always suggest anxiety on many levels— which I shall explore—linked to the felt contradictions and ambiguities of the contemporary world: "It looks, therefore, as though romance were simply replacing the world of ordinary experience by a dream world, in which the narrative movement keeps rising into wish fulfilment or sinking into anxiety and nightmare. To some extent this is true" (Frye 1976: 53).

At the opposite extreme is the elevation of the "point of epiphany," a term drawn from Frye's *Anatomy of Criticism*, of which the most common setting is the mountain top, "the symbolic presentation of the point at which the undisplayed apocalyptic world and the cyclical world of nature came into alignment" (1957: 203). This elevated position has close links with the imperial explorer's preferred position as "monarch-of-all-I-survey" described by Pratt (1992: 205-206), which implies power and position over landscape and, by inference, its peoples. It is also a position of vantage frequently used by Haggard, usually to extol the beauties of the open panorama that lies before the viewer. The following example from *King Solomon's Mines* is typical of this position, but others can be found in most of Haggard's African romances (as will be later discussed):

Behind and over us towered Sheba's snowy breasts, and below, some five thousand feet beneath where we stood, lay league on league of the most lovely champaign country. Here were dense patches of lofty forest, there a great river wound its silvery way. To the left stretched a vast expanse of rich undulating veldt or grass land, on which we could just make out countless herds of game or cattle, at that distance we could not tell which. This expanse appeared to be ringed in by a wall of distant mountains. To the right the country was more or less mountainous, that is, solitary hills stood up from its level, with stretches of cultivated lands between, amongst which we could distinctly see groups of dome-shaped huts. The landscape lay before us like a map, in which rivers flashed like silver snakes, and Alp-like peaks crowned with wildly twisting snow-wreaths rose in solemn grandeur, whilst over all was the glad sunlight and the wide breath of Nature's happy life. (1992: 104-105)

Such a vantage point implies that the viewer may be tempted to attempt "the elevation of Icarus" (Noyes 1992: 163) with all its danger—a telling comparison, for the conflict within Icarus between desire and fear is the stuff of legend. Noyes elaborates on the tension implicit on this "point of epiphany" contextualised within the imperial gaze: "The conflict arising out of the initial apprehension of boundless space initiates a tension within the entire corpus of colonial discourse. In the colonial setting, desire is invariably articulated as torn between dissolution in this boundless space and confinement within boundaries—boundaries which allow it to be represented as desire" (1992: 167).

Here is the conflict between Said's manifest and latent levels of discourse within the imperial framework: the desire to possess through information, as well as through the gaze, and the anxiety that this may not be possible. It is a conflict visually evident in Baines's painting "Bird's-eye view of the Victoria Falls from the West" (1874) referred to in chapter 2 and repeatedly in text in Haggard's romances.

Desire, too, in an erotic sense, is also part of the "mental landscape" of Frye's romance world, also evidenced in Haggard's reference to "Sheba's snowy breasts" in the passage from *King Solomon's Mines* just quoted. Frye suggests that the point of epiphany "may be presented in erotic terms as a place of sexual fulfillment, where there is no apocalyptic vision but simply a sense of arriving at the summit of experience in nature" (1957: 205). Haggard's frequent references to the "laps" of mountains, which offer the masculine ego a position of vantage coupled with intense satisfaction (and yet also feelings of precariousness), seem to illustrate this idea. This is most evident in the description of Ghost Mountain in *Nada the Lily*, which offers an extended example of such satisfaction combined with fear. In the following passage, Umslopogaas and Galazi in turn describe the mountain:

So Umslopogaas rose and crept through the narrow mouth of the cave. There, above him, a great grey peak towered high into the air, shaped like a seated woman, her chin resting upon her breast, the place where the cave was being, as it were, on the lap of the woman. Below this place the rock sloped sharply, and was clothed with little bushes. Lower down yet was a forest great and dense, that stretched to the top of a cliff, and at the foot of the cliff, beyond the waters of the river, lay the wide plains of Zululand . . . from time to time between the tops of trees I saw the figure of the grey stone woman who sits on the top of Ghost Mountain, and shaped my course towards her knees. My heart beat as I travelled through the forest in dark and loneliness like that of the night, and ever I looked round searching for the eyes of the *Amatonga* . . . great spotted snakes crept from before my feet . . . and always high above my head the wind sighed in the great boughs with a sound like the sighing of women. ([1892] 1949: 112-114)

Linked to this sexualising of the African landscape in terms of Frye's "idyllic world" is the "identification of the mistress' body with the paradisal garden" (1976: 153). For Haggard, writing within the masculine imperial romance form, the love interest of the sexual quest is partially transferred onto the landscape, there being "not a *petticoat*" (Haggard 1992: 9), that is, no domesticated white woman, advisable or even desirable in the genre of his time, as previously quoted. He allows a far more powerful love affair between his protagonist and the land than with any woman, with whom love affairs are shown to be inevitably transitory, unlike that with the land which is eternal. Desire is projected onto the landscape, which frequently assumes a female form, alluring yet dangerous as in the paradisal myth. The intensely sexualised landscape of *King Solomon's Mines* offers us a view at one point of the mountains named Sheba's Breasts "modestly veiled in diaphanous wreaths of mist." After seeing this, Quatermain declares "this new land was little less than an earthly paradise" (1992: 125-126). Both *Jess* and *The Ghost Kings* offer specific references to the Garden of Eden: "'It is like the Garden of Eden, isn't it, with the sea thrown in. There are all the animals, and that green tree with the fruit on it might be the Tree of Life, and—oh; my goodness, there is Adam!'" (1908a: 46).

Descent to the "demonic or night world" of romance offers by contrast a dark, anxiety-ridden, still sexualised landscape. Frye draws parallels between the methodological universe of the romance and the macrocosmic body "with analogies to the human body. The stars, sun and moon present an analogy to a human brain, especially when they are taken to be images of the intelligence of a creating god. At the bottom of this macrocosmic world we find the organs of generation and of excretion, which are emphasised in proportion as this part of the mythical universe is made demonic" (1976: 119).

Perhaps as much as Haggard's African romances are known for their paradisal landscapes, so are they known for the night world of caves, labyrinths and underground rivers they describe as a counter balance to the sunlit world above. The characteristic state of the protagonist in this other world is the dream or nightmare—Horace Holly in *She* exclaims: "No nightmare dreamed by man, no wild invention of the romance, can ever equal the living horror of that place" (1991: 200). That powerful interpreter of dreams, Freud, recognised the importance of the dreamy underworld of *She*, recommending it to a patient as "A *strange* book, but full of hidden meaning" and finding its landscape even intruding into *his* dream wherein he had to cross a chasm on narrow planks, after which he woke in a "mental fright" (Freud [1953] 1983: 586). In the same passage, Freud also refers to *Heart of the World* (1896), another of Haggard's novels about a lost city. In Freud's dream, the topography of both *She* and *Heart of the World* become entwined:

The boggy ground over which people had to be carried, and the chasm which they had to cross by means of boards brought along with them, were taken from *She*; the Red Indians, the girl and the wooden house were taken from *Heart of the World*. In both novels, the guide is a woman; both are concerned with perilous journeys; while *She* describes an adventurous road that had scarcely ever been trodden before, leading to an undiscovered region. (Freud 1983: 587-588)

Mazlish points out that Freud and Haggard, exact contemporaries in terms of their birth year, overlapped in many areas: both had an interest in archaeology, in the struggle between civilisation and savagery and, most notably, both men "held idealized views of women and had an intense interest in sex" (Mazlish 1993: 731). Haggard, prior to Freud, had recognised that "sexual passion is the most powerful lever with which to stir the mind of man, for it lies at the root of all things human; and it is impossible to over-estimate the damage that could be worked by a single English or American writer of genius, if he grasped it with a will" (1887: 176). Years later, in his diary for 1916, Haggard repeated his anxieties on the subject of "sexual passion." Writing about A.C. Benson, author of *Thy Rod and Staff*, Haggard stated that Benson "speaks with some horror of all the sexual business. Doubtless he is right in a way; it is, at any rate in highly civilized conditions, the source of our worst woes" (Haggard, L. 1951: 251). What Haggard did not allow to reach his conscious mind was the extent to which his own works were driven by desire, and how this desire of an imperial age, with its tensions and ambiguities, is present in his African landscapes.

All the foregoing points on the imperial romance, its form and Haggard's opinions on the matter, lead to the centrality of landscape to the romance form and to Haggard, with his powerful landscapes, as one of the imperial romance's most influential and popular practitioners: "Landscape might be seen more profitably as something like the dreamwork of imperialism unfolding its own movement in time and space from a central point of origin and folding back on itself to disclose both utopian fantasies of the perfected imperial prospect and fractured images of unresolved ambivalence and unsuppressed resistance" (Mitchell 1994: 10).

Before space can be changed into place, it needs to be anchored by words; thus (as I have shown in chapter 2) explorers and travellers and later empire builders used the power of the word to contain the unknown. What they mapped, charted, measured and described were the new lands they saw. From this mass of information emerged ideologically charged visual landscapes—what this work has already referred to as "rival geographies" (Said), an "ideological geography" (Hofmeyr), a "psychological terrain" (Etherington), a "mental landscape" (Frye), a "fictive geography" (Rich 1982-83: 59), a "dreaming landscape" (Haggard). The British Empire at its peak in particular, was a time of textuality fed by the Victorian mania for information, always in the name of Progress. Boehmer refers to colonisation in the nineteenth century as "a metaphoric and a cartographic undertaking. New spaces were interpreted visually and verbally, both as grids and triangulations, and as sentences retracing the travellers' routes" (1995: 49).[3] Landscape, created through description in novels or books of science, can therefore act as a text to be read, though not transparently as it is inevitably ideologically encoded, but with caution.

Landscapes anywhere can be viewed as texts which are constitutive of discursive fields, and thus can be interpreted socio-semiotically in terms of their narrative structure, their synecdoches, and recurrence. . . .The way that these concepts are articulated with reference to different times and places will of course, vary greatly. Nevertheless, the thrust of the interpretive method will be the same—to uncover the underlying multivocal codes which make landscapes cultural creations, to show the politics of design and interpretation, and to situate landscape at the heart of the study of social process. (Duncan 1990: 184)

Thus I return to the point with which I began—the importance of fiction to the understanding of a culture—more specifically, the centrality of landscape within the fiction of Empire, especially the imperial romance, to an understanding of the ambiguities and desires of the age, as translated within Haggard's African romances. In the next chapter, I will chart a topography of Haggard's African landscape as he repeated it through his African romances, particularly those prior to 1892 when his mapmaking vision seems most sustained and intense, but not excluding reference to some that come after that date. I hope to show how Haggard created an idiosyncratic yet also symptomatic African space, which through repeated patterns he turned into what de Certeau calls "a practised place" (1984: 117); a space-turned-place permeated with desire and nostalgia, yet deeply fissured by doubts and anxieties characteristic of his age.

NOTES

1. Bunn perceptively discusses the significance of the positioning of this house in Haggard's dream landscape: "By imagining his house placed centrally in this evocative locale, Haggard unconsciously elevates his taste as a romance writer to the point where he alone is qualified to reveal profound, unexplored mysteries to his audience" (1988: 7). This supports my point that, despite his repeated denigration of romance writing as an older man, he did not underestimate his own proficiency as a romance writer. As a point of interest, the house Hilldrop still stands and was declared a national monument in 1981 (Coan 1997: 53).

2. Etherington points out that the Quatermain of Haggard's later African romances is not the no-nonsense character of his earlier, fresher romances. He notes that the later Quatermain was, in fact, closer to his creator than the earlier version with whom Haggard identified:

As the embodiment of pragmatism and common sense, a crusty old hunter made a perfect foil for outrageously improbable events. He represented skeptical Everyman. Fantastic happenings were more believable because he narrated them. The Allan of the later romances with his "spiritual longings," his previous existences, his country house weekends and numerous lady friends cannot fulfill that function. (Etherington 1984: 75)

3. Not only was Empire a time of textuality, but also of intertextuality whereby writers, particularly of the adventure romance, acknowledged the influence of one by another; for example, the correspondence between Haggard and Robert Louis Stevenson, whose *Treasure Island* Haggard acknowledged as being his prompt for *King Solomon's Mines*; also the close friendship and mutual influence of Haggard and Kipling. In 1887 Haggard was elected to the Savile Club, where many leading writers of the day gathered on Saturdays for luncheon and literary discussion. (See also on this point Boehmer 1995: 47-48.)

CHAPTER 4: HAGGARD'S AFRICAN TOPOGRAPHY

> What gave Rider Haggard's romances their power and popularity in the closing decades of the nineteenth century . . . was the way such stories as *King Solomon's Mines, Allan Quatermain*, and *She* gave powerful expression, through symbolical journeys into Africa and the past (which are often the same thing), to late Victorian obsessions with evolution and race, and with psychology and sexuality.
> —Dennis Butts, introduction to *Allan Quatermain*, xiii

> The geographies of adventures . . . enable writers and readers to remove themselves from the messy realities and textured experiences of here and now, enabling them to imagine alternatives, other possible worlds, departures from the *status quo*.
> —Richard Phillips, *Mapping Men and Empire*, 168

One of Haggard's first biographers, Morton Cohen, wrote that "[f]or many Englishmen, Africa became the Africa of *King Solomon's Mines*" (1960: 94). What Haggard continued to do after this, his first successful African romance, was to work the same canvas, repeating certain features, embellishing, adding until he had created an instantly recognisable "Africa" for his readers. In the same way that certain writers are always linked to fictional or real landscapes about which they have written, so too is Haggard, despite his other novels set elsewhere, finally tied to a kind of generic Haggardesque "Africa": "Novels themselves aid in making the landscapes that they apparently presuppose as already made and finished. Mississippi is partly what it is because of Faulkner's Yoknapatawpha novels. Dorset has been made what it is in part by way of Hardy's Wessex, Salisbury by way of Trollope's Barset novels, London by Dickens, Paris by Balzac and Proust, and so on" (Hillis Miller 1995: 16).

My contention is that we could add "Africa by Haggard" to the above list, such is the link drawn in the popular imagination. The aim of this chapter is to construct a composite topography of Haggard's Africa as it emerges from his African romances, showing through its manifest and latent levels the ambivalent desire its creator felt for its contours. What I will attempt, in a self-conscious contemporary and post-colonial explorer's fashion, is to flesh out Haggard's ideological mapping of the African land he loved so much that he repeatedly covered the same ground with his pen. In his African romances, he took a real geophysical place, with current and past verifiable historical events to which he frequently referred, and moved the whole into a series of "imaginative geographies of desire" (Jacobs 1996: 34), as this chapter will describe. Writing of Africa intermittently for his whole writing career of just over forty years, Haggard sustained a remarkably constant construction of Africa, perhaps because of, rather than despite, a changing political climate at home. At odds, post-Shepstone, with Britain's handling of territories in South Africa and the changing policy particularly towards the Zulu people, Haggard drew a largely nostalgic landscape even from his earliest African romance. Old before his time, he left South Africa at the age of twenty-five already disillusioned with British party politics and in particular with Gladstone's handing back of the Transvaal to the Boers. This political disillusionment predated *King Solomon's Mines*; thus the way was already prepared for a vision of a pre-Gladstonian, nostalgic African canvas, that persisted throughout his writing career. Periodically Haggard sounded the note of his disillusionment, as in the prefatory dedication to Shepstone/Sompseu (Haggard's spelling; nowadays spelt Somtseu) in *Nada the Lily*:

It is many years even since I was a boy, and followed you when you went up among the Boers and took their country for the Queen.

Why did you do this, my father? I will answer, who know the truth. You did it because, had it not been done, the Zulus would have stamped out the Boers... Perhaps it had been better to leave it, since "Death chooses for himself," and after all there was killing—of our own peoples, and with the killing, shame.

Enemies have borne false witness against you on this matter, Sompseu, you who have never erred except through your kindness. Yet what does that avail? When you have "gone beyond" it will be forgotten, since the sting of ingratitude passes and lies must wither like the winter veldt. (1949: vi)

Certainly, the contours of Haggard's African topography are at their freshest and clearest in the pre-1892 romances. Though this image of Africa drew on earlier explorers' accounts (as I have shown), the picture struck the reading public with a curious nostalgic yet contemporary clarity, as is verified by their phenomenal sales. The gradually diminishing sales figures of his later romances are evidence that the topography had lost some of its allure and that the imperial dream that underpinned the whole had, even in Haggard's mind, lost its lustre and moment. Haggard acknowledged this in his autobiography written a few years before he died.

Be it good or be it bad, the best that I can do in the lines of romance and novel-writing is to be found among the first dozen or so of the books that I wrote, say between *King Solomon's Mines* and *Montezuma's Daughter* [1893]. Also I would add this. A man's mind does not always remain the same. People are apt to say of any individual writer that he has gone off, whereas the truth may be merely that he has changed, and that his abilities are showing themselves in another form. Now, as it happens in my own case, in the year 1891 I received a great shock [the death of his only son, Jock]; also subsequently for a long period my health was bad. Although from necessity I went on with the writing of stories, and do so still, it has not been with the same zest. (1926 vol. 2: 12)

The seven early African romances—*King Solomon's Mines, She, Jess* (though not strictly speaking a romance as I shall shortly establish), *Allan Quatermain, Maiwa's Revenge, Allan's Wife* and *Nada the Lily*—thus bear the stamp of a youthful political disapproval but also the energy of a young, newly married man, later with a beloved son, recalling the vitality of a land he had recently, against his desires, felt he had to leave.

Certainly in his earlier romances, what Haggard achieved for his readers was a more completely "African" landscape than any fiction writer before him, which was no doubt aided by his physical sojourn in South Africa. However, it is important to keep in mind that Haggard wrote when physically *outside* Africa, thus enabling a more exotic landscape of the imagination enhanced by the desire that separation engenders. Thus Olive Schreiner could respond to Andrew Lang's criticism of *The Story of an African Farm* as being too dour and unadventurous with these words: "It has been suggested by a kind critic that he would better have liked the little book if it had been a history of wild adventure; of cattle driven into inaccessible 'kranzes' by Bushmen; 'of encounters with ravening lions, and hair-breadth escapes.' This could not be. Such works are best written in Piccadilly or in the Strand" (Schreiner [1883] 1971: 27-28).

Haggard and Schreiner met first in 1885, later on a few other occasions, and exchanged a small correspondence. Prior to their first meeting, Haggard sent Schreiner a copy of his first novel, *Dawn*, and expressed interest in making Schreiner's personal acquaintance, saying "Your book [*The Story of an African Farm*] made a great impression upon me" (letter 21 October 1884). He again singled out this work of Schreiner's in his essay "About Fiction," in which he calls it a work "written from within, and not from without." However, in this case he is not referring to geographic location but to the book's "impression of being the outward and visible result of inward personal suffering on the part of the writer;" it is a book "written from the heart" (1887: 180). Haggard later remarked in a letter to his brother Jack that he was attracted by Schreiner's intellect, pronouncing her rather patronisingly to be "my intellectual superior," but admitting that he was repelled by her "complete and overpowering atheism" (17 February 1885). On one occasion he encouraged her to be more "cheerful" in her subject matter, advice that she rejected from one whom she obviously considered too florid and sensational a writer. The advice she gives to a writer in the preface to *The Story of an African Farm* would be rather to "squeeze the colour from the brush . . . dip into the grey pigments . . . paint what lies before him" (Schreiner 1971: 28). Strange associates as they may seem, both Haggard and Schreiner in their different styles and geographical locations were engaged in the same project at one level: "Both Olive Schreiner and Rider Haggard were working on central questions of their age by showing (although sometimes indirectly) how the European nurtured individual tried to meet the challenge of a 'primitive' and totally other environment" (Maclennan and Christie 1973: 10). Both were engaged in the issues of their age, projected in part onto an African terrain that for both featured far more strongly than mere backdrop, though the distance between the spectacular city of Kôr and the plain farm in the Karoo is vast.[1]

Perhaps in an attempt to make the distance to Kôr seem not quite so fanciful, many of Haggard's African romances employ the device of a framing "Editor" who interrupts the narrative in the tone of a Victorian gentleman-amateur scientist. This Editor satisfies the manifest informational impulse of the Victorian reader with corroborating—or corrective—facts and figures, specifications and details on aspects of Quatermain's unscholarly accounts of African adventures. His tone varies from broadly informative and opinionated, as in this note on Chaka, "The Zulu Napoleon, one of the greatest geniuses and the most wicked man who ever lived. He was killed in the year 1828, having slaughtered more than a million human beings.—Ed." (1949: 21); to pedantically corrective as in "Mr Quatermain does not seem to have been aware that it is common for animal-worshipping people to annually sacrifice the beasts they adore. See Herodotus, ii, 42—Editor" (1995: 148); to an interesting, very long footnote in *Marie* that combines an extraordinary level of manifest and latent Africanism. The subject that warrants such intense interest from the Editor (and presumably, Haggard must have thought, also the readers) is a gun, "a very beautiful hair-triggered small-bore rifle fitted with a nipple for percussion caps, then quite a new invention" (1959: 64). The gun as a symbol of masculinity and assertiveness, especially in the context of an imperial age where the gun doubled up on empire's margins as both a provider of food for the pot and as protection against the savages, is a well-worn cliché. What strikes the post-colonial reader of the Editor's footnote is the attention lavished on details of this particular gun that falls into Quatermain's hands and the intimacy implied between the owner and weapon. The footnote itself extends over two pages and ranges in tone from the informational, with specialist detail such as "[w]ithout the ramrod, which is now missing, it weighs only 5 lbs. 3¾ oz. The barrel is octagonal, and the rifled bore, designed to take a spherical bullet, is ½ in. in diameter," together with further details as to the name and address of the manufacturer plus year of manufacture, to passages laden with a kind of latent desire for the imperialist male dream of facing the wilderness alone with only one's loyal gun for companionship.

On the lock are engraved a stag and a doe, the first lying down and the second standing
... it is an extraordinarily well-made and handy gun, finished with horn at the end of
what is now called the tongue, and with the stock cut away so as to leave a raised
cushion against which the cheek of the shooter rests.

It is easy to understand that in the hands of Allan Quatermain this weapon . . . was
capable of great things within the limits of its range, and that the faith he put in it at
the trial of skill at the Groote Kloof, and afterwards in the fearful ordeal of the shooting
of the vultures on the wing upon the Mount of Slaughter, when the lives of so many
hung upon his marksmanship, was well justified. (1959: 64-65)

The feminising and sexualising of this gun is clear, with descriptive words such as "very beautiful," "nipple," "tongue," together with the doe engraved in relation to the stag on the stock, plus mention of a "cushion" for the (male) shooter to "rest" his cheek against. Furthermore, Quatermain makes the link between gun and woman explicit later in the narrative when he relates that "the natives . . . named this particular gun Intombi which means a young girl, because it was so much slimmer and more graceful than other guns" (1959: 158). Despite its elegance and precision, the gun requires a masculine ownership and competence to achieve its potential.² Similar tensions are evident in Haggard's frequent sexualising of an African "bodyscape"/ landscape, which I shall discuss later in this chapter. The Editor then functions as a kind of peculiarly Victorian safety-net of facts and corroboration, a sane, steady voice assuring the readers of their known world in the face of the extraordinary narratives the books tell. The Editor "cannot be precisely identified with Haggard" (Etherington in Haggard 1991: xvii) though he is obviously one part of Haggard—perhaps the ordered, precise and overbearing streak that he occasionally exhibited—while his dominant romantic strain formed the material that the controlling Editor failed to keep within bounds. As Bristow comments, "Two different kinds of masculinity, then, are endorsed at both the centre and the margins of the book. As each novel demonstrates, these men need each other" (1991: 136).

To proceed to Haggard's African topography itself, my method will be to deal with the particular characteristic elements that Haggard creates and repeats in order to build up a composite whole. The repetitive nature of Haggard's landscapes allows one to draw from the whole range of his African romances, though as said before, those written pre-1892 enunciate all of Haggard's most interesting and original ideas. The previous chapters have shown the arena in which Haggard was operating as a romance writer, drawing on pre-existing myths of Africa, together with his own important personal African experience in an ambivalent imperial age. What the composite Haggard topography of Africa shows is landscape onto which the desires and fears of an age, through one of its most representative writers, are projected.

AFRICA AS VAST EDEN

Despite the many hardships Haggard's heroes face in Africa, their first apprehension of the land is frequently of a kind of pre-lapsarian paradise.

Quatermain, travelling with Captain Good and Sir Henry Curtis as three intrepid Englishmen, gives voice to this position in Haggard's first successful romance, *King Solomon's Mines*:

> The brook, of which the banks were clothed with dense masses of a gigantic species of maidenhair fern interspersed with feathery tufts of wild asparagus, babbled away merrily at our side, the soft air murmured through the leaves of the silver trees, doves cooed around, and bright-winged birds flashed like living gems from bough to bough. It was like Paradise.
>
> The magic of the place, combined with the overwhelming sense of dangers left behind, and of the promised land reached at last, seemed to charm us into silence. (1992: 109)

Later he repeats this assertion, incorporating a more materialistic eye: "This new land was little less than an earthly paradise; in beauty, in natural wealth, and in climate I have never seen its like" (1992: 126). Two aspects of the "Africa-as-paradise" view emerge here—one is that Africa can be a haven, a tonic, for the world-weary Englishman in an industrial age; and the other is the growing recognition of the land's natural resources, its "wealth," which could be brought to fruition by dint of some hard labour in the not too distant future. Here is Haggard on the potential of the Transvaal, where he promises a nineteenth-century imperial paradise still to come:

> Those plains, too, which for centuries have lain idle and unproductive, will before long supply the greatest corn markets with grain; for, save in some places where water is scarce, the virgin soil is rich beyond comparison. Yes, before us lies the country of the practical future, of the days when the rich man will have his estate in Switzerland to gratify his eyes, and his estate in the Transvaal to fill his pockets. This vast land will one day be the garden of Africa, the land of gems and gold, of oil and corn, of steam-ploughs and railways. It has an assured and a magnificent future. (1899b: 399)

Haggard would contradict himself frequently on this issue of "improving" the land. In his nonfictional works this is his constant theme: the necessity of making something of the "empty" lands in the colonies—but in his romances, he frequently sounds warning notes about the damage to both land and indigenous peoples' ways that such incursions could make. It is a debate between Haggard the Victorian imperialist and Haggard the romance writer that is unresolvable and a mark of "the vulnerability of imperialist and colonialist power.... They [these cultures of domination] are always anxiously regrouping, reinventing, and reinscribing their authority ... against their own internal instability" (Jacobs 1996: 29). The issue of Haggard's view of the "empty" land and possible improvements to it will be taken up more fully later in the chapter, for in the view of "Africa-as-paradise" the industrial age does not normally intrude. Indeed, adventure fiction of the kind Haggard wrote celebrated "a pre-industrial past, and particularly after mid-century, the nostalgia implicit in this fiction fulfilled industrialized reader's desires for Edenic, unspoiled beauty—generally rendered in such explicitly male terms as 'the virgin track,' or 'the unpenetrated forest'—and for an arena for manly, heroic action, uncomplicated by the complex moralities of a modern, democratic world" (White 1995: 62-63).

This is quite clear in an extended passage from *The Ghost Kings*, in which Haggard offers the British reader a picture of Paradise tamed reminiscent of the Baines painting "Bird's eye view of the Victoria Falls from the West," described in chapter 2:

> It was a singularly beautiful spot, for to the east of them, about a mile away, stretched the placid Indian Ocean, while to the west, overshadowing them almost, rose a towering cliff, over which the stream poured itself, looking like a line of smoke against its rocky face. They had outspanned upon a rising hillock at the foot of which this little river wound away like a silver snake till it joined the great Tugela. In its general aspect the country was like an English park, dotted here and there with timber, around which grazed or rested great elands and other buck, and amongst them a huge rhinoceros. (1908a: 44)

Everything is ordered, the animals benign, the grass almost trimmed for the benevolent park owner, who seems to be the reader at the moment of reading. A few pages later, specific reference is made to the scene resembling "the Garden of Eden" and to the unwelcome intrusion of Adam/Ishmael noted by Eve/Rachel Dove in an ironic reversal of the Biblical story. Rachel observes that "he came into our Garden of Eden and shot the buck" (1908a: 49) upsetting the paradisal equilibrium. In this rather heavy-handed, allegorical section, Ishmael, we are reminded, "dwelt in the wilderness . . . and was a wild man whose hand was against every man's" (1908a: 48). He is an Englishman "gone native" in the African paradise, dressed in animal skins and living in a remote stronghold with his native wives. Though in this romance Ishmael's actions make him the villain, "going native" is not always condemned in Paradise— Quatermain is tempted by Mameena in *Nada the Lily*, Good by Foulata in *King Solomon's Mines*, Leo by Ustane in *She* and that epitome of an English gentleman–knight, Sir Henry Curtis, *does* marry Nyleptha and remain as benevolent dictator in "one of the most beautiful stretches of country that the world can show" (1995: 140) in *Allan Quatermain*.

A more complex variation on the Adam/Eve in Paradise theme is extended throughout *Jess* and serves to underscore the political allegory of the tale. A tale, in Haggard's mind, of political shame, since its subject is the retrocession of the Transvaal to the Boers in 1881, *Jess* is cast as an allegorical tale of fated lovers in Paradise lost. In this vein, Rich sees *Jess* as an "interesting reflection of the uncertain state of the white settler mind in the 1880s in South Africa before the major burst of British imperial expansionism in the 1890s leading up to the Anglo-Boer War of 1899-1902" (1984: 125). Written soon after the actual retrocession, the narrative is laden with nostalgia for an earlier, less troubled Eden and a resigned sense of fatalism.[3] The scene in which Captain John Niel spies on Jess Croft asleep in Lion's Kloof is heavy with desire and warning. The virginal Jess is almost hidden in this secluded, secret place by "ferns, the last mostly of the maiden-hair (*Capillas Veneris*) genus" and "thousands upon thousands of white arums ... which were now in full bloom" together with "a bush ... completely covered with masses of the most gorgeous scarlet bloom" (1900a: 48). As Jess' purity, symbolised by the whiteness of the massed arums, is tainted by the physical desire she feels for Niel and he for her—symbolised by the blood-red bush flowers—so is the "divine climate and virgin soil of the Transvaal" (1900a: 113) turned to a sullied wilderness by Britain's shameful retreat:

Then they [Jess and John Niel] up-saddled and went on across the lonely, desolate veldt. No human being did they see all that long day. The wide country was tenanted only by great herds of game that went thundering past like squadrons of cavalry, or here and there by coteries of vultures, hissing and fighting over some dead buck. And so at last the twilight gathered and found them alone in the wilderness. (1900a: 318)

Indeed, Jess is explicitly linked to Eve, when naked, drying her clothes in the sun, she regrets betraying her sister Bessie, also in love with Niel, thus: "The poor girl shook her damp hair over her face and sobbed in the bitterness of her heart, as Eve might have sobbed when Adam reproached her" (1900a: 313). Jess as an outcast in the wilderness has been linked by Rich to Schreiner's Lyndall in *The Story of an African Farm*. Both can be seen as intellectual women ill-fitted to their social surroundings and, given Haggard's appreciation of Schreiner's book, together with their correspondence in 1884 and 1885, it is not inconceivable that Haggard had a figure such as Lyndall in his mind when creating Jess. Rich describes Jess as "an alien figure in the harsh African landscape [who] reflects the uncertain and ultimately tragic status of a thinking female in a colonial society, paralleling Lyndall in *The Story of an African Farm* or even Olive Schreiner's own career" (1984: 124). The only place where Jess is totally "at home" in the novel is in the safe, secret and yet, paradoxically, sexually charged space of Lion's Kloof. As Rice notes, Haggard draws repeatedly on the "myth of Africa as a corrupt Eden," with the Transvaal in particular soon to become wilderness for the English at that time (1981: 1). Jess, Rice maintains, lives in a world of "deep and unresolved inner conflict concerning mortality and the meaning of life for which Africa stands as the metaphor" (1981: 5). In *Jess*, as in *The Story of an African Farm*, the landscape is characterised by "overwhelming intransigence" (1981: 7), though Haggard as romancer, and not realist writer, kept revisiting the site of paradise lost. *Jess* can be read, then, on one level as a cautionary tale of paradise lost—John Niel nearly loses his only chance of domestic contentment with Bessie (fair, sweet) through his sexual and intellectual attraction to Jess, the fallen Eve (dark, moody). Jess is consistently associated with upheaval and the wilderness— whether in Lion's Kloof with its sexual undertones; the war camp in Pretoria; or in "The Palatial" (Haggard and Cochrane's bachelor residence in Pretoria, popularly known as "Jess' Cottage" after Haggard's literary fame was established) where Niel and Jess play at a temporary, illicit domesticity (as Haggard himself might once have done as a young man), in Muller's tent in which Jess murders Muller; and finally in her death in the cave in Lion's Kloof, "her bridal bed" (1900a: 364). Bess, in contrast, is *always* resident at Mooifontein, the paradisal farm, and when it is destroyed by fire, she moves to an even more domesticated space, "a large estate in Rutlandshire" on which Niel is appointed "land agent... which position he fills to this day, with credit in these times" (1900a: 367-368). The last line is Haggard's critique of his own faltering agricultural world in England.

Keeping in mind, however, that *Jess* was written post-1892 when Haggard's spirits both personally and politically were depressed for some period of time, Africa as a less complicated Paradise is most evident in his earlier romances. A typical scene from the "Africa-as-paradise" theme in Haggard encompasses vast lands which are sun-drenched and thundering with huge herds of game. Quatermain waxes lyrical in this passage from "A Tale of Three Lions," in rather purple prose:

The sunny streams babble like Nature's children at his feet; high above him in the purple sunset, are domes and minarets and palaces, such as no mortal man has built, in and out of whose flaming doors the angels of the sun seem to move continually. And there, too, is the wild game, following its feeding-grounds in great armies, with the springbuck thrown out before for skirmishes; then rank upon rank of long-faced blesbuck, marching and wheeling like infantry; and last the shining troops of quagga, and the fierce-eyed shaggy vilderbeeste. (1951: 186)

This is a stage on which the spirit of adventure can be tested and reaffirmed, "an exotic paradisal landscape functioning on colonists as a moral agent that destroys the weak and wicked, but purifies and nurtures the good and the strong in the beauties and richness of its bosom" (Hutchings 1981: 2). Imperialism in Britain in the late nineteenth century provided the context and the motive for the intrepid man to venture out to the colonies and see what he could make of himself in the sun. As Quatermain proudly boasts, "Englishmen are adventurers to the backbone; and all our muster-roll of colonies, each of which will in time become a great nation, testify to the extraordinary value of the spirit of adventure" (1995: 101).

For a nineteenth-century British (white, Christian, male) adventurer to survey the immensity of the paradisal colonial holdings, the preferred position was from a position of vantage, the *bird's-eye view*. Pratt has called this convention, frequently used by nineteenth-century explorers and travel writers, the "monarch-of-all-I-survey scene" (1992: 205-206). The position adopted by the viewer is regal, aloof[4] and powerful for one can see the land passively laid out before one, yet not be seen in any equivalent manner: "Like the supervisor in the Panopticon, the writer who engages this view relies for authority on the analytic arrangement of space from a position of visual advantage. The writer is placed either above or at the center of things, yet apart from them, so that the organisation and classification of things takes place according to the writer's own values" (Spurr 1993: 16-17). The gaze, then, is never neutral, for it always selects and orders what is seen according to the gazer's own preconceptions and desires. Haggard's African romances frequently employ this aerial perspective, which recalls his Zulu name which when translated means, "the tall one who walks on the mountain-tops," as I mentioned earlier. As early as 1875 he used this convention to dramatic effect in a letter home to his mother in which he described the view from Chief Pagate's kraal: "The view is superb; two thousand feet below lies the plain encircled by tremendous hills bush-clad to the very top, while at the bottom flashes a streak of silver which is the river. There is little of what we admire in views in England, but Nature in her wild and rugged grandeur" (1926 vol. 1: 59).

This is a debate that the Olympian gazer in Haggard's African romances frequently repeats: the tension between the two kinds of landscape—the English type, known and already ordered; and the African type, "wild and rugged," attractive yet threatening. Here is the ambivalence again within Haggard. For an imperialist, one way to render the African landscape ordered and "admirable" in a British aesthetic sense is to tame the land (and, by implication, its peoples), yet as a romantic and occasional private doubter of imperialism's aims he wished it to be left in its wild and rugged state. This is evident in these contradictory passages taken from three novels published over two short years: Quatermain in *King Solomon's Mines* pronounces, "To my mind, however beautiful a view may be, it requires the presence of man to make it complete" (1992: 35-36); Niel in *Jess,* looking at the "untamed beauty" of a view, concludes that "however desirable the presence of civilised man might be in the world, it could not be said that his operations really add to its beauty" (1900a: 23); while Quatermain in *Allan Quatermain* asserts from his perch high in a look-out tree, "It is a glorious country, and only wants the hand of civilised man to make it a most productive one" (1995: 57). Involved in the great imperial project, even though only a very junior cog in the vast machinery of Empire, Haggard could see that "improvement," order and progress—the great nineteenth-century watchwords—would ruin the mystery of his landscape of desire: "In scanning projects in the spatial sense—as landscape panoramas—this eye *knows itself* to be looking at prospects in the temporal sense—as possibilities for the future, resources to be developed, landscapes to be peopled or repeopled by Europeans" (Pratt 1985: 125). In Haggard's nonfictional work this is his repeated call—for British people to go to the colonies and make use of the land, but in his romances he is uneasy about the implications this would have for those "safe and secret" places he desired. I will return to this point later on in the chapter.

Generally, however, in the early romances Haggard's use of "a proconsular sweep of vision" (Pierce 1975: 16) is free from the presence of man, civilised or otherwise—excepting of course that of the gazer, who is invisible to himself, and glories in the panorama placed before him for his benefit:

The landscape lay before us like a map, in which rivers flashed like silver snakes, and Alp-like peaks crowned with wildly twisted snow wreaths rose in solemn grandeur, whilst over all was the glad sunlight and the wide breath of Nature's happy life.

Two curious things struck us as we gazed. First, that the country before us must lie at least five thousand feet higher than the desert we had crossed, and secondly, that all the rivers flowed from south to north. (1992: 105)

The voice of manifest Africanism is clear here in the informational details of altitude and river flow direction, together with the classificatory image of the map. Specific geographical detail is provided in a complementary passage in *Allan Quatermain*, describing from an aerial perspective a "wonderful and beautiful lake [which] lay, according to our aneroid, at a height of no less than 11,450 feet above sea-level, and its climate was quite cold, and not at all unlike that of England" (1995: 106-107). Further attempts "to create an illusion of geography, territory and place" (Rodgers 1997: 109) for his fanciful tales were made by Haggard through the device of a literal map, which he provides in *King Solomon's Mines*, and the Sherd of Amenartas in *She*.[5] Yet despite the lengths to which Haggard went to provide a pseudo-scientific, scholarly framework for his romances, he is *also* at pains to keep his terrain within the realm of myth and dream; thus "[f]or his purposes ... the vaguer he was about African geography the better" (Etherington in Haggard 1991: xxiv).

Pierce points to a further ambivalence in Haggard's bird's-eye view scenes written at the moment of late empire. He comments on how the "Olympian situation is never sustained" in Haggard's romances which, he contends, corresponds to "that pessimism which was as important an element of fin-de-siècle imperial feeling as pride of possession or conviction of the right to rule" (1975: 21). Haggard was doubtful of the durability of the British Empire, and thus, while he usually always includes a "monarch-of-all-I-survey" scene in the early stages of his African romances, that dominant position is never sustained. The monarch descends from his lofty position to face hardship on the plains of empire and emerges generally victorious but wiser, never jingoist. This passage from *She* carries a note of the trials that inevitably follow the rush of adrenalin afforded by an aerial view:

It took us an hour and more to cross the cup of the volcano plain, and another half hour or so to climb the edge on the farther side. Once there, however, the view was a very fine one. Before us was a long steep slope of grassy plain, broken here and there by clumps of trees mostly of the thorn tribe. At the bottom of this gentle slope, some nine or ten miles away, we could make out a dim sea of marsh, over which the foul vapours hung like smoke about a city. (Haggard 1991: 79)

She is Haggard's work that most concerns itself with sombre questions of power and the rise and fall of civilisations; therefore such contrasts of aerial and terrestrial positioning are appropriate in their symbolism.

Haggard is unusual among nineteenth-century adventure writers in not only giving bird's-eye view scenes to his white male protagonists but also occasionally to his female and black characters. Neither grouping, however, achieves quite the same majesty of vision or security of tenure as the white man. Otter, who is Leonard Outram's black servant in *The People of the Mist*, is given a panoramic scene to describe, which he does with astonishment as "he was not much given to the study of scenery" ([1894] 1973b: 309), implying perhaps that the indigenous black man does not see the aesthetic or practical value of land in the same way as does the white man. Mopo in *Nada the Lily* is more sensitive to the aesthetic panorama before him but translates it into a prophetic scene of horror: "So I wandered out from the kraal that was named Duguza to the great cleft in the mountains yonder, and sat down upon a rock high up in the cleft, so that I could see the wide lands rolling to the north and the south, to my right and to my left. . . . The sun sank redly, flooding the land with blood; it was as though all the blood that Chaka had shed flowed about the land which Chaka ruled" (1949: 173).

Since he is one of Chaka's subjects, Mopo's elevation here does not afford him power but only anxiety. A scene from *Benita*, in which the heroine of the same name is given a bird's-eye view scene, is fissured with Haggard's ambivalence about women in positions of power. Benita is suggestively placed on a phallic-shaped cone, which exacerbates her precariousness:

It was a dizzy place, for the pillar leaning outwards, its point stood almost clear of the water-scarped rock, so that beneath her was a sheer drop of about four hundred feet to the Zambezi bed. At first the great height made her feel faint. Her eyes swam, and unpleasant tremors crept along her spine, so that she was glad to sink to the floor, whence she knew she could not fall. By degrees, however, she recovered her nerve, and was able to study the glorious view of stream and marshes and hills beyond. ([1906] 1986a: 270)

Benita's ambivalent position closely resembles the "contradictory voices" in Mary Kingsley's travel accounts (discussed in chapter 2) and is deeply symptomatic of the uncertain, changing positions of women in late nineteenth-century England.

AFRICA AS WILDERNESS

If one classic element of Haggard's African topography is Africa as vast sunlit Eden, then another is the theme of Africa as wilderness. The wilderness he draws, however, has both positive and negative elements: in the positive sense, wilderness represents nature as opposed to civilisation; in the negative version wilderness becomes the alienated heart of darkness. To take the positive view of wilderness first, Africa as unspoilt nature offers the jaded, civilised Englishman a chance to recharge his spirits, rediscover himself. Haggard, critical of the new commercial middle classes in pursuit of wealth in England, makes his alter ego Quatermain both constitutionally and ideologically a restless wanderer. At the start of *Allan Quatermain*, the hero who is saddened by his boy's recent death (which similar bereavement was soon to happen to his creator in reality) gives expression to his wanderlust:

The thirst for the wilderness was on me; I could tolerate this place no more; I would go and die as I had lived, among the wild game and the savages. Yes, as I walked, I began to long to see the moonlight gleaming silvery white over the wide veldt and mysterious sea of bush, and watch the lines of game travelling down the ridges to the water . . . no man who has for forty years lived the life I have, can with impunity go coop himself in this prim English country, with its trim hedgerows and cultivated fields, its stiff formal manners, and its well-dressed crowds. He begins to long—ah, how he longs!—for the keen breath of the desert air; he dreams of the sight of Zulu impis breaking on their foes like surf upon the rocks, and his heart rises up in rebellion against the strict limits of the civilised life. (1995: 9-10)

This is a desire-laden passage written by one who had recently left the less restricted life of a settler in a "new" land and was now uneasily adapting himself to a far more circumscribed environment in all ways—politically, physically and mentally. The physical and spiritual limitations of his English life are strikingly captured by his daughter. She writes of his circumstances around the time of the publication of *Allan's Wife* (1889) two years later:

Rider made up his mind that the adventurous part of his life was behind him. That in future his path lay at home, on the small Norfolk estate bordered by the River Waveney and the wide green valley which ran down between the two counties from the town of Bungay to Beccles. In the square Georgian house where his wife had been born, set amidst its shady lawns and beech trees and walled garden. On the little farm consisting of some two hundred and forty acres of heavy land, with its antiquated buildings, neglected pastures and dilapidated fences. Not a very wide or romantic prospect, or very promising material to fill the life of a man of his temperament and ambitions unless he had a political career as well, and that had failed him. (Haggard, L. 1951: 173)

Small wonder—given the number of circumscribing adjectives, "walled," "bordered," "small" and "square" in this passage—that Haggard repeatedly sent his heroes out to Africa to the wilderness to escape such limitations. Occasionally on these adventures, the heroes come across intrepid settler families or missionaries in whose group is a white girl frequently described as a kind of "nature's child" which is meant as a mark of great approval. Flossie Mackenzie in *Allan Quatermain* is the daughter of Scottish missionaries and a "true child of the wilderness" (Haggard 1995: 57) who "had more courage, discretion, and power of mind than many a woman of mature age nurtured in idleness and luxury" (1995: 95). Rachel Dove, similarly a missionary's daughter, is also "nature's child, if in a better and a purer sense than Byron uses that description" (1908a: 42); while Hope in *The Holy Flower*, the daughter of an eccentric American butterfly collector named "Brother John" and his wife Elizabeth, "had grown up a lady in the true sense of the word. After all, why should she not, seeing that her mother, the Bible and Nature had been her only associates and sources of information" (1915: 252). The obvious Christian thread linking these girls lends the wilderness an improving possibility: in the same way that the wilderness can "improve" civilised man, so can it provide an uncluttered, natural environment for a young girl to grow up in, provided, of course, she remains within her nuclear Christian family. This is a clear set of double standards, unavoidable given the mores of the age—the essence of the English male adventurer in the wilderness is his lack of formal ties both secular and religious; whereas the white female generally does not have such latitude. To do Haggard justice, however, he does allow certain of his white female characters a chance to challenge the wilderness—witness Rachel's travels to the land of the Ghost Kings and Benita's adventurers with the Bambatse.

The great positive virtue then of the wilderness is the potential it offers for adventure. In its most recreational form, adventure for the hero involves hunting wild animals in which the wilderness abounds: "Haggard's novels set in Africa tend to treat the continent as a vast nobleman's park [6] teaming with game, big and little, waiting to be shot. While the slaughter of wildlife in *She* is mild compared with that in *King Solomon's Mines* and *Allan Quatermain*, the eye of Haggard's imagination is ever alert for wild game" (Etherington in Haggard 1991: 224).

While I would disagree with Etherington's description of the passivity of the animals (for the whole point of a hunting adventure is that the quarry must be dangerous and therefore render the action exciting), there is no doubt as to the "slaughter" in Haggard's wilderness. What in the 1990s is environmental carnage is for Haggard and his readers a hundred years ago is a good "bag" for the day. The following elephant hunt from *King Solomon's Mines* is typical of many such passages in Haggard's romances: "Now was our opportunity, and firing away as quick as we could load we killed five of the poor beasts, and no doubt should have bagged the whole herd had they not suddenly given up their attempts to climb the bank and rushed headlong down the nullah. We were too tired to follow them, and perhaps also a little sick of slaughter, eight elephants being a pretty good bag for one day" (1992: 60). It must be noted, however, that in later life Haggard turned his back on hunting saying that "the destruction of the lower animals for the sake of sport, has become abominable to me" (1926 vol. 2: 105), and indeed published an anti-blood sports novella *The Mahatma and the Hare* in 1911; but this is certainly not apparent in the early romances in which hunting is clearly relished, as the above passage attests.

The wilderness, however, has a negative aspect, and that is the varying difficulty and hazards of the terrain that the hero must overcome before achieving the purpose of his quest. Haggard's inventiveness knew no bounds in the construction of obstacles to be conquered, as they always are, in his African romances. The movement of the hero is always from the known and the British—whether "Home" or a British settlement on the coast—to the unknown African interior. On one level, the journey is an arduous physical one in which several African helpers may lose their lives, and on another level it is a psychological test of nerves for the Englishman. It is "a trek from the known into the unconscious unknown self" where the characters move "progressively through a symbolic landscape from physical tests to moral tests" (Etherington 1978: 76-77). The journey usually leads backwards in time as in this primordial scene from *She*:

> To the right and left were wide stretches of lonely death-breeding swamp, unbroken and unrelieved so far as the eye could reach, except here and there by ponds of black and peaty water that, mirror-like, flashed up the red rays of the setting sun... And then ourselves—three modern Englishmen in a modern English boat—seeming to jar upon and look out of tone with that measureless desolation. (1991: 47)

The travellers struggle through deserts, swamps, mountains, plains teeming with dangerous animals and inhospitable tribes, and the movement is "northward, ever northward" (1908a: 277). By the time of one of Haggard's post-1892 romances, *The People of the Mist* (1894), the perilous voyage had become for the writer rather hackneyed: thus in the space of two pages a synopsis of a journey lasting twelve weeks is given, and it summarises the kinds of perils the intrepid Englishman would have to undergo: Leonard Outram, a disinherited Englishman, accompanied by Juanna, daughter of a British trader, her maid Soa as guide/chaperone and the faithful Otter, shoot rapids, march through "a land uninhabited by man, the home of herds of countless game," "northward and upward through a measureless waste," scale an "unexplored plateau that separates southern from central Africa" where "the loneliness was awful," survive fever, starvation, enter a lion-infested forest, walk for seven days "through a plain strewn with sharp stones," then cover miles of a "dreary rolling veldt" and finally arrive at "a huge cliff... a thousand feet in height," which marks their arrival at the home of the People of the Mist (1973b: 146-147).

In *Allan's Wife*, this challenging terrain is allegorically called the "Bad Lands," "a great expanse of desolate land, stretching further than the eye could reach, and bordered far away by a line of purple hills.... To look back on it is like a nightmare" (1951: 77-78). This extract hints at not only the physical, but also the psychological strain that Quatermain undergoes in the early romances, and certainly that Leo and Holly undergo in *She*. "Africa-as-wilderness" in this sense signifies the challenge darkest Africa afforded to the Victorians: "As the Victorian mind tried to ground itself in its role as the colonizer of the 'new' lands, it was threatened with the abysses, cliffs, swamps and sands, not only of the southern lands it was colonizing, but of its own psyche" (Carter in Darian-Smith et al. 1996: 3).

Remarkably, the hero always overcomes these hardships, generally to return to Britain—though *Allan Quatermain* breaks the pattern that Haggard was later to stick to, as Sir Henry Curtis remains in Zu-Vendis to rule with Queen Nyleptha, and Quatermain dies in Zu-Vendis at the book's end. The returning adventurer is often filled with nostalgia for the wilderness he has left, despite its dangers. Brother John (*The Holy Flower*) back in England "spends a lot of his time wandering about the New Forest... trying to imagine that he is back in Africa" (1915: 319), while John Niel, back in Britain with the placid

Bessie, yearns instead for Jess, who is the tragic outsider, the loner, symbolised in the following extract by the freedom of the remembered (African) night skies:

> He is not a man much addicted to sentiment or speculation, but sometimes when his day's work is done, and he strays to his garden gate and looks out at the dim and peaceful English landscape beyond, and thence to the wide star-strewn heavens above, he wonders if the hour will ever come when once more he will see those dark and passionate eyes, and hear that sweet remembered voice. (1900a: 308)

To keep the wilderness, especially in its negative aspect, at bay, Haggard's African topography frequently features *the enclosure*. The small cultivated patch of ground in the midst of the wilderness is a feature of Haggard's African romances, as it is indeed of other colonial writers' works, in which the garden, bearing powerful connotations of paradise and order, is shown in sharp contrast to the turbulence beyond. Boehmer describes this feature in colonial writing as the creation in the fruitful but wild colonial lands of "a whole collection of green spots ... replicas of the Kentish garden county" (1995: 53). The symbolic value of the garden, the cultivated land, as a victory of civilisation/order over wilderness/chaos is thus evident: "Nature is neutralised in the garden to become an object of detached contemplation. The garden is not, has never been, a product of nature but a *symbolic structure of meaning*. In the post-lapsarian world, the garden is the return of nature through art" (Pugh 1988: 103, my emphasis).

Garden making is an attempt to impose a structure upon an existing topography, to change a small corner of it to suit oneself. Haggard, by all accounts, was an enthusiastic gardener both at home and in Africa—his daughter comments on this in her description of her father at "The Palatial," also known as "Jess' Cottage," the small house that he and Cochrane shared during the British occupation of Pretoria: "Rider, being Rider, at once made a garden, planted roses, and a vineyard in front, and a screen of blue gums around it. He also wrote to his mother asking her to send him nuts and acorns from his favourite beech and oak trees in the park at Bradenham, so that he might grow 'English trees'" (Haggard, L. 1951: 75).[7]

The largely autobiographical *The Witch's Head* has the main character Ernest Kershaw (Haggard) described in similar vein: "Even if he only stopped a month in a place he would start a little garden: it was a habit of his" (1890: 336). Ironically, despite Haggard's frequently voiced dissatisfaction with England and its "trim hedgerows and cultivated fields" (1995: 9), it is mostly an English kind of garden that he creates in the Africa which he valued for its freedom from constraints. Ideologically, perhaps one could say that this is another manifestation of the contradiction between Haggard the public imperialist and the private doubter—while he yearned for Africa to remain untouched and unspoiled, he contrived to create an artfully natural English spot for himself within it. Of course while England was in control of the

Transvaal, things were for Haggard as they should have been, politically speaking. Thus the garden of "The Palatial" is a cornucopia of plenty: "The grounds themselves were planted with vines, just now loaded with bunches of ripening grapes, and surrounded with a beautiful hedge of monthly roses that formed a blaze of bloom. Near the house, too, was a bed of double roses, some of them exceedingly beautiful, and all flowering with a profusion unknown in this country. Altogether it was a delightful little spot, and . . . seemed perfectly heavenly" (1900a: 169-170). Returning to this same garden in 1914 as part of the Royal Commission investigating the state of the Dominions, with the Transvaal long returned to the Boers, the Anglo-Boer wars and Zulu Wars now past, all of which Haggard felt dated back to poor political decisions in Britain, Haggard's words on his garden seem symbolic of promise wasted:

The garden is a terrible sight, a mere tangle, the whole two acres of it. Of the vines we planted only one or two survive climbing up trees. The roses are all gone . . . Standing among those noxious growths I seemed to forget all the intervening years and grow young again. I saw the walls rising. I saw the sapling gums, the infant vines and the new planted roses and gardenias . . . I went away with a sad heart. Oh! Where are they who used to pass in and out through that humble gate? (1914a: 87-88; 2000: 130)

A more sudden dilapidation overtakes another type of enclosure in *Jess*: the farmhouse of Mooifontein, the fictional version of Haggard's first marital home, Hilldrop. Both Pocock's description of Hilldrop and Haggard's fictional version of Mooifontein have already been referred to, together with comments on Haggard's unconscious sexualising of the scene and references to the civilisation/wilderness theme on which I will now expand. It is a picture of plenty and order, again "a delightful spot," a haven of productivity:

All along its front ran a wide verandah, up the trellis-work of which green vines and blooming creepers trailed pleasantly, and beyond was the broad carriage-drive of red soil, bordered with bushy orange-trees laden with odorous flowers and green and golden fruit. On the farther side of the orange-trees were the gardens, fenced in with low walls of rough stone, and the orchard full of standard fruit trees, and beyond these again the oxen and ostrich kraals, the latter full of long-necked birds. To the right of the house grew thriving plantations of blue-gum and black wattle, and to the left was a broad stretch of cultivated lands, lying so that they could be irrigated for winter crops by means of water led from the great spring that gushed from the mountain-side high above the house, and gave its name of Mooifontein to the house. (1900a: 22-23)

Everything has its place, with Silas Croft, the owner-farmer, as benevolent dictator over the whole.[8] The picture is pre-lapsarian and recalls Haggard's own pride in his achievements at Hilldrop in brickmaking and haymaking, and his early domestic happiness with his new bride and first-born child, the precious Jock: "The presence of the white man [Silas Croft] domesticates the wild country into a safe pastoral one; here a man may live and work like an original Adam, creating and refashioning an Eden—trapped in a time warp—to his own image" (Low 1996: 38). Yet neither the idyll at Mooifontein nor at Hilldrop could last. Croft's farm is burnt down by the Boers as part of the Boer uprising against the British in the Transvaal following retrocession, and the Haggards felt forced to leave Hilldrop for fear of an imminent Anglo-Boer outbreak. Both Silas Croft and Haggard leave South Africa in the belief that, at that point politically, "this is no country for Englishmen" (1900a: 367) and return reluctantly to England.

It must be remembered however, that *Jess* is not a pure romance but for Haggard "a bit of history put into tangible and human shape" (1926 vol. 1: 265), in other words, an historical romance. This is evident in his use of landscape which, while used allegorically, is also rooted in autobiographical reality. Thus "while using a number of romance modes in *Jess* . . . Haggard still anchored the novel in a solid South African terrain in a manner different from his more commonly known romances" (Rich 1984: 125). In *Allan Quatermain* and *Allan's Wife*, for instance, the enclosures brought to the foreground are less obviously rooted in Haggard's own history and more closely allied to the ideals of romance "commonly symbolized by some kind of paradise or park like the biblical Eden, a world in which a humanity greatly reduced in numbers has become reconciled to nature" (Frye 1976: 172). Yet despite their origins in Haggard's fancy, their ideological implications remain rooted in the late nineteenth-century preoccupation with Africa. Both enclosures mentioned—the Mackenzie mission station in *Allan Quatermain* at which Quatermain rests on his way to Zu-Vendis, and the Carson compound in *Allan's Wife* where Quatermain meets his wife, Stella—have their origins in the desire for colonial settlement in Africa, the idea of colonial land "as property, and with it inevitably the appropriation and enclosure of land" (Young 1995: 172).[9]

The Mackenzie mission station is reached after a ten-day trek inland from Lamu, an island off Kenya, and a perilous canoe trip up the Tana River in which Quatermain, Sir Henry Curtis, Good and Umslopogaas are attacked by murderous Masai tribesmen. The first view of the Mackenzie family marks them as separate from the wilderness that Quatermain and company have just struggled through: "A gentleman, a lady, and a little girl . . . walking in a civilised fashion through a civilised garden, to meet us in this place" (1995: 40). They then proceed to the mission enclosure, which is in microcosm a British paradise in Africa, a British protectorate hierarchically organised and feudally arranged. On the lower slopes of the hill (for the topography mirrors the power relations) are the "Kaffir gardens" full of indigenous crops of mealies, pumpkins, potatoes and also containing "neat mushroom shaped huts" whose occupants come "pouring out" to greet the visitors. The road up the hill is lined with orange trees "positively laden with golden fruit." As an aside, Haggard pursues a level of informational discourse typical of Africanism by letting the reader know the altitude: "about 5,000 feet above the coastline level" on the "uplands below Mt. Kenia," stressing the incredible productivity of the soil and climate. Higher up the hill the party is shown a "splendid quince fence," which marks the border with Mackenzie's private enclosure within which is his "private garden," church and house (1995: 41). This garden is symbolically far more English than the African gardens lower down. Quatermain, no doubt speaking for Haggard, exclaims:

> I have always loved a good garden, and I could have thrown up my hands for joy when I saw Mr. Mackenzie's. First there were rows upon rows of standard European fruit-trees, all grafted; for on the top of this hill the climate was so temperate that very nearly all the English vegetables, trees and flowers flourished luxuriantly... strawberries and tomatoes (such tomatoes!) and melons and cucumbers, and, indeed, every sort of vegetable and fruit. (1995: 41)

Protecting this enclosure is Mr. Mackenzie's "magnum opus," a huge ditch and wall that took him and "twenty natives" two years to dig and to construct. The effort was worth it, for Mackenzie says "I never felt safe till it was done; and now I can defy all the savages in Africa" (1995: 42). The image of the manor complete with moat and drawbridge is sustained by the method of entry into the inner sanctum—the party crosses "over a plank and through a very narrow opening in the wall," which seems a very much tamed and domestic version of the crossing over the chasm into the place of the Fire of Life in *She*. This small opening leads immediately to Mrs. Mackenzie's "domain—namely, the flower garden" filled significantly with "roses, gardenias, or camellias (all reared from seeds or cuttings sent from England)." Flossie, the Mackenzie daughter, has a little "patch" devoted to indigenous plants, "some of which were surpassingly beautiful." Quatermain's interest in one in particular, the Goya lily whose beauty is fabled, sends Flossie off on an expedition to procure him one that ends in her being kidnapped by the Masai. The Mackenzie house is "massively built" but unremarkable. The whole enclosure is dominated by a vast phallic fir tree, "a beautiful tapering brown pillar without a single branch" for seventy feet whereafter the top boughs offer shade to the house. Mackenzie uses this tree as his "watch tower" as it affords a bird's-eye view of terrain within "fifteen miles or so" (1995: 42-43). This enclosure is evidence of the wilderness tamed and mastered within its borders, yet ever vigilant for the possibility of attack from without. It marks a triumph of English planning implemented by black African labour and aided by the natural fertility of the soil together with temperate climate. It is at one level Haggard's and Empire's dream of making the wilderness into a Garden of Eden now lost at "home," yet it is also a dream that cuts across the latent desire for a free, uncivilised wilderness to escape the confinements of that same "home":

> Yet there is an ambivalence and contradictory movement in Haggard's version of the African pastoral. On the one hand, Africa is represented within the Judaeo-Christian myth of the garden as the place where the original perfection of man can be recovered; on the other, Africa is also presented as an anti-garden where man's presence in the landscape merely heralds impending corruption. (Low 1996: 39-40)

The enclosure at Baboon Head in *Allan's Wife* is hierarchical in a manner similar to the Mackenzie compound, with Mr. Carson at the head, accompanied by Stella, Quatermain's future wife. Though it has no moat surrounding it, Quatermain has to struggle through the appropriately named "Bad Lands" to reach the Carson settlement, which is "embraced . . . in the arms of the mountain" that backs it. Again, the settlement is arranged in tiers with the "Kaffir kraals, built in orderly groups" on the lowest level and the Carson dwellings higher up surrounded by the ubiquitous groves of orange trees. The dwellings, shaped like beehive huts, are built of "blocks of hewn marble" by an ancient people. At this point the Editor figure breaks in with a learned footnote about ruins of such kraals being found in the "Marico district of the Transvaal," built necessarily by "a white race who understood building in stone and at right angles" for "it required more than Kaffir skill to erect the stone huts." Haggard's African landscapes are littered with ruins of ancient white civilisations, as I shall show later; suffice it to say here that these white marble structures, because built by an ancient white race, validate Carson's own dominance in this enclosure. Again there is a "beautifully planted" garden with "many European vegetables and flowers" growing in it. All in all, it is "the best farm I have ever seen in Africa" created again by British initiative and planning, African labour and "marvellous soil and climate." Carson says, "I found this spot a wilderness" after "renouncing civilization"; in Africa he has created something rather more idealistic than Mackenzie, whose enclosure is described in rather more prosaic terms than Carson's quasi-spiritual realm. Carson is known as the chief of the "Children of Thomas," a labouring force of about a thousand Africans, and the farm is run on a cooperative basis, with Carson reserving "only a tithe of the produce" (1951: 91-101).

This is Haggard's vision of the muscular Christianity that he was to encourage in his positive report on the Salvation Army settlements in the United States in *The Poor and the Land* (1905), and which he would repeat in *The After War Settlement and Employment of Ex-Servicemen* (1916). The African wilderness could be made to yield up its bounty by dint of planning and labour, could be held back from these hard-working small fiefdoms even at the risk of relinquishing some of the exhilarating yet threatening freedom promised by the wilderness of latent Africanism.

AFRICA AS DREAM UNDERWORLD

Bhabha refers to Said's Orientalism as "on the one hand, a topic of learning, discovery, practice; on the other, it is the site of dreams, images, fantasies, myths, obsessions," which is given further specificity by Said's use of the terms "manifest" Orientalism to describe the first option Bhabha offers above, and the term "latent" Orientalism to describe the second. The split between these two strands (though they overlap) within Orientalism Bhabha finds analogous to "the dreamwork" (Bhabha 1994: 71), which refers to the split between a person's conscious intentions/actions and unconscious desires, frequently manifested in the shape of dreams. I have already noted that in the discourse of Africanism there are similar manifest and latent strands and that these are evident in Haggard's African romances. Within Haggard's African topography, the latent strand of desire underpins the whole. This is quite evident in the kind of dream underworld featured in many of his romances, together with many references to a kind of altered dream state that the protagonist enters into prior to entering this underworld: "Over and over Haggard's adventurers liken their experiences to dreams as they leave the actual geography of Africa ... for landscapes that obviously have more affinity to the world of fantasy than the real one" (Brantlinger 1988: 246).

Quatermain, lying face down in a canoe shooting along an underground river in pitch darkness, recalls that the experience seemed "faint and unreal. Indeed, the whole thing overpowered my brain, and I began to believe that I was the victim of some ghostly spirit-shaking nightmare" (1995: 111). In a later romance, Quatermain again takes a canoe trip on a river, aptly named the Black River, which acts as a conduit between the known and unknown world, and again he slips into a dream-like trance: "an impression of nightmare stole over me; I felt as though I were a sleeper taking part in the drama of a dream. ... It was a haunted sleep, however, for I dreamed that I was entering into some dim Hades where all realities had been replaced by shadows, strengthless but alarming ... I began to think or dream that I must be dead and waiting for my next incarnation" (1972: 101-102). Holly enters the Kingdom of Kôr asleep in a litter carried by Amahagger bearers and awakes into a dream landscape, a "strange spot" (1991: 56), while Quatermain asserts in *The Holy Flower*: "Still, I hold that all this is a phantasy; that we live in a land of dream in which nothing is real except those things which we cannot see or touch or hear" (1915: 156).

In his autobiography, Haggard described a recurring set of what he called "dream-pictures" (1926 vol. 2: 167-172), pictures which came to him "between sleeping and waking," an ambivalent time when one hovers between two states. He ascribes the origin of his dream-pictures to either a memory of a previous incarnation or a "racial" ancestral memory or an overworked "subconscious imagination." Of the five *tableaux vivants* he describes, one is set in ancient Britain, one in sub-Saharan Africa, and one in Egypt, while the other two do not have clearly identifiable settings. Haggard describes these dream-visions in detail, showing his and the nineteenth century's interest in what would have been called spiritualism or mysticism, leaving the reader, however, with a cautionary note about dabbling in such matters: "But it is at best a dangerous sea to travel before the time. The swimmer therein will do well to keep near to this world's sound and friendly shore lest the lights he sees from the crest of those bewildering, phantom waves should madden or blind him, and he sink, never to rise again. It is not good to listen for too long to the calling of those voices wild and sweet" (1926 vol. 2: 172)

It was a warning he did not heed, at least in his African romances, which accounts in part for the success of his tales—his dream landscapes, which are so modern in their air of alienation, fragmentation and sexual anxiety, struck a chord in his readers, themselves at the end of one century and age, and nervously looking towards the next. Gilbert and Gubar attribute Haggard's success with the "dreamlike story" of *She* to the fact that it was "as if he had been narrating their own dreams for them and to them" (1989: 25). They see the kingdom of Kôr as an outpost of death's dream kingdom in its threats to dismantle the "living empire of England" (1989: 22) while Cornelia Brunner, a pupil of Jung's, describes *She* as successful because it so clearly portrayed Haggard's anima, through which he acted as "a mediator for the urgent, yet still unconscious, problems of his time" (quoted in Manthorpe 1996: 148). Jung had suggested to Brunner that she study *She*, which particularly interested him as it was written in longhand, in a blistering six weeks and was thus for him a fascinating example of a dream-text with the anima dominant. Both Freud and Jung used the language of landscape to describe features of the human psyche and strategies to understand the mind's workings—dreams being for Freud the "royal road to the unconscious"—and both saw in Haggard's dream landscapes a means to understanding not only the man but his age.[10]

The dream landscapes in which Haggard's characters find themselves "recall the dream visions of sleep" (Etherington in Haggard 1991: xxxv) based on, yet also different from, any known African environment. The dream landscape may be paradisal, as is the one Holly first sees when awakening from his sleep in the litter: "Before us was a vast cup of green from four to six miles in extent, in the shape of a Roman amphitheatre. The sides of this great cup were rocky, and clothed with bush, but the centre was of the richest meadow land, studded with single trees of magnificent growth, and watered by meandering brooks. On this rich plain grazed herds of goats and cattle" (1991: 56). This is a scene that simultaneously recalls pastoral Arcadia and a nineteenth-century imperial dream of Africa, an oasis surrounded by the wilderness, as the word "cup" implies. As Etherington points out, the access to this dream landscape is through a rocky defile, a device often used by Haggard "to mark a passage into the land where fantastic things happen" (1991: 218). A similar emergence from a rocky cleft into an oasis-like arena occurs in *Allan's Wife*, where Quatermain and the child Tota, searching for Stella, who has been kidnapped, come upon "an extraordinary scene":

We were in a great natural amphitheatre, only it was three times the size of any amphitheatre ever shaped by man, and the walls were formed of precipitous cliffs, ranging from one to two hundred feet in height. For the rest, the space thus enclosed was level, studded with park-like trees, brilliant with flowers, and having a stream running through the centre of it, that, as I afterwards discovered, welled up from the ground at the head of the open space. (1951: 143-144)

Again there is the cup-like protectorate, this time reminiscent of an English park in the summer. More often than not, however, the dream landscape is not paradisal but rather nightmarish, corresponding to Frye's "demonic or night world," as I shall now demonstrate.

Instead of the sunlit plains of the aboveground world, Haggard's dream landscape more frequently creates *a nightworld of underground caves and tunnels*. In *Allan Quatermain* it is the journey to Zu-Vendis that illustrates empire's nightmare. Instead of the adventurers in a sense "swallowing the world," an assumption of their right to do so, they endure "the nightmare of being swallowed by the world's dark places" (Brantlinger 1988: 246-247). Their trip on the underground river in total darkness is a deathly experience: "rushing along, as we were, through the bowels of the earth, borne on the bosom of a Stygian river, something after the fashion of souls being ferried by Charon" (1995: 114). The next ordeal they encounter is the terrifying Rose of Fire, a jet of ignited gas shooting up through the water. Even in his trance-like state, Quatermain speculates in a scholarly way that the lethal jet before them is probably the result of "some spontaneous explosion of mephitic gases" (118). Then the explorers encounter a recurring Haggardian terror: the river emerges to run between "two frightful cliffs which cannot have been less than two thousand feet high" casting the whole scene in dense gloom with deathly imagery: "Here and there ... grew ghostly patches of long grey lichen, hanging motionless to the rock as the white beard to the chin of a dead man" (119). This rocky abyss is populated by giant crabs, which attack Quatermain's company and then fall upon each other. In an interesting passage, Quatermain describes them thus: "Strange as it may seem to say so, there was something so shockingly human about these fiendish creatures—it was as though all the most evil passions and desires of man had got into the shell of a magnified crab and gone mad" (1995: 122).

Curtis echoes this same comparison in his anti-imperialist speech at the book's end, in which he argues for the "total exclusion of all foreigners from Zu-Vendis" in the interests of maintaining "the blessings of comparative barbarism." He says:

I have no fancy for handing over this beautiful country to be torn and fought for by speculators, tourists, politicians and teachers, whose voice is as the voice of Babel, just as those horrible creatures in the valley of the underground river tore and fought for the body of the wild swan; nor will I endow it with the greed, drunkenness, new diseases, gunpowder, and general demoralisation which chiefly mark the progress of civilisation amongst unsophisticated peoples. (1995: 281-282)

It is a passage in which Haggard's contradictory imperialist leanings are evident—on the one hand, Haggard exhorted his countrymen to settle in the colonies, and yet he lamented the changes that the inevitable culture clash would bring. The irony, of course, is that Curtis is himself a "foreigner" in Zu-Vendis, but because he is an English gentleman he is unquestionably the right person to rule the locals and to protect them from other "foreigners" such as he. This is a scenario slightly different from the ending of *King Solomon's Mines*, which ends on a similarly anti-imperialist and anti-materialist note but leaves Kukuanaland in charge of Umbopa/Ignosi who, however, "has many of the qualities of the English gentleman—honour, dignity and courage" (Street

1975: 59). Haggard, like many of his English readers, deplored the crass commercialism of his times and yearned imaginatively to escape to a simpler, unsullied place and age where a new start could be made. This is what he creates in *Allan Quatermain*, which has been read by some as an "allegor[y] of imperialism" and as a "literary symptom of cultural neurosis" (Christie, Hutchings and Maclennan 1980: 20,23). The nightmare journey to this haven also carries allegorical overtones and corresponds to the first main stage of Frye's analysis of the romance—the perilous journey. In this sense the rose of fire, the burning river, then the black cliffs and crabs correspond to "a kind of purgatory before the entry into the Paradise of Zu-Vendis" (Bursey 1972: 116-117), a test in which both mind and body are tested to prove them worthy. That they are worthy is confirmed by the paradisal dawn that greets them after they are reborn out of the dark tunnel, with the sun depicted as a bridegroom who "embraced the night and covered her with brightness, and it was day" (1995: 124).

The nightmare journey in *Allan Quatermain* might lead to a place of life and promise as in Zu-Vendis, but frequently in Haggard's topography it leads to a place of death and uncertainty. In *The People of the Mist*, the journey leads the Europeans to "a haunted land" (1973b: 152) while in the little known *Black Heart and White Heart*, the two protagonists of the title, enter the Home of the Dead forest, which is a rotten Eden: "It was a gloomy place indeed; great wide-topped trees grew thick there shutting out the sight of the sky; moreover, the air in it which no breeze stirred, was heavy with the exhalations of rotting foliage. There seemed to be no life here and no sound—only now and again a loathsome spotted snake would uncurl itself and glide away, and now and again a rotten bough fell with a crash" (1903a: 27).

However, the most frequently used locus in Haggard for the imperialist nightmare of being swallowed up is the cave. Though I will concentrate on the use of caves in *King Solomon's Mines* and *She*, there are caves of terror in many of Haggard's romances. Nearly all are womb-shaped, reached via a vagina-like tunnel, but all are wombs of death and destruction to be escaped from with all possible haste. In *Allan's Wife*, Stella is imprisoned in a "small cave, shaped like a pickle bottle and coming to a neck at the top end" where it is stoppered by a hymen-like boulder, access to which is gained via a "narrow, water-worn passage" (1951: 144-145). Nada dies of starvation and madness in a cave the entrance to which is between "the knees of the Old Witch" (1949: 282), unable to shift the boulder that seals the cave. There is no joy for the fated lovers Umslopogaas and Nada in this womb-shaped cave, but only joy in the masculine arena of battle which, in comparison to matters of the heart, is uncomplicated. Umslopogaas and Galazi yearn to "one day find a land where there are no women [and no treacherous caves?], and war only, for in that land we shall grow great" (1949: 285-286). Quatermain in *Heu Heu* squeezes through a cave's very small "opening" within the "lips" of which "was a narrow tunnel." He closely avoids falling into "a great chasm in the floor of the tunnel" (1972: 19) but in his near fall loses his front tooth. The cave he reaches houses a rock painting of the monster, which is a grotesque version of Neanderthal man—"The brow, however, was disproportionate to the rest of the face, being prominent, massive and not unintellectual" (1972: 29).

This passage echoes part of Darwin's legacy to the late nineteenth century: the fear of humankind's origins in bestiality and thus the displacement of such fear onto other, darker races. Haggard's Darwinian monster is all the more fearful because it is an intelligent monster, capable therefore of surprising humankind, here in the shape of Quatermain. Caves are also evident in *Wisdom's Daughter,* written to narrate Ayesha's life prior to *She,* and again the rock becomes flesh: "We climbed up a cleft in that wall and entered a hidden fold of rock; invisible from below. Following this fold we came to the mouth of a cave" (1923: 219). This cave is the last dwelling place of the seer Noot, who is guarded by "some gnome from the Under-World appointed by the Powers which ruled in that dark place" (1923: 221). The caves in *Benita* start above ground and are located at the base of the phallic cone of granite within the Bambatse fortress. They contain the mummified dead Portuguese missionaries and their followers, dead for three hundred years but some still well preserved.

King Solomon's Mines has caves both above and below ground. The frozen, preserved corpse of Dom José da Silvestra, together with his treasure map drawn in his own blood, is found in a high-altitude cave located on "the springing slope of the nipple" (1992: 95) of one of Sheba's mountain breasts. Ventvögel, "the poor Hottentot" (1992: 101), unlike the Europeans, is unable to withstand the rigours of the night spent within the cave, but the others proceed through various adventures, the most testing of which take place in the subterranean mines and caves of King Solomon. These caves pose a great threat to Quatermain, Curtis and Good because they are not only a literal Place of Death, being the burying place of the Kukuana kings, but also a place of psychological disorientation:

We were buried in the bowels of a huge snow-clad peak. Thousands of feet above us the fresh air rushed over the white snow, but no sound of it reached us. We were separated by a long tunnel and five feet of rock even from the awful chamber of the dead; and the dead make no noise. The crashing of all the artillery of earth and heaven could not have come to our ears in our living tomb. We were cut off from all echoes of the world—we were as already dead. (1992: 286-287)

In true adventure story fashion, Gagool the witch has shown the three white men their dreams—the treasure consisting of masses of ivory, old gold coin and chests of uncut diamonds, which will make them "the richest men in the whole world" (1992: 278)—and their nightmares, firstly in the form of the grisly spectacle of the stalactite dead kings seated around the table, and secondly in the form of their own imminent demise. British courage and strength in pulling open the stone trapdoor lead them down a passage where they briefly fall into an "African Styx" (1992: 296) and then into a close tunnel from which they push their way out: "Suddenly something gave and we were all rolling over and over and over through grass and bushes, and soft, wet soil" (1992: 297). McClintock sees this an "an extraordinary fantasy of male birthing, culminating in the regeneration of white manhood" (1995: 248).

In addition to their regenerated state, Quatermain had prudently filled his pockets with diamonds, thus ensuring their fortunes. The first diamond in South Africa was discovered in 1867, precipitating a great rush of interest in South Africa and its riches; thus *King Solomon's Mines* within its story answers the British readers' avid anticipation of the treasure to be found in Africa, together with the nightmare vision of entrapment in the Dark Continent through greed. In the diamond mines, the diamonds are conveniently there for the taking, already dug out of the soil by long-ago hands, masking the effort that lies behind their excavation. The British adventurers through their courage and intelligence have earned the right to take what is lying about in the caves that have been conquered, although they almost die in their efforts.

Hofmeyr describes the cave in adventure tales set in Africa as "the heart and 'essence' of Africa, which becomes both extraterrestrial and subterranean" (1980: 200), and thus it seems appropriate that *She*, which contains the most extensive reference in Haggard's works to caves, should be set in the land of Kôr, "which suggests various connotations (core, coeur, Cora; the centre, the seat of passion, and [Kore] the queen of the underworld)" (Bristow 1991: 140). It is also a place of death, as the numberless mummies in Ayesha's caves attests, with one in particular—the body of Kallikrates, Ayesha's lover of old—held in especial reverence. Haggard's reflections on his boy Jock's death seem preempted in his most famous character Ayesha and her morbid longing for the dead: [11] "There is no human passion like the passion for the dead; none so awful, none so holy, none so changeless. For they have become eternal, and our desire for them is sealed with the stamp of their eternity" (Haggard, L. 1951: 156-157).

What could be called Haggard's necrophilia is everywhere evident in Ayesha's domain in the subterranean caves. From the cup-like plain, Leo and Holly ascend to "the mouth of a tremendous cave, measuring about sixty feet in height by eighty wide," which is the beginning of a "vast catacombs." This first cavern in covered with bas-relief sculptures depicting various gruesome Amahagger practices and contains columns inscribed with markings that look "Chinese" in part (1991: 89-91). The allusion to foreign non-African civilisations and their ruins in Africa is a favourite Haggard device, which will be discussed later. Ayesha shows Holly a vast cave that is a giant "charnel-house, being literally full of thousands of human skeletons, which lay piled up in an enormous gleaming pyramid, formed by the slipping down of the bodies at the apex as fresh ones were dropped in from above" (1991: 122). These "grotesquely horrible caricatures of humanity" were all victims of a great epidemic, hence their jumbled condition. Holly is taken into other smaller, interleading caves to see some of the many embalmed dead wrapped in linen.

shown a mother and child: "So sweet was the sight although so awful, that
⌐fess it without shame—I could scarcely withhold my tears," and a pair of
vers, "Wedded in Death," among other examples of the embalmer's art (122-
24). Holly is led around the embalming room, together with its grisly illustrations, and gives a long, learned footnote on the tree that is the source of the embalming fluid. Perhaps the most perverse example of this book's fascination with death and the dead is the Amahagger use of mummies as individual flaming torches to light up an entertainment put on for Leo and Holly. Holly informs the reader that each corpse took "about twenty minutes" to burn down, after which "the feet were kicked away" and another installed (146).

Haggard's use of such precise detail and the amount of space he allows to lengthy descriptions of this vast mausoleum of caves points to a morbid fascination with death, even prior to Jock's death. He ascribes to Holly his own contradictory mix of attraction and repulsion to death when he gives Holly these words: "There was something very terrible, and yet very fascinating, about the employment of the remote dead to illumine the orgies of the living; in itself the thing was a satire, both on the living and the dead" (1991: 145). Bhabha describes Haggard's necrophilia as a sign of "disturbance" within the narrative, an "estrangement" between the book's authority and its underlying tensions. There is a basic ambivalence in such a moment in "the English book" between the illusion of authority and a "hollowness" that undermines this. Thus "[these moments] mark the disturbance of its authoritative representations by the uncanny forces of race, sexuality, violence, cultural and even climatic differences which emerge in the colonial discourse as the mixed and split texts of hybridity" (Bhabha 1994: 113).

In a book such as *She*, set in a fearful underworld and written at a time when the decline of England was a popular fear, such disturbance of the narrative is inevitable. Prone to depression, Haggard gave full rein to a number of his anxieties in the underworld of *She*. Numerous references are made to the mortality of humankind, the transience of empires, the desire for immortality and the ultimate impossibility of this together with "the terror of an unstoppable progress towards nothingness in a Darwinian universe governed by chance and conflict" (Etherington in Haggard 1991: 230).

Ayesha herself is testimony to the rise and fall of civilisations and to the attempt to triumph over time, only ultimately to fail. In an age of religious doubt, Haggard created a character who symbolised the mystical hankerings after reincarnation, immortality, eternal youth and psychic phenomena of the late nineteenth century. Seen also by some critics as representing the New Woman in her emancipation, Ayesha offers a challenge to the masculine adventurers. *She* was published in 1887, the year of Queen Victoria's Golden Jubilee, and while Queen Victoria is described by Holly as having no real political power—for although the queen "was venerated and beloved by all right-thinking people in her vast realms," in fact "real power rested in the hands of the people" (1991: 169)—Ayesha would doubtless "assume absolute rule over the British dominions, and probably over the whole earth" (170). Part of the book's appeal, therefore, could be in the "combination of desire and anxiety aroused in male readers by its heroine, Ayesha, who, as the all-powerful ruler . . . was a type of the New Woman" (Gregory 1994: 83). Given Ayesha's complex appeal, even though her physical frame finally withers away, her powerful presence is still sufficiently dominant to provide the impetus for at least three further Haggard novels.

AFRICA AS SEXUALISED BODYSCAPE

One of the best known aspects of Haggard's African topography in post-colonial analyses of his writing is the extent to which Haggard used "the imperial setting to tap a level of yearning which, by contrast, seems almost indecent in its disregard for the standards of middle-class behaviour" (Bivona 1990: 80). It appears that unconsciously Haggard projected a good deal of his latent sexual desire and that of his age, which was one of determined public prudery, onto his feminised African landscapes. Writing in a time of domestic propriety at home, it seems inevitable that the exotic imperial lands would be seen imaginatively as offering an escape and a site of desire, both political on the manifest level and sexual at the latent level: "The landscape of potential empire becomes the landscape of pornographic fantasies and of sexual terrors" (Stott 1989: 84).

It is important to stress that Haggard did not consciously intend to create these highly sexualised landscapes, and this is what perhaps gave his romances such popular appeal for his Victorian readers. Indeed, his readers seemed by and large to be unaware of what today appears as obvious landscape sexualisation—Haggard was praised during his 1914 visit to South Africa as "one who for 30 years has been giving to the English-speaking world volume on volume of healthy, wholesome and thoroughly entertaining literature, in no page of which is there anything of a degrading or unmanly tendency" (Coan 1997: 47). Haggard was a highly respectable member of the landed gentry, a farmer, a tireless participant in various government commissions, and eventually knighted for his services to the empire. He had more than once publicly[12] denounced lasciviousness in writing. When his "modern" novel *Beatrice* (1890) was criticised by some for apparently criticising the institution of marriage, Haggard responded, "I have always felt that the author of books which go anywhere and everywhere has some responsibilities. Therefore I have tried to avoid topics that might inflame even minds which are very ready to be set on fire" (1926 vol. 2: 15). In his essay "About Fiction," he acknowledged that "sexual passion is the most powerful lever with which to stir the mind of man, for it lies at the root of all things human," and criticised the French Naturalist school:

It is not so much a question of the object of the school as of the fact that it continually, and in full and luscious detail, calls attention to erotic matters. Once start the average mind upon this subject, and it will go down the slope of itself. It is useless afterwards to turn around and say that, although you cut loose the cords of decent reticence which bound the fancy, you intended that it should run *uphill* to the white heights of virtue. (1887: 176-177)

It is interesting to note that Haggard uses a landscape image in this passage to illustrate his lecture on morality in writing, for it is onto the seemingly innocuous landscape rather than the people within it that the fears and desires of this late-Victorian gentleman and, by extension, his readers, are projected. As Etherington notes: "In Africa . . . the beasts which Victorians feared to encounter in themselves could be contemplated at a safe remove" (1984: 50), though perhaps he could have included their desires too, as Africa in writing of the time is always locked into the binary opposites of paradise/wilderness, pleasure/pain.

Africa, it should be noted, is generally feminised in late Victorian adventure tales and Haggard is no exception, although in a few of his romances the landscape is masculinised. In *Allan Quatermain*, for example, Mount Kenia is described in distinct phallic undertones as "a glittering white glory, its crest piercing the very blue of heaven." It is named by the natives the "Finger of God," which implies its overpowering masculinity (plus, incidentally, the belief that God must be white) but it is for all that curiously dead: "that white old tombstone of the years" (1995: 51-52). Mount Kenia, however, comes very much to life in a highly erotically charged dawn scene, when "a beam from the unrisen sun lit upon his heaven-kissing crest and purpled it with blood" whereupon "the sky above grew blue, and tender as a mother's smile" (1995: 83), which promptly deflates the eroticism. The phallic granite cone in *Benita* has already been commented on briefly. It is a "great cone . . . shaped by the hand of man out of a single gigantic granite monolith of the sort that are sometimes to be met with in Africa." It can be ascended by steps in order to reach the top, which "was fashioned in the shape of a cup, probably, for the purposes of acts of worship and sacrifice" (1986a: 255). In both instances of the masculinisation of the landscape here quoted, Haggard has endowed the places with a spiritual significance: both Mount Kenia and the Bambatse cone are to be venerated. In contrast, the feminisation of imperial landscapes was largely a result of Empire work being mostly a masculine activity of assuming dominance over less powerful opponents and spaces. Thus in a strongly patriarchal age the lesser half of a power equation would inevitably be feminised—"as Europe is to Africa, so is man to woman" (Bristow 1991: 133). As the feminised, less powerful partner, African landscape was open to a powerful discourse of latent sexuality: "African landscape is to be entered, conquered, its riches are to be reaped, enjoyed. The phallic semiology accompanies the imperialist topoi, a conjunction based on the assumption that if explorers are 'manly' then what they explore must be female" (Torgovnick quoted in Gregory 1994: 131).

The soon to be clichéd use of phrases to describe African land, such as "virgin" territory that had yet to be "penetrated," attests to the implicit if unconscious sexualising, specifically feminising, of African landscape in books of Empire, and it is to Haggard's "bodyscapes" that I now turn.

Predictably, Haggard's African romances published by 1892 are the most erotically charged, written as they were at great speed and shortly after Haggard's return from South Africa. Of these romances, the one most commented upon in terms of a sexualised geography is *King Solomon's Mines* (Patteson 1978, Bunn 1988, McClintock 1990, 1995, Bristow 1991 among others). The prompt for the narrative in this work is the device of a treasure map (already briefly mentioned in chapter 2) that points the way to Solomon's mines in Kukuanaland, the mythical Ophir of the Bible. The map has come into Quatermain's hands from a descendant of José da Silvestra, who died looking for the fabulous wealth of the mines. As Bunn points out, the map together with the information it contains passes down "a line of male inheritance" (1988: 10) and provides the male adventurers with a European grid to decode the mysterious, because unknown, landscape before them. Haggard attempts to impart to his map a further masculinist framework through the compass points drawn on the top right corner—the compass being "the icon of Western 'reason', technical aggression and the male, militarized possession of the earth" (McClintock 1995: 3)—giving the explorers a proper sense of direction. In this sense, "The map, a visual representation from an imaginary bird's-eye perspective, imaginatively controls and possesses the geography of the interior. Representing the land from an imaginary bird's-eye perspective . . . the map is a gendered image. It naturalises the masculine authority of the colonial map-maker, making him the 'monarch of all he surveys'" (Phillips 1997: 85).

However, the relationship between the map and the landscape is not here a purely hypothetical one, as the map Quatermain holds is an unconscious but obvious "bodyscape" of a recumbent woman lying upside down, turned literally on her head as Bunn (1988), the first scholar to comment on this, pointed out. The place where the head would have been is marked "Pan bad water," which portrays female intellect in a negative and dangerous light; instead the quest path moves northward through Queen Sheba's breasts, on either side of which the "arms"/mountain range lie outstretched in a passive gesture of acceptance. The pages describing Sheba's breasts would have been, I am sure, the most well-thumbed section in any schoolboy's edition of *King Solomon's Mines* (keeping in mind that it is dedicated "to all the big and little boys who read it") for their description is quite graphic. In fact, Bristow points out the narrative pictures "parts of the female anatomy that, banished from public view in Britain, could be found in obscene publications. Yet, as this story is a romance, it assumes that it will not be confused with the male genre it closely resembles: pornography" (1991: 133). Quatermain unconsciously reinforces the sexualised nature of what he sees by declaring himself "impotent" before even the "memory" of the mountains—thus the gazer is momentarily unmanned by the terrible attraction of what his imagination has superimposed onto these twin peaks. Despite his impotence, this is what Quatermain recalls seeing:

These mountains standing thus, like the pillars of a gigantic gateway, are shaped exactly like a woman's breasts. Their bases swelled gently up from the plain, looking, at that distance, perfectly round and smooth; and on the top of each was a vast round hillock covered with snow, exactly corresponding to the nipple on the female breast .... For awhile the morning lights played upon the snow and the brown and swelling masses beneath, and then, as though to veil the majestic sight from our curious eyes, strange mists and clouds gathered and increased around them, till presently we could only trace their pure and gigantic outline swelling ghostlike through the fleecy envelope. (1992: 85-86)

The repetition of "swelled/swelling" no fewer than three times in this passage (not to mention in other texts such as the "pass or nek between two swelling hills" that leads to Ishmael's enclosed kraal in *The Ghost Kings* 1908a: 99), speaks not only of Haggard's self-admittedly careless writing, but also of an unconscious prurience. What is at work here is a projection of Quatermain/Haggard's desire for, yet fear of, female sexuality projected onto an unknown landscape, corresponding to the fact that "for the Victorian patriarchy women were as much an image of ontological uncertainty as the unknown interior" (Bunn 1988: 12). Africa in particular (as discussed in chapter 2) came to represent for the nineteenth century a zone of erotic possibility, given its climate, the scanty dress of some of its peoples and, to the European mind, lax morals. Yet, despite being in Africa, Sheba's breasts do not seem to represent black female sexuality as much as white female sexuality with dark (black) possibilities: "Thus this story of the exploration and penetration of Africa expresses white masculine fears about white female sexuality: that beneath the veneer it is a sexuality that corresponds to the myth of black female sexuality, primitive, sadistic, active and death-threatening" (Stott 1989: 81).

The peaks tower "up in awful white solemnity" while the cliff that connects them is "precipitous." The nipple is a frozen symbol of succour that particularly fascinates Quatermain, as he returns to describe it again and again: a little further on from the above passage, the one nipple is "crowned . . . with a diadem of glory" above its "springing slope" (1992: 94-95). These breasts, however, are not life giving but in fact deadly close up, especially near the erogenous nipple zone, for it is here that the cave housing the frozen body of José da Silvestra is discovered, and it is also in this cave that Ventvögel freezes to death. Female sexuality is wonderfully attractive from a safe "monarch-of-all-I-survey" perspective, but potentially deathly once the distant aerial perspective is forsaken for a close encounter.

Once past Sheba's breasts, the travellers follow the map which leads them up Solomon's Road, over the woman's torso and across a burning desert, "past a navel-like, life-giving well" (Patteson 1978: 121) and finally to Kukuanaland.

Their goal is a suggestively triangular treasure cave area marked by "three great snow-capped mountains" called the "Three Witches," which are "sheer and precipitous, instead of smooth and rounded" (Haggard 1992: 134) like Sheba's breasts. One is obviously past the pleasurable if frozen part of the female anatomy and near the place of ultimate treasure yet also extreme danger—the treasure mines, if vaginal, are more reminiscent of Freud's vagina dentata that any less complicated site of pleasure. To add to the forbidding air, the mines are guarded by three colossi: "The female form, which was nude, was of great though severe beauty. . . The two male colossi were . . . draped, and presented a terrifying cast of features, especially the one to our right, which had the face of a devil" (258). These three "Silent Ones"—whose possible Phoenician origin is the subject of Quatermain and Curtis's learned speculation—guard these mines, which also double up at the "Place of Death" where the Kukuana kings are preserved in the grisly fashion already described in an earlier section in this chapter. The escape route from the caves is an anal back passage—predictably "in the bowels of the mountain" (298)—from which the intrepid adventurers emerge chastened and covered in primal ooze, "smeared all over with dust and mud, bruised, bleeding" (298). Yet the terrifying experience is finally shown to be worth it both psychologically, for they have proved their manhood in surviving this encounter with female sexuality, and materially, for Quatermain's diamonds once sold enrich the three of them. Quatermain is able to acquire property in England from the proceeds: "there is a place for sale quite close which would suit you admirably" (319) writes Curtis once back home, the implication being that any property in Sir Henry Curtis's neighbourhood, that of the aristocracy, must be substantial indeed. Politically too, the adventure in Kukuanaland has been successful if life-threatening at times: Quatermain and company as prototype British imperialists have succeeded in installing a legitimate ruler in the landlocked Kukuanaland, which is to be cut off from the outside world with access only allowed to the three British men: "a rudimentary colonial state has emerged which maintains a British monopoly and establishes trade and legislative barriers that control the flow of imperial traffic" (Bunn 1988: 15). All in all, then, it appears that in this, Haggard's first successful romance, he established what was to become a typical part of his African topography, a sexualised "bodyscape" in which the "adventure story's displacement of woman returns in the form of the geography of the land" (Low 1996: 49). Though *King Solomon's Mines* technically contains no "petticoat," it is everywhere displaced onto the seemingly innocent landscape,[13] which always takes the part of a powerful protagonist, deceptively impassive, immobile, at times beautiful, yet always potentially destructive.

It is not surprising that *She*, written so rapidly, is also characterised by a highly sexualised landscape—it has never, together with *King Solomon's Mines*, been out of print and in its day achieved record sales figures. It has been translated into numerous languages and several times made into a Hollywood film. In the great success *She* achieved, "Haggard, one is tempted to say, has pulled out all the stops without exactly knowing he is seated at the keyboard" (Millman 1974: 51). Probably this success can in great part be attributed to the very powerful figure of Ayesha with her sexual frankness and freedom from convention, her political expedience and ambition. As previously noted, she corresponds to the late nineteenth-century New Woman, attractive yet threatening to the old-style Victorian man whom Haggard represented. The landscape of Ayesha's kingdom, Kôr, acts as a kind of objective correlative to these tensions and desires. Indeed Gilbert and Gubar go so far as to draw a parallel between the "internal landscape" of woman described by the American gynaecologist Sims in 1845 and the "dreamlike landscape" of Haggard's *She*, in which "ideas about female power that were increasingly popularised throughout the nineteenth century" have their counterpoint (1989: 33-34). In "Orientalism Reconsidered," Said compliments Gilbert for her insights in an essay on *She*, presumably an early version of the essay published by Gilbert and Gubar in 1989, noting in particular that she shows "the narrow correspondence between suppressed Victorian sexuality at home, its fantasies abroad, and the tightening hold on the male late nineteenth century imagination of imperialist ideology" (Said 1985: 23).

The early, perilous journey over the swamp to Kôr has already been commented on in the context of Africa as dreamworld. The overlap between dream, the unconscious and a sexualised "bodyscape" is evident, and from the moment of entry into the hidden valley of Kôr, the reader, with Leo and Holly, has entered a *paysage moralisée*. As Etherington notes:

It does not require much imagination to see the female body . . . dominating the topography of *She*. The narrow passes between the beautiful shrubbery suggest the loins of a woman. The two extinct volcanic mountains where most of the action occurs suggest breasts standing up from the broad African plains. The ancient channel cut to drain the crater lake is most strongly reminiscent of the birth canal from which the waters burst at the moment of parturition. (Etherington in Haggard 1991: xxxiv)

In an echo from *King Solomon's Mines*, the travellers cross "*swelling* grassy plains"[italics added] (1991: 54), and altogether the aboveground terrain is manageable, even welcoming. With entry to Ayesha's subterranean kingdom of caves, the insecurity of the two British men—Holly the Oxford don, and Leo his handsome ward who is the reincarnation of Kallikrates, Ayesha's lover of antiquity—begins in earnest. The aboveground hazards of swamps, wild animals, and hostile natives are the standard fare of adventure tales and had Haggard left it there, the book might have stayed at the "boy's own adventure" level. However, in the caves ruled by the wise temptress Ayesha, day is turned into night, a time of fears and seductive possibilities, and time stands still as it has in a sense for thousands of years for Ayesha, made immortal by the Flame of Life. The way to this Flame provides one of Haggard's most highly eroticised passages, again doubtless done unconsciously. Leo, Holly, and Job, Holly's manservant and source of comic relief, have to follow the fearless

Ayesha by balancing on a narrow spur of rock, which spans a vast, sunless chasm buffeted by huge gusts of wind. The narrow bridge of rock resembles "nothing that I can think of so much as the spur upon the leg of a cock in shape" (1991: 179) and its phallic connotation is strengthened the further the four crawl along it, until, with Ayesha leading the terrified men behind her, "like a living thing, the great spur vibrated with a humming sound beneath us" (180). The spur ends just short of reaching the other side, "a sugarloaf-shaped cone" on which a clitoral "glacier stone" (181) rests. At the precise moment of the day when a shaft of sunlight illuminates the scene, the nerve-wracking final few steps on a fragile plank over the abyss can be made. In this truly terrifying passage, Haggard is in his most imaginatively fearful space—at the heart of male and female sexuality[14]—and it is significant that Ayesha not only leads the way confidently, but exhorts the men to follow her example: "'It is safe,' she called. 'See, hold thou the plank! I will stand on the farther side of the stone so that it may not overbalance with your greater weights. Now, come, oh Holly, for presently the light will fail us'" (182).

Once successfully across the perilous abyss the party find themselves, after traversing a short passage, in a "rocky chamber . . . warm and dry—a perfect haven of rest compared to the giddy pinnacle above, and the quivering spur that shot out to meet it in mid-air" (184); they are in fact in the mystic Noot's cave, near the "very womb of the Earth" (189), which houses the Flame of Life. Ayesha, Leo and Holly have resolved to enter the Flame in order to gain immortality in order for the physical union between Ayesha and Leo to be made possible. Ayesha describes her anticipation of the Flame in physical terms as she now undresses—"now for thee I loose my virgin zone" (188)— whereas Holly, as chaperone to the bridal couple, uses a more spiritual vocabulary: "It was as though the bonds of my flesh had been loosened, and left the spirit free to soar to the empyrean of its native power" (190). As it transpires, Ayesha's second encounter with the Flame proves fatal, as she shrivels up into a Darwinian nightmare of man's origins, a monkey. In the reversal of what could have been a consummation scene, Ayesha loses her beauty, wisdom and sexual power in a tragedy that yet, given her threatening potential, has some measure of relief about it. Millman says of this scene: "The Victorian ban on explicit sensuality has here created something akin to a sexual act, governed by prose which abruptly suggests cathartic release" (1974: 55). The male voyeurs of this scene all "swoon" away (Haggard 1991: 194), and Job even dies of shock at what he has witnessed. Leo is inconsolable, having lost his first love, and joins the growing list in the Haggard canon of men doomed to yearn eternally after their irrevocably lost first love, in much the same way as Haggard always pined after Lilly Jackson. Holly, once recovered from the shock of witnessing Ayesha's spectacular demise, is able to accept her death as perhaps for the best, politically, for "Ayesha strong and happy in her love, clothed in immortal youth and goddess beauty, and the wisdom of the centuries, would have revolutionised society, and even perchance have changed the destiny of Mankind" (1991: 195). Perhaps Haggard is implying that the New Woman taken to extremes would prove too dangerous on a latent, sexual level and also on a manifest, political level. Gilbert and Gubar see a possible parallel in this regard between Ayesha and Schreiner's Lyndall in *The Story of an African Farm* (1883), illustrating Haggard's ambivalence towards strong, successful women. They suggest that "what might have been Schreiner's utopia—a 'world elsewhere' in which Lyndall could survive and thrive—became Haggard's dystopia, a dystopia that dramatically integrates nineteenth century fears about the rise, and the redefinition, of female power with imperialist worries about the claims of colonized peoples and Christian fears about the challenges posed by alternative theologies" (1989: 35). This is confirmed by the return journey of the surviving members of the party, Leo and Holly, for when they have made their desperate leaps across the awesome chasm, Leo's attempt dislodges the clitoral rock, which thereafter bars any future access to Noot's cave and the Flame of Life and entombs Ayesha's body in this womb of the world. Billali's words of farewell to Leo and Holly, once he has escorted them across Kôr's encircling swamps, may be taken on many levels:

"But if ever ye come to your country, be advised, and venture no more into lands that ye know not, lest ye come back no more, but leave your white bones to mark the limit of your journeyings. . ." We watched them winding away with the empty litters like a procession bearing dead men from a battle, till the mists from the marsh gathered round them and hid them, and then, left utterly desolate in the vast wilderness, we turned and gazed around us and at each other. (1991: 207)

All three of Haggard's most famous African romances end with a warning to would-be English adventurer-imperialists, but this warning is probably the bleakest. In *King Solomon's Mines* safe passage in the future is granted to the heroes should a return visit be planned, whereas in *Allan Quatermain*, though other explorer-imperialists are not welcome, Zu-Vendis is left in the capable hands of a British aristocrat and his lady-love. In *She*, however, the brush with matters sexual and political has been far more dangerous and intimate, and thus no superficially happy ending is possible for Haggard. Holly's description of himself once out of the final caves seems to sum up well the effect of the book's probing into such ambivalent matters: "There was something beside ugliness stamped upon my features that I have never got rid of until this day, something resembling that wild look with which a startled person wakes from deep sleep more than anything else that I can think of" (203-204). In this book, it seems Haggard engaged with his dreams and nightmares projected in part on to a sexualised geography; the book's popularity suggests that these were not peculiar only to Haggard.

Wisdom's Daughter, published in 1923, post-World War I and in a less sexually repressed age, literally goes over some of the same ground as *She*, and it is interesting to compare Haggard's descriptions of similar geographical spaces in both books. The romance is an account of Ayesha's early life, her love affair with Kallikrates the Greek, and his with Ayesha's rival, Amenartas. Ayesha rules over Kôr as a priestess of Isis but in order to claim Kallikrates's love once and for all, she resolves with Philo, one of her court, to visit the Flame of Life guarded by Noot, together with Kallikrates and his pregnant wife Amenartas, in order to enter the forbidden fire. Again, we as readers watch Ayesha and her followers as they face for the first time the dreadful chasm in darkness and make the crossing on the rocky spur. Writing nearly forty years after *She*, Haggard reinforces the eroticism of the crossing of the chasm in darkness, giving—if unconsciously—more explicit language to Ayesha as narrator, which is to be perhaps expected in a less prudish age: "At length we came to the end of that long needle which thrust itself thus into the dark stuff of space, and as we did so all light went out of the sky above, leaving us plunged in blackness. I seated myself upon the throbbing point of rock, clinging to Philo who had done likewise" (1923: 220).

Again, we read of the "huge, trembling stone" joined to "that fearsome spar" by a narrow wooden plank "which bridge rose and fell and rocked as the great stone trembled on its farther side" (220-221). This sexually charged zone still holds fears and yet desire for Haggard, it appears. A more pronounced change is present in the description of the Flame of Life, which now assumes an explicit phallic quality, with Ayesha's entrance into the fire described as a marriage union. On this occasion, Ayesha has persuaded Kallikrates and Amenartas to accompany her to the Flame, which she plans to enter and thus gain immortality and eternal beauty, which would prove irresistible to the mortal Kallikrates. On her first visit with Philo to the cave, Ayesha describes the Flame as having "blood-red, splendid arms that stretched towards me as though to clasp me to that burning breast" (227), and on the second visit when she enters the fire, Haggard gives us a passage that would not be out of place in a soft-porn novel: "It swelled and grew and now I had entered into womanhood and in my heart were strange, uncomprehended longings. It took a fiercer note and I bethought me of the beating of the hoofs of horses as, mounted on my crested stallion, I rushed across the desert like the wind" (259).

Ayesha's punishment for such an action is to lose Kallikrates, who stabs himself rather than follow her into the fire. He prophesies for Ayesha a life of lonely bitterness, which is indeed her lot. It would be two thousand years before Kallikrates's reincarnation, Leo, visits Ayesha at Kôr in *She*. Though *Wisdom's Daughter* does not have the power of *She*, the passages just analysed bear witness to Haggard's continuing projection of sexual anxieties and desires onto an eroticised (and fantasised) African landscape: "If at first glance, the feminizing of the land appears to be no more than a familiar symptom of male megalomania, it also betrays acute paranoia and a profound, if not pathological, sense of male anxiety and boundary loss" (McClintock 1995: 24).

Nada the Lily (1892) is Haggard's song of praise to the Zulus of the *ancien régime*, his aim being "to convey, in a narrative form, some idea of the remarkable spirit which animated these kings [Chaka, Dingaan] and their subjects, and make accessible in a popular shape, incidents of history which are now, for the most part, only to be found in a few scarce works of reference" (1949: ix). As an extension of Haggard's above intention, one critic also reads it as "a tribute to expiate the British people's guilt over their 'liquidation' of the peoples of South Africa, especially the Zulus" (Adewumi 1977: 106). Dedicated to Shepstone, it also seeks to vindicate "the way the Shepstonian system sought to reach into a Zulu world to discover the principles by which it might best establish its authority" (Hamilton 1998: 119). Haggard states in his preface to the novel that he will "for a time forget his civilisation, and think with the mind and speak with the voice of a Zulu of the old régime" (1949: x) and it is indeed remarkable for the age that Haggard does try to create a completely Zulu world peopled entirely by black characters, although admittedly seen through a paternalistic prism. Laurens van der Post saw Haggard as "the first to take the African into the fellowship of the imagination," a writer who had "admitted [the African] to our home of many mansions, a legitimate tenant at last of the human imagination" (quoted in Sévry 1992: 9), a pronouncement which in itself sounds unfortunately and unconsciously patronising. However, despite his stated intention to speak with a Zulu voice, when it comes to certain descriptions of the landscape it is very much the voice of Haggard that the reader hears. Particularly (as previously briefly mentioned), the passages dealing with Ghost Mountain show a high degree of sexualisation, witness in part to Haggard's private anxieties about women's sexuality but now specifically cast in terms of black women's sexuality, given the "Zulu-ness" of the tale. While Haggard believed he had been a Zulu and loved a Zulu woman in one of his previous incarnations—in one of his "dream visions" discussed earlier, he sees himself in a scene with his black companion and their children, he is attacked, speared and retreats to his hut "where I fall into the arms of the woman and die" (1926 vol. 2: 168-169)—his descriptions of Ghost Mountain project an image of a deathly, fearful and primordial sexuality onto the landscape. Perhaps this is due in part to the mountain being associated with "an aged woman" (1949: 81) with whom any sexual contact might be considered taboo, even incestuous. Unlike the supine woman of the map in *King Solomon's Mines*, whose "swelling" breasts soar heavenward promising—superficially at least—a youthful fertility, the woman-mountain in *Nada the Lily* sits upright, solid, "her chin resting upon her breast" (112), her face turned down to her lap, unable or unwilling to meet the male gazer's eye. Galazi the Wolf, who saves Umslopogaas from the lions, describes his first encounter with the mountain. He sees the reputedly haunted Ghost Mountain as "a seated woman" with a cave "being, as it were, on the lap of the woman." This pubic/womb area is "clothed with little bushes" (112) and guarded by a protective hymen-like stone as are various feminised caves in Haggard—Stella's cave in *Allan's Wife*, Noot's cave in *She* and the entry to the holy site of the Tree of Life and Death in *The Ghost Kings,* "a kind of cleft . . . not more than two feet in width, across which cleft were stretched strings of plaited grass" (1908a: 302). Galazi recounts how at night, he makes his way to this cave, which is situated between "the knees of the stone Witch, which are the space before the cave" (1949: 115) in great fear of the grey wolves that live there and of the "great spotted snakes" (114) of this lapsed corner of Eden. However, he manages to defeat the wolves, which are in fact ghosts of evil men, and there is no doubting his show of masculine bravado before the fearful cave: "I walked to the mouth of the cave proudly, as a cock walks upon the roof" (116). The cave houses the dessicated corpse of a man described in Haggard's usual necrophiliac detail, together with the leaders of the wolf pack, whom Galazi kills. The ghost of the dead man instructs Galazi, the victor, to "climb to the breasts of the stone Witch, and look in the cleft which is between her breasts" (121). He does so and finds "as it were, a crack in the stone twice as wide as a man can jump" (122) in which are "the bones of men" (123), victims of the wolves who guard the Ghost Mountain.

Haggard's characteristic nervous tic of "as it were" (quoted above)[15] as he describes a sexualised site is much in evidence in these descriptions of Ghost Mountain: "The cave was ... as it were, on the lap of the woman," "I had ... come, as it were, to the legs of the old stone Witch," etc. This little phrase is an unconscious hiccup before Haggard engages with his imagined terrain. Significantly, Galazi is hailed on his return to the village, draped in the bloody fresh skins of wolves, as one who has "won the lap of her who sits in stone forever" (126), a euphemism for sexual intercourse also used later in the book—the Zulu princes Dingaan and Umhlangana are described as ones who "drink beer and sleep in the laps of their wives" (180), while both Galazi and Umslopogaas are "ghosts who live in the lap of the old Witch" (197). The image of "lying in laps" may be an echo from *Hamlet*, who cruelly jests with Ophelia, "Lady, shall I lie in your lap? . . . Do you think I meant country matters?" (Shakespeare, *Hamlet* III, ii,108-112), a work with which Haggard would surely have been familiar. Be that as it may, the woman-Ghost Mountain is a fearsome and ambivalent sexual partner in this book. She is a contradictory mix of haven for Galazi and Umslopogaas, yet tomb—for Nada dies within the womb-like cave having pushed the hymen rock too far and thus locked herself within, after which Ophelia-like she goes mad—a blend of attraction yet revulsion. The mountain is, however, consistently labelled a "witch," thus demonising this feminised site and casting her beyond the realm of the normal and into a supernatural realm of night fears. She is "a place of dead men" (1949: 119). Nada is the only woman brought to her for refuge, whereupon in jealous rage, the woman-mountain easily extinguishes the light from one who is loved by Umslopogaas, who, together with Galazi, ought to be hers. This tragic end is recalled in *The Ghost Kings* in a scene where Dingaan is allowed to "see" his own death reflected in a bowl of water:

I see a mountain whereof the top is like the shape of a woman, and between her knees is the mouth of a cave. Beneath the floor of the cave I see bodies, the body of a great man and the body of a girl.... I see a man, a fat man came out of the cave.... Two other men seize him.... They drag him up the mountain to a great cleft that is between the breasts of her who sits thereon.... They hale him to the edge of the cleft, they hurl him over. (1908a: 272-273)

This scene occurs, as Dingaan describes it, at the end of *Nada the Lily*. Ghost Mountain is thus unremittingly linked to the feminine and to the deathly, and though I have shown passages from other texts that link the feminine to a more attractive landscape prospect, there is also the contradictory pessimistic tension pulling beneath. As Bunn observes: "Haggard's texts produce fictive landscapes ideologically, but they do so under the shadow of contradiction and neurosis. The figure of Woman in the colonial text seems to me the point at which most of the contradictions become visible" (1988: 23).

AFRICA AS HOME TO ANCIENT WHITE CIVILISATIONS

One of the most recurrent features in Haggard's African topography is the proliferation of ruins of ancient, supposedly white, civilisations, which is in fundamental conflict with a primary myth of imperial adventure stories: *the myth of the empty landscape*. Reference has already been made to the use of this myth by nineteenth-century explorers and scientists in constructing a discourse of Africanism in chapter 2, and also briefly, earlier in this chapter, to Haggard's ideas on improving the empty wilderness. I should like to look in more detail now at Haggard's contradictory position on the "empty land" myth, which supported the image "of a huge unpeopled wilderness lying north of the Limpopo, a new land that waited only for the settlers to stir it into life" (Chennells 1982: 160).[16] Though Haggard in his romances might have left the border of the empty land of the imagination where Chennells suggests it is, in his nonfictional writing some of the vacant land potentially lies further south.

In an effort to encourage emigration to South Africa, Haggard wrote in *A Farmer's Year*: "Why should people continue to be cooped up in this narrow country, living generally upon insufficient means, when yonder their feet might be set in so large a room?" (1899b: 397). The "room" he was discussing was the Transvaal with its "vast spaces of rolling veld stretching away north, south, east, and west, without a tree, a house, or any sign of man, save here and there a half-beaten waggon track" (399). Of course, just over twenty-five years before, angered and disappointed by the retrocession of the Transvaal to the Boers, Haggard had left that self-same "room" declaring it "no country for Englishmen" (1900a: 367), but years of living in cramped England made him see the benefit again of wide, open spaces. Again, repeating his message in *The After War Settlement and Employment of Ex-Servicemen*, a document written to encourage emigration to the colonies, Haggard drew on the myth of the empty land: "I have recently travelled around the Empire. It has been to me like scene after scene drawn up before my eyes—ever new vastnesses, ever new possibilities, ever new richness waiting to be seized" (1916b: 48).

From an imperialist and capitalist point of view, it was important that colonies such as South Africa and territory to the north should be seen as virtually empty, for then "colonial landscape is produced as one possible level of spatiality onto which desire may be mapped in the service of social production" (Noyes 1992: 8). Only space seen as empty can be filled without guilt. Even more desirable is empty land previously unworked; in other words, "virgin" territory so beloved of the imperialist romance, "for if the land is virgin, colonized peoples cannot claim aboriginal territorial rights, and white male patriarchy is violently assured as the sexual and military insemination of an interior void" (McClintock 1995: 30). Now, while Haggard is mostly partial to "virgin" territory, he is in no doubt as to what McClintock calls "aboriginal territorial rights" as he makes clear on a number of occasions, notably in this passage from *Cetywayo and His White Neighbours*:

It seems to me, that as they [the "natives"] were the original owners of the soil, they were entitled to some consideration in the question of its disposal, and consequently and incidentally, of their own. I am aware that it is generally considered that the white man has a right to the black man's possessions and land, and that it is his high and holy mission to exterminate the wretched native and take his place. But with this conclusion I venture to differ. (1888: 269)

What Haggard does see as a legitimation of colonisation of empty space— which, however, may have "original owners"—is if the land is not worked or is uncultivated, for then the coloniser may actually improve the land, which also appealed to Haggard, the farmer and gardener. Thus as practical imperialist, he could write with missionary zeal in *The Poor and the Land* of the "beautiful but useless foam" of the Zambesi which "when it is harnessed, will drive every engine within a thousand miles." The "Zambesi Falls," as Haggard calls them, previously "unserviceable to man, will one day be at work continually" bringing the benefits of the industrial age to citizens in Pretoria and Johannesburg. He exhorts the capitalist power of the imperial centre to make use of such "waste forces of Benevolence" so that "they are applied to the salvation of the poor, and so dedicated to the welfare of the earth" (1905b: x-xi). In a passage taken from *The Last Boer War*, Haggard describes the Transvaal as a potential Little England in conjuring up the English potential of African landscape: "The capabilities of this favoured land are vast and various. Within its borders are to be found highlands and lowlands, vast stretches of rolling veldt like gigantic sheep downs, hundreds of miles of swelling bushland [with its erotic implications], huge tracts of mountainous country, and even little glades spotted with timber that remind one of an English park" (1900b: 8).

What is needed to transform the empty land into productive land is labour, and this is where a related myth of native laziness comes into play, for if the indigenous inhabitants do not work such obviously fertile land, then they "waste" it and thus forfeit their right to it. As Pieterse points out, "the claim of native laziness therefore was simultaneously a claim to the legality of colonialism" (1992: 91). Haggard's approach to "native laziness" is a little more complicated, however, because of "an anxiety about the easy fit between native and land which is evident in all his African romances" (Low 1996: 70). Low goes on to point out how this "easy fit" was, ironically, superficially enhanced by the British establishment of African reservations in Natal in which "the Natalian natives are seen as existing in a pre-lapsarian garden of plenty managed by the colonial administration" (70). Quite rightly, Haggard always pictures male Zulus as warriors, not farmers, in both his nonfiction and his romances; it is the white missionaries in their enclosures and their largely invisible black labourers that make the land work: "The missionary imported ploughs and taught them [the 'natives'] to improve their agriculture, so that ere long this rich, virgin soil brought forth abundantly. Their few cattle multiplied also in an amazing fashion, as did their families, and soon they were . . . prosperous" (1908a: 85-86).

As I pointed out previously, however, there is always an underlying ambivalence on this question of improving empty land in Haggard. While his public imperialist discourse urged such Victorian "improvement," his desiring, romantic discourse longs for a "safe and secret place" (made safe perhaps by an ultimate, framing British authority), a land that is wild yet inviting to the true seeker: "a more tractable face that returns the European's gaze, echoes his words, and accepts his caress" (Pratt 1985: 127). Therefore, though Haggard admired the Zulus in particular and uses them extensively in his African romances, he also needed the notion of unoccupied "waste" land as a lodestone for his adventurers in an exaggeratedly vast Africa. The following passage from *Marie* is a rare one in that it combines all of the features so far discussed— the "empty land" myth yet also the acknowledgement of a prior claim by indigenous inhabitants; the ideal of improving the land and yet also the "safe and secret" position of space safeguarded; and the simultaneous, contradictory image of the Zulus as both ruthless warriors and yet also pliant labourers. It is the contradictory romantic imperialist's dream—Haggard could be speaking of himself as a once idealistic youth, newly married at his South African farm, Hilldrop. In this passage, Allan Quatermain has found the site near the Mooi River for himself and the Boer girl, Marie Marais, to settle once they are married:

Enclosed in this loop were some thirty thousand acres of very rich, low-lying soil, almost treeless and clothed with luxuriant grasses where game was extraordinarily numerous. At the head of it rose a flat-topped hill, from the crest of which . . . flowed a plentiful stream of water fed by a strong spring. Half-way down this hill, facing to the east, and irrigable by the stream, was a plateau several acres in extent, which furnished about the best site for a house that I know in all South Africa. Here I determined we would build our dwelling-place and become rich by the breeding up of great herds of cattle. I should explain that this ground, which once, as the remains of old kraals showed, had belonged to a Kaffir tribe killed out by Chaka, the Zulu king, was to be had for the taking. Indeed, . . . there was more land than we could possibly occupy. . . . I pegged out an estate of about twelve thousand acres for myself, and selecting a site, set the natives to work to build a rough mud house upon it which would serve as a temporary dwelling. ([1912] 1959: 187)

The remains of the "Kaffir" huts are the only trace of prior indigenous settlement and, like their tenure, eventually almost no trace at all would remain except the crumbling and overgrown stones from which the huts were built. And thus it is in Haggard, that the indigenous inhabitants leave little or no trace of their passing. Like John Niel's servant, Jantjé the Hottentot in *Jess*, all they do is write on the earth in temporary signs, soon to be obliterated: "Look, Baas, I draw a circle in the sand with my foot, and I say some words so, and at last the ends touch. . . . An old witch-doctor taught me how to draw the circle of a man's life and what words to say. . . . And now, look, I rub my foot over the circles and they are gone, and there is only the path again" (1900a: 88-89).

The story is undoubtedly different when it comes to the remains of ancient white civilisations in Haggard's romances. The great imaginative impetus for Haggard's typical inclusion of ancient ruins of non-African peoples in his books was undoubtedly the "discovery" of Great Zimbabwe by Mauch in 1870. As Murray points out, "Haggard, like the great archaeologists of the nineteenth century, assumed the strength of a relationship between the human, earth and life sciences, that would explain the past and give it popular meaning and value" (Murray, T. 1993: 181). The popular view of these impressive stone ruins was that they were built in antiquity by a people of Phoenician origin who were overrun by an indigenous African people. Haggard, in his preface to Wilmot's book *Monomotapa (Rhodesia)* (1896) puts forward this view, dominant at the time—he asserts that "the ruins of Zimbabwe . . . are undoubtedly of Phoenician origin," the inhabitants being taken over after some few hundred years by "savages [who] were of the Zulu section of the Bantu race; at least they stamped out whatever civilisation, Christian or Mohammedan, still flickered in Monomotapa so completely that even native tradition is silent concerning it, and once more oblivion covered the land and its story" (Wilmot 1896: xiv-xv).

As Jantjé's foot erased the marks he made in the sand in the passage above (quoted from *Jess*), so too is the history of these ruins erased under black dominance. The belief in a "white" origin for the ruins was due in part to then current nineteenth-century studies in anthropology and ethnography that differentiated between Saharan and sub-Saharan peoples, the former being Arabic and considered more civilised that the latter. Saharan peoples, being paler in colour, were taken to be more refined, whereas sub-Saharan, darker people were assumed to be savage, literally and morally darker, dwelling in a darkened African interior. While Haggard's writing seems "at moments to hint at a form of cultural relativism in which African tribal society and "Africanness" might be compared on at least neutral terms with white Anglo-Saxon society" (Rodgers 1997: 111), there is evidence that, contradicting this cultural relativism, Haggard seems to have believed in some moments in a hierarchy of races. In the diary Haggard kept of his fact-finding trip to Southern Africa as part of a Royal Commission looking into the state of the Dominions, he wrote, after visiting Great Zimbabwe, that it was "to my mind so very absurd, that this gigantic fortress and the other ruins were built by Kaffirs in the middle ages. How he [Professor McIver, a supporter of the 'black built' Great Zimbabwe theory] can think so after seeing them I cannot imagine, especially as I remember that the Portuguese writers of 3 centuries ago say that the Natives of that day asserted that they were the work of the Devil in unknown antiquity" ([1914a] 2000: 31). The telltale impersonal "them" speaks of a racism that does occasionally emerge in Haggard, especially when describing races other than the Zulu, although his ability to see the relative merits of other races generally "enabled him to escape the vice of racial prejudice to which so many of his contemporaries succumbed" (Sandison 1967: 31).

The novel *Elissa* was Haggard's attempt to dramatise the rise and fall of the civilisation of Great Zimbabwe. It was "a romantic sketch" (1917: viii) first published serially in *The Long Bow*, then published in book form in the United States in 1900 and reprinted thereafter in the United Kingdom. In the preface he repeats his ideas on the origins of the ruins; that it is "almost beyond question that Zimbabwe was once an inland Phoenician city" and that it was perhaps "weakened by luxury and the mixture of races, that hordes of invading savages stamped it out of existence beneath their blood-stained feet" (vii-viii). The narrative tells of the illicit love of Prince Aziel, a Hebrew, for Elissa, a priestess of Baaltis and daughter of the governor of Zimboe (Zimbabwe), a city under threat by the tyrant King Ithobal, who demands Elissa in return for the city's safety. Ithobal is described as being of mixed race, of which Haggard is always most critical, believing as did current thinkers, that this led to the degeneration of races: "The brow, nose and cheek-bones were Semitic in outline, while the full, prominent eyes, and thick, sensuous lips could with equal certainty be attributed to the negroid stock" (28).[17] The ending of the novel is suitably tragic as it describes Zimboe's downfall—Elissa converts to Christianity but finally commits suicide rather than be taken by the wicked heathen Ithobal, who also dies when shot by one of Aziel's arrows: "And thus, because of the fateful and predestined loves of Aziel the Prince, and Elissa the priestess and daughter of Sakon, three thousand years and more ago, the ancient city of Zimboe fell at the hand of King Ithobal and his Tribes, so that today there remains of it nothing but a desolate grey tower of stone, and beneath, the crumbling bones of men" (243).

This passage recalls one of Haggard's abiding interests—the rise and fall of empires in a kind of Darwinian cycle of change and flux, which further explains the littering of his African topography with ruins. In an echo of the passage in *She* in which Holly discusses the rise and fall of many civilisations in Africa, Quatermain speculates in *Heu Heu* that "Africa is a very ancient land, and in it once lived many races that have vanished, or survive only in a debased condition, dwindling from generation to generation until the day of their extinction comes" (1972: 114). *King Solomon's Mines*, which specifically draws on the biblical Ophir for setting, describes Solomon's Great Road leading from Sheba's breasts in terms of an archaeological layering of civilisation—the "wide turnpike road" is described as "a sort of Roman road" in which "no difficulty had been too great for the Old World engineer who designed it." At one point the road tunnels through a ridge, the sides of the tunnel being "covered with quaint sculptures mostly of mailed figures driving in chariots," which leads Sir Henry Curtis to remark that, in his opinion, "the Egyptians have been here before Solomon's people ever set a foot on it" (1992: 105-108). The three colossi who guard the entrance to the diamond mines recall for Quatermain the "false divinities" Solomon worshipped, who were also the gods of "the Phoenicians, who were the great traders of Solomon's time" (258-259). Such passages allow Haggard to show off his classical knowledge, as he does throughout his *oeuvre*, usually through the device of the "Editor." However, one can perhaps detect a deeper reason for Haggard and his contemporaries' penchant for placing non-African ruins in Africa. The desire this strategy expresses is a validation of the British presence in Africa, for if foreign civilisations had once established themselves in Africa, then a historical precedent had been set for Britain to do likewise. As Macherey proposes in *A Theory of Literary Production*, "The journey is disclosed as having ineluctably happened before. To explore is to follow, that is to say, to cover once again, under new conditions, a road already actually travelled... The conquest is only possible because it has already been accomplished" (McClintock 1990: 119; 1995: 243).

In the case of Great Zimbabwe, for example, "Haggard's message was that of the British South Africa Company: Britain was the heir to Phoenicia and British colonization of southern Africa was justifiable" (Tangri 1990: 296). Tangri's equation, however, doesn't take into account Haggard's ambivalent feelings about the British presence in South Africa, which has already been explored—Haggard, while promoting a British settler presence in Africa, also worried about the impact this would have on the indigenous peoples on a practical level, and also on the fragile Africa of his imagination. Again and again, however, Haggard points to a prior "white" presence in Africa (the common fantasy of Haggard's time being that the Egyptian civilisation, as the start of humanity, was white): The huge temple of the ruined city of Kôr is "almost as large as that of El-Karnac, at Thebes" (1991: 173), the Pongo envoys in *The Holy Flower* are "tall, light-coloured men with regular and Semitic features, who were clothed in white linen like Arabs" (1915: 176), the Makalanga people in *Benita* have "no negro blood, but rather that of some ancient people such as Egyptians or Phoenicians; men whose forefathers had been wise and civilised thousands of years ago" (1986a: 234), and so one can continue throughout Haggard's romances. Quatermain, wondering about the origins of the Zu-Vendi people, suggests that "their architecture and some of their sculptures suggest an Egyptian or possibly an Assyrian origin," and goes on to let the reader know that "it is a well-established fact that there have been many separate emigrations of Persians from the Persian Gulf to the east coast of Africa up to as lately as seven hundred years ago. There are Persian tombs at Kilwa, on the east coast, still in good repair, which bear dates showing them to be just seven hundred years old" (1995: 155-156).

A long and learned footnote by the Editor follows in which the theory is forwarded that the Zu-Vendi are "descendants of the Phoenicians" (156). The Editor gives geophysical reasons for this, adding that "to this day a very extensive trade is carried on between the Persian Gulf and Lamu and other East African ports as far south as Madagascar" (156). Quatermain goes on to describe the customs of the Zu-Vendi, allowing Haggard an extended opportunity to indulge in some cultural relativism whereby the ways of England, supposedly civilised, and Zu-Vendis, supposedly savage—though greatly tempered by its Phoenician antecedents—can be compared. Haggard is able thus to criticise aspects of British society he disliked, especially what he considered to be an exaggerated materialism: "The law of England is much more severe upon offences against property than against the person, as becomes a people whose ruling passion is money" (159). The use of foreign, "uncivilised" peoples by Haggard in his romances to criticise defects in the British political and social life of the time is commented on by Etherington: "In fact, the point of bringing colour and ancient ruins into the romances is not to make statements about race but to make statements about us, about our psychology, our past. Ruins of vanished white civilizations are there to remind us that Africa is our interior self" (1977a: 193).

Not only, then, are the ancient "white" ruins in Haggard's Africa a historical precedent for Britain's own presence in Africa, but they could also act as a demonstration of the inevitable transience of empires, including Britain's own, together with a reminder of civilised Britain's intimate relationship with a savage Africa in which the classical world, humankind's cradle, had also once had its roots. Thus Haggard's ruins fulfill a number of functions, both on the manifest level of Africanism as places to classify, catalogue and speculate about in an informed manner, and as sites of desire and fear on a latent level— desire for legitimacy and yet fear of too close a relationship with savagery. Hence, as an aside, all those beautiful black but "light skinned" women in Haggard's romances who are of savage Africa but also of an ancient "civilised" strain—Foulata (*King Solomon's Mines*), Ustane (*She*), Mameena (*Child of Storm*), Noie (*The Ghost Kings*), Sihamba (*Swallow*), Nada (*Nada the Lily*) and Nanea (*Black Heart and White Heart*), whose description summarises this type:

Her naked bronze-hued figure was tall and perfect in its proportions; while her face had little in common with that of the ordinary native girl, showing as it did strong traces of the ancestral Arabian or Semitic blood. It was oval in shape, with delicate aquiline features, arched eyebrows, a full mouth that drooped a little at the corners; tiny ears, behind which the wavy coal-black hair hung down to the shoulders, and the very loveliest pair of dark and liquid eyes that it is possible to imagine. (1903a: 34)

Finally, in Haggard, the ruins mark imperialism's anxious "interrogation of its own historical origins, and of the relations between exploitation and civilization" (Chrisman 1990: 50) in a profoundly contradictory manner. Africa is seen as both "primordial and secondary (having been preceded by an ancient white civilization); as both fundamentally antagonistic towards, and supportive of, the imperial project" (Chrisman 1992: 3).

In the face of those who see Haggard as a typical imperialist adventure writer, Haggard produces a paradoxically complex African topography onto which he projects some of his own qualifications about Britain's imperial future in Africa, introducing thereby "an adversarial element, a contentious note, not present before" (White 1995: 82). It is a fictional topography that would resonate deeply in his own age, as this passage from *The Natal Witness* (27 March, 1914) illustrates: "Who shall say how many strong and sturdy pioneers have been attracted from the pleasant Homeland to help in winning the African wilds to civilisation as a result of romantic interest aroused in them when as boys they read and revelled in these romances? Haggard did more to advertise South Africa to the world when it was less known than any man of his time" (Coan 1997: 48), and in subsequent years, as the next chapter will show.

NOTES

1. The Haggard/Schreiner correspondence is briefly referred to in several critical works on Haggard including the chapter on *She* in Gilbert and Gubar 1989: 35-36, 51-53; Cohen 1960: 90; and Hofmeyr 1980: 133. Haggard's letter of 17 February 1885 to his brother Jack discussing Schreiner is reproduced in Lewsen, P. "Olive Schreiner: Selected Documents" published in the *Brenthurst Archives* vol. 1(1) 1994: 7-29 Houghton: The Brenthurst Press. There is also Haggard's letter of 21 October 1884 to Schreiner, the original of which is held in the Harry Ransom Research Center, the University of Texas at Austin.

2. A comparable (and better known) passage wherein the hero's weapon is particularly feminised and sexualised is, of course, that dealing with Umslopogaas and the Groan-Maker battle axe. Again, while paying homage to the weapon's deadliness, the ultimate male dominance of the owner is established:

But Umslopogaas held up the great Groan-Maker, the iron chieftainess, and examined its curved points of blue steel, the gauge that stands behind it, and the beauty of its haft, bound about with a wire of brass, and ending in a knob of a stick, as a lover looks upon the beauty of his bride. Then before all men he kissed the broad blade and cried aloud: "Greeting to thee, my Chieftainess, greeting to thee, Wife of my youth, whom I have won in war. Never shall we part, thou and I, and together we will die, thou and I, for I am not minded that others should handle thee when I am gone." (Haggard 1959: 147)

3. Katz (1987) sees Haggard as being much preoccupied with Gladstone's policies in the Transvaal in the eighties and nineties and claims that these preoccupations appear not only in *Jess* but also in *The Witch's Head, Colonel Quaritch, V.C.*, and *The Way of the Spirit*. She comments on the importance for Haggard of the landscape as a screen on which to project ideology: "What is significant about these early works is their presentation of the voice of the moribund gentry and the way the imperial

landscape lent itself to the diffusion of sentimental pastoral impulses. Haggard's attraction to Empire was based partly on a reaction to the forces of free trade, Liberalism, and industrialization—ironically, all that had made Empire possible— which were eroding the landowning tradition and changing the face of England" (Katz 1987: 50-51).

4. The contradictory desire to be separate from the panorama before the gazer, and yet closer to experience it more directly, is "a contradiction that world exhibitions, with their profusion of exotic detail and yet their clear distinction between visitor and exhibit, were built to accommodate and overcome" (Mitchell 1989: 231). Haggard clearly engaged with both desires as he frequently used the bird's eye view separatism from landscape yet also got his characters physically involved in the hazards of their environment. He also regularly attended the various World Exhibitions brought to London and was thus familiar with the "land/culture as spectacle" displays.

5. Not only did Haggard create the treasure map and pottery sherd in his fictions, but he went to great lengths to create these artefacts in reality. Together with his sister-in-law, he physically made a map for *King Solomon's Mines*, artificially aged it and had it inked. The sherd in *She* was also physically made up by Haggard and his sister-in-law, with various scholars commissioned to provide the medieval Latin and old English translations inscribed upon it (Haggard 1926 vol. 1: 251; see also Etherington in Haggard 1991: 214). His pride in the degree of authenticity of these objects is evident in a story he was fond of telling concerning an old lady travelling in a train compartment with Haggard en route to taking the map to his publisher to be bound with the manuscript. The woman was reading *King Solomon's Mines* and was much taken with the picture of the map. Haggard took out the original map drawn on linen and studied it too, whereafter he exited the train leaving the old lady quite dumbfounded (Haggard 1892: 14).

6. Etherington's reference here to Haggard's African wilderness resembling in its positive aspect "a vast nobleman's park" is interesting for the way in which it foregrounds Haggard's frequent reference to "parkland" in Africa. Etherington suggests that "such vistas were an impetus to colonization and imperialism, inasmuch as they suggested the possibility of country estates open to acquisition by adventurous spirits" (in Haggard 1991: 225). Appleton in *The Symbolism of Landscape* suggests another intriguing reason for the appeal of parkland to the viewer/reader:

If there is a type of environment which we as a species can recognise as our natural habitat, it has to be the savannah.... This is now generally agreed by the anthropologists to be the kind of environment in which the first recognizable hominids made their home; ... the power of attractions ... which drew them towards this favorable kind of landscape, has not been eliminated from our genetic make-up but has survived—in Jungian terminology—as an archetype, whose influence is still to be seen in many ways, not least in the wide-spread attraction which people feel towards "parkland," an idealised contrived arrangement of well-spaced trees within a tidily groomed grassland. (1990: 15)

7. See also Haggard 1900c: 112-119 for Haggard's own description of the creation of the garden at Jess' Cottage, Pretoria. On the question of creating gardens in the colonies as domestic spaces, it is interesting that Haggard was known for his intense interest in gardening, usually seen as a woman's domain. For example, Ranger, in an article entitled "Landscape Gendering in Zimbabwe" remarks in relation to colonial Rhodesia: "As in Australia, the women created oases of civilised domesticity, green lawns and flower-gardens; they moderated essential male violence" (1994: 7). Certainly Haggard's gardening efforts in South Africa were then an exception to the norm as

described here by Ranger, who also draws on Chennells to make this point (Chennells, A. 1991 "Cultural Violence During the Pax Rhodesiana: The Evidence from Rhodesian Fiction." Conference on Political Violence in Southern Africa, Oxford).

8. Boer-owned farms in Haggard's African romances are similarly hierarchical, if more severely disciplined—see, for example, Maraisfontein in *Marie* and Botmar's Transkei farm in *Swallow*. The farmers own the land by virtue of the fact that they work it and have "created" cultivated land out of raw nature: "The farm pyramidal structure, presided over by the Boer owner, translates nature into an order based on wealth and power; in Eden, and in the hundreds of farms of South African fiction, the garden of myth finds its practical, historical actualization" (Oboe 1994: 143).

9. Haggard, it must be noted, was in favour of returning to the system of smallholding farming in England in an effort to provide the small farmer with a stake in the land. The long succession of Enclosure Acts of Parliament had transformed the sociological and topographical map of England by legislating for the enclosure of common land into larger and larger estates, squeezing out the smallholder. What Haggard campaigned for in his agricultural writings was "to revive a regime of smallholdings... returning the larger farms created by a century of Enclosure Acts to an earlier condition. It meant the active encouragement of local difference, even in a sense of return to the picturesquely primitive" (Carter in Darian-Smith 1996: 29). This radical move from one who, after all, was a member of the landed gentry, can be traced back to Haggard's firm belief in the restorative value for people of working the land.

To large classes of this country the land means a place that is green and full of cows in the summer, and brown and full of mud in winter; to another class it means a place where there are weekend parties and pheasant shoots; and to a third and more select class, a place where they can go hunting for votes. But the land is a great deal more than all these things. It is the nursery of peoples.... Therefore the land is the most vital of all the problems with which we have to deal. (Haggard 1916b: 47)

Haggard had support for his position on smallholdings from Joseph Chamberlain whose "three acres and a cow" policy was in similar vein—after reading a copy of *Rural England* that Haggard had sent to him, Chamberlain replied: "I judge from what you say that we are very much at one [on agricultural matters]. I am, and always have been, in favour of Small Holdings" (quoted in Cohen 1960: 175).

10. See Etherington (1978: 71-88) for a more detailed discussion of this issue. Gilbert and Gubar also refer to this article in their discussion of Freud's interest in Haggard's work, particularly *She*: "It is certainly likely... that, as Norman Etherington has argued, the very topography as well as the motion and direction of Haggard's quest-plots helped Freud conceptualize the psychic geography that was to be so crucial to his theory of 'layered personality'" (1989: 43).

11. Haggard's lifelong preoccupation with Jock's untimely death has a bizarre echo in *Maiwa's Revenge* in Maiwa's preoccupation with her child's death in a lion trap. She keeps one of the child's hands "which evidently had been carefully dried in the smoke" in a pouch about her waist ([1888]1965: 70). Maiwa's revenge against the child's father is called the War of the Little Hand in recognition of the pathetic (and grisly) hand Maiwa carries as remembrance of the child lost.

12. There is very little surviving record of how Haggard felt about his own sexuality or sexual life. He made one such rare reference in a note written on 15 November 1918, where he writes: "He [Kipling] thinks that imagination such as mine is the sign and expression of unusual virility, a queer theory that may have something in it" (Cohen

1965: 107). The telltale "may" suggests that Haggard privately agreed with Kipling. In a letter written to his wife Louie, en route to Tasmania on board ship in foul weather, he admitted his depressed spirits in a very uncharacteristic manner: "This kind of solitary confinement is not gay. All one's failures and failings rise before one in a melancholy procession till one is sick of contemplating them... No wonder the people make love to each other furiously, for physical warmth I imagine, as much as anything else. However it is supposed to be very healthy" (19 March 1916, unpublished letter, Norfolk Record Office). Many of Haggard's letters to his wife refer to his loneliness and melancholy—it seems that they increasingly spent time apart while Haggard was on business or researching his novels, or Louie away visiting relatives. Etherington (1984) tries to make a case for Haggard's possible incestuous longing for his mother, accounting thus for Ayesha's power over Leo in terms of Haggard's very deep love for his mother, but it seems to me that Haggard's longings were for a closer marital and sexual bond with Louie, and this is part of the fuel that goes into his sexualising of African landscapes.

13. In an interesting translation of the original map of *King Solomon's Mines* into a concrete woman's shape, one film version of the book has the map engraved on the body of a small nude female sculpture. The trail again leads through the breasts to the pubic area of the diamond mines:

The camera voyeuristically tilts down on the female body/map, scrutinizing it from the excited perspective of the archaeologist and the antique dealer. The road to the utopia of capital involves the deciphering of the map, the comprehending of the female body; the legendary twin mountains and the cave metaphorize the desired goal of the hero's mission of plunder. The geology and topography of the land are also explicitly sexualized to resemble the anatomy of a woman. (Shohat 1991: 47)

Significantly, Foulata is replaced as love interest in this version by a white woman, the archaeologist's daughter, who falls in love with Quatermain. The deciphering of the map and the final attainment of the treasure parallel the development to closure of the couple's love affair.

14. Showalter, among others, describes the sexual ambience of *She* as being particularly homosocial, beginning with the all-male community of Cambridge (Holly, Leo, Job) with which the book opens. These male adventurers seek out Ayesha as one who holds the secret of life, the "Ur-Mother," one whose power is eventually broken. With Ayesha's death, "the space is charted for unbroken male bonding and creativity.... The vast popularity of *She* suggests how powerfully it spoke to a male community" (Showalter 1991: 87). Showalter also comments on the sexualisation of Haggard's African landscape, though she stresses the homoerotic potential of the text: "They penetrate Kôr ... as if it were a masculine body, through the rear cave entrances into the 'bowels of a great mountain'" (86). Although there are undoubtedly homoerotic elements in Haggard's work, and indeed much adventure fiction of the time, I would argue that Haggard's topography is feminised by a male heterosexual viewing eye, and that thus the underlying sexual dynamic of the text is predominantly heterosexual.

15. Variations of this "nervous tic" when describing sexualised landscapes occur elsewhere in Haggard's romances, an example of which is found in this extract from *Heu Heu*: "We were through the lip of the mountains, *if I may so call it* [italics added], and had entered a stretch of unbroken virgin forest, a veritable sea of great trees that occupied the rich land of the plain and grew to an enormous size and tallness" (1972: 106).

16. Chennells points out that most explorer-adventurers and settlers would have realised that the Southern Zambezian plateau "was thickly populated and populated by a people who were skilled agriculturalists" (1982: 170). He quotes, among others, Selous on the size and prosperity of numerous black tribes resident on the plateau prior to the Ndebele raids at the beginning of the nineteenth century. Haggard himself wrote of the Zulu and other tribes resident in Zululand under Chaka's rule in *Nada the Lily*, set also at the beginning of the nineteenth century. In his contradictory vision of southern Africa as both empty and peopled, Haggard seems to imply that the African landscape is so vast that *despite* the presence of indigenous dwellers, there is still land to spare.

17. Haggard also attributed this Semitic/negroid mix occasionally, and rather unusually, to the Zulus, giving the lie here to the strong anti-Semitism usually attributed to Haggard since he was always so admiring of the Zulu people: "Probably they [the Zulus] are Semitic, or semi-Semitic in their origin, since they retain sundry of the customs of the Jews and kindred people. Thus they celebrate a feast of the first-fruits, and have somewhat similar regulations as to clean and unclean food and so forth" (1908b: 764). The article this passage is drawn from is entitled "The Zulus: the Finest Savage Race in the World," which encapsulates Haggard's attitude to the Zulus—they were undoubtedly savage, hence their appeal for him, but the best of all possible savages. In an extract from "A Journey through Zululand," Haggard speculates on the possible Semitic blood of a very light-skinned Zulu chief's daughter: "Here without doubt the old Arab blood—or was it Semitic or Somali?—still declared itself after a score or a hundred of generations" (1916a: 87).

CHAPTER 5: THE HAGGARD LEGACY

> In a strange, oblique way the last eighty-five years of South African fiction has [*sic*] been an extensive footnote to Rider Haggard. We had to wait until 1972 before we got a serious "literary" novel about explorers [Fugard, S. *The Castaways*]. His allegorical battle of love and hate, light and dark, energy and entropy, the cry of the smothered soul for release from rational anguish—all these are still with us. His work is visionary, touching on the primordial experience.
> —Don Maclennan and Sarah Christie, *Dream Life and Real Life,* 35-36

Although the above extract from Maclennan and Christie's unpublished work *Dream Life and Real Life* (1973)[1] will make some hackles rise, there is an element of truth in the observation it makes. Though Haggard's influence on successive British romance writers and colonial civil servants is well known, his influence on South African writers is less well documented, though it has been profound. Speaking of the mark Haggard made on his countrymen and women, Graham Greene remarked:

If it had not been for that romantic tale of Allan Quatermain, Sir Henry Curtis, Captain Good, and above all, the ancient witch Gagool, would I at nineteen have studied the appointment list of the Colonial Office and very nearly picked on the Nigerian Navy for a career? And later, when surely I ought to have known better, the odd African fixation remained. . . . Wasn't it the incurable fascination of Gagool with her bare yellow skull, the wrinkled scalp that moved and contracted like the head of a cobra that led me to work all through 1942 in a little stuffy office in Freetown, Sierra Leone? (1969: 15)

C.S. Lewis, in an essay written in the 1960s entitled "The Mythopoeic Gift of Rider Haggard," asked why "obstinately, scandalously Haggard continues to be read and re-read" (1984: 128). He came to the conclusion that Haggard's continued popularity rested "on an appeal well above high-water mark" derived from a "great myth" (131) that Haggard had developed in his African romances. Most South African academics, while noting Haggard's influence on South African literature, have been less positive, seeing him primarily as a conservative, imperialist writer, and have not always noted his contradictory, complex position on central ideological positions of his age. Thus Stephen Gray sees Haggard, quite correctly, as part of a boys' adventure story lineage stretching from Captain Marryatt and R.M. Ballantyne, through Buchan and Stuart Cloete, to Wilbur Smith, but states that it would be a "tedious business" to discuss them separately as they all "conform so rigidly to established patterns" (1979: 111).

Though Haggard certainly used the formulaic adventure model, his interest for my purposes lies in the manner in which he projected doubts about his age and person onto the imaginative geography he constructed in these romances; in this sense he is not as straightforward a "potboiler" writer as Gray seems to imply. Gray comments on the influence of this tradition on South African literature, on its "awesome power and undying appeal" and sees merit in "trying to define it more closely," which seems to contradict his earlier position. He hopes thereby to "arrive at a more clear definition of the literature [South African English Literature] as a whole" (111). Hofmeyr comments as well on Haggard's ongoing popularity, evident in "the strength and longevity of an ongoing reproductive ideology concerning Africa, that still claims many ardent supporters" (1980: 218), and attributes this popularity to "the reactionary image of Africa and its inhabitants that Haggard created" (218). Paul Rich, in an essay entitled "Romance and the Development of the South African Novel" that discusses *Jess* at some length as well as novels of Buchan, Paton, Gordimer and Coetzee, reinforces the perception of the durability of the romance form and of Haggard as one of its exponents. He writes: "romance formulas remain deeply embedded within the South African literary experience and it may, indeed, take generations of urban living before the nostalgia for the pastoral and idyllic is finally driven from the heart" (1984: 135).

It seems, however, that, as Rich points out, nostalgia is a particularly powerful force in what might be called the "Haggard legacy" in South African letters. As McClure observes on the importance of nostalgia in the late imperial romance: "Most writers in the mode respond to the threat of global modernization by finding some way to return to the earlier, more heroic days of imperial adventure . . . they produce nostalgic historical novels about these earlier days . . . [for example] increasingly fantastic romances like H. Rider Haggard's, set on 'new frontiers' in the most remote parts of the globe" (McClure 1994: 11).

In this chapter, though I will discuss quite diverse South African writers who claim to have been influenced by Haggard, I will note the role of nostalgia in the depiction of, specifically, a South African topography. Nostalgia relates very strongly to Said's notion of a latent discourse that runs parallel to a manifest discourse on Orientalism. Said points out that though changes may occur on the manifest level of discourse about a place—historical, economic and social changes, scientific discoveries that refine "knowledge" or information of peoples and spaces—the latent level remains generally unaltered: "Whatever change occurs in knowledge of the Orient is found almost exclusively in manifest Orientalism; the unanimity, stability and durability of latent Orientalism are more or less constant" (Said 1995: 206).

Furthermore, Said maintains that the geography of the Orient is central to the latent and unchanging characteristics of Orientalism. If we apply the same terms to what could be called a discourse of Africanism, as I suggest in chapter 1, the dual discourse theory of Said's can be very helpful. While South Africa has undergone profound changes in the twentieth century in many areas—historically, politically, economically, socially—to which the manifest level of discourse bears witness, there remains a barely changing latent level of nostalgic discourse about Africa, certainly in terms of landscape, that is evident in an ongoing tradition of romance adventure tales, the lineage of which Gray outlines. It seems then, that Haggard captured not only the *Zeitgeist* of his age in his African romances, but also left for succeeding generations of South African writers and readers a legacy of nostalgia for a kind of Africa cast forever in amber, a mythical Africa particularly echoed in the geographies of his successors. In fact, the more the manifest level of discourse has changed, the more the latent nostalgic desire for Haggard's "safe and secret" (1894: 762) African spaces has survived. At the end of the twentieth century, with South Africa profoundly politically altered, with violence on the increase and the urban jungle becoming more than a metaphor, perhaps it is no wonder that Wilbur Smith—billed by many as Haggard's current successor—is the world's biggest popular seller, with over a hundred million sales to his credit (Smith 1997b: 72). This chapter will trace this "Haggard legacy" in twentieth-century South African literature—especially as regards use of landscape—in those romance writers most directly connected to him, in whom the latent level of discourse is loudest, being foregrounded.[2] I will also consider those who might in popular terms be called "potboiler" writers, together with aspects of twentieth-century popular culture in South Africa that show evidence of Haggard's influence. Although this may disappoint some who disdain such writing in favour of other, more "serious" writers of romances, my contention is that the popularity of such writers and their possible influence demand they be taken seriously.

JOHN BUCHAN: *PRESTER JOHN* (1910)

Before turning to the South African writers, however, it is worth mentioning John Buchan, who directly continued the imperialist "boy's own" adventure tradition in his influential and popular work set in South Africa, *Prester John* (1910). Though he lacks Haggard's contradictory and at times doubtful approach to imperialism, Buchan's interest for this book lies in his repetition, in a work that would become a popular classic, of some of Haggard's characteristic handling of African spaces. For readers who had been enchanted by Haggard's Africa—in the same way as they had been by "Kipling's India, Stevenson's Pacific Islands and Gilbert Parker's Canada" (Bursey 1972: 25)— *Prester John* offered a slightly different political (manifest) message but an unchanging backdrop of latent desire. Of Haggard's most immediate successors, John Buchan and *Prester John* bear Haggard's imprint most clearly. A few critics have already made this connection. Tucker in an early work on African literature, remarked that "the influence of Rider Haggard lives on in *Prester John*" (1967: 185), and Couzens claims Haggard's *She* to be "a vast unacknowledged source for . . . Buchan" (1979: 53), while Linnemann sees Buchan's nostalgic description of the North-Eastern Transvaal that follows as an example of "Rider Haggard's Africa" (1972: 13): "The heavy tropical scents which the rain brought out of the ground, the intense silence of the drooping mists and water-laden forests, the clusters of beehive Kaffir huts in the hollows, all made up a world strange and new to the sight and yet familiar to the imagination. This was the old Africa of a boy's dream, and there is no keener delight than to realise an impression of childhood" (Buchan 1903: 122).

Though Buchan cites Stevenson and Kipling as the authors he read as a boy (1941: 40, 202), it seems clear in a work such as *Prester John*, with its hidden diamond treasure, scenes of high adventure, powerful black male central character and, above all, landscape descriptions, that he had also read some of the early Haggard African romances, or at the very least was aware—because of their enormous popular success—of the African world they depicted. In some ways too, Buchan in his public service career followed Haggard's example but with more success, his career being crowned by the position of Governor General of Canada (1935-1940) and the title of Baron Tweedsmuir of Elsfield. Buchan was a first class student at Oxford and had begun to study for the Bar when he was recruited in 1901, at the age of twenty-six, to what was known as Milner's "Kindergarten" in the Transvaal. The task of this group of bright young men was to help Milner with the reconstruction of South Africa at the end of the second Anglo Boer War: to get the Boer farmers back on the land, to clear up the refugee camps, to start the mines working again and, in an echo of Haggard's dream, to bring settlers from Britain to the Transvaal in the hope that the colony might become predominantly British.

Buchan's specific brief was to deal with problems of land settlement through a specially constituted Land Settlement Department, which he headed. Like Haggard in his youth, he was obliged by his work to ride back and forth over the countryside, leading him in his autobiography entitled *Memory Hold-The-Door* to declare: "But it is the land itself which holds my memory. . . . This has much to do with the climate, which I take to be the best in the world. . . . I resolved to go back in my old age, build a dwelling, and leave my bones there" (Buchan 1941: 115, 118, 120). In particular he dreamed of settling one day in an area called the Wood Bush in the North-Eastern Transvaal (now Northern Province). What he described is Haggard's Hilldrop on a grander scale:

There is a piece of flat land, perhaps six acres square, from which a long glen runs down to the Letaba. There I shall have my dwelling. In front there will be a park to put England to shame, miles of rolling green dotted with shapely woods, and in the centre a broad glade in which a salmon-river flows in shallows and falls among tree-ferns, arums and bracken. . . . In front I shall have a flower-garden, where every temperate and tropical blossom will appear, and in a sheltered hollow an orchard of deciduous trees, and an orange plantation. Highland cattle, imported at incredible expense, will roam on the hillsides. My back windows will look down 4,000 feet on the tropics, my front on the long meadow vista with the Iron Crown mountain for the sun to set behind. . . . I shall grow my own supplies, and make my own wine and tobacco. . . . There will be wildfowl on my lake, and Lochleven trout in my waters. And whoever cares to sail 5,000 miles, and travel 1,500 by train, and drive 50 over a rough road, will find at the end of his journey such a palace as Kubla Khan never dreamed of. (Buchan 1903: 119-120)

It is a youthful vision (written at the end of his stay in South Africa, aged twenty-eight) of "Africa-as-paradise," the enclosed garden settlement safe within the broader savage wilderness, the white imperialist's desire for a "safe and secret" place in the heart of Africa. A Scot, Buchan has made himself at home with Lochleven trout and Highland cattle in the glen; it is a gentleman's country retreat where even nature is ordered and in its place. In a sense this extended fantasy was inspired by Milner's resettlement plan for the Transvaal. Rich comments on the "aristocratic dreams" that a new life in Africa could engender: "Land settlement in a colony such as the Transvaal offered opportunities for the establishment of new landed estates and the fostering of a cult of individual heroism" (Rich 1981: 9). The wide open spaces of South Africa promised much for the son of a minister of the Free Church of Scotland of modest income.

With Couzens, I would agree that—as one can see in the above extract from Buchan's nonfictional work, *The African Colony*—in *Prester John* "his descriptions of nature, his pattern of geography, are not totally ideologically neutral" (Couzens 1979: 54). All in all, *Prester John* is a highly ideologically charged work. The story centres on David Crawfurd, a young Scotsman who comes to South Africa to make a living, and the Reverend John Laputa, a charismatic black preacher and political head of a rebellion to overthrow whites in an area east of Pietersburg known as the Wood Bush. Laputa's sign of authority is a fabulous necklace of ancient rubies "which may once have burned in Sheba's hair" (Buchan 1956: 105) and his hideout is a huge mountain cave where his followers have amassed a fortune in diamonds smuggled out of the Kimberley mines. Setting himself up as a descendant of Prester John, the mythical Christian king of Ethiopia, Laputa can be seen as an early incarnation of what came to be later known in the apartheid years as "die swaart gevaar," an educated and thus dangerous black firebrand who could lead gullible blacks to overcome the minority white settlers. Couzens points out that there had been numerous instances of black resistance to white settlement in the Transvaal in the second half of the nineteenth century. Buchan would have been aware of these, as well as of the then popular fears of "Ethiopianism" or black aspirations to political glory using missionary churches as fomenting grounds.³ What is quite clear in *Prester John* is the way in which the political struggle between blacks and whites is projected on to the novel's geography—it is an allegorical struggle of highlanders versus lowlanders. In *The African Colony* Buchan had already sounded this drum. Describing his beloved Wood Bush area, he says:

It is England, richer, softer, kindlier, a vast demesne laid out as no landscape gardener could ever contrive, waiting for a human life worthy of such an environment. But it is more—it is that most fascinating of all types of scenery, a garden on the edge of a wilderness. And such a wilderness! Over the brink of the meadow, four thousand feet down, stretch the steaming fever flats. From a cool fresh lawn you look clear over a hundred miles of nameless savagery. (1903: 126)

Crawfurd, like some of Haggard's adventurers, feels the lure of the places of "nameless savagery." He nearly succumbs to Laputa's power, but manages to resist and return "home" with a wealth of diamonds to show for his exploits. Laputa's death produces a brutal catharsis that releases Crawfurd from his thrall. The narrow escape from savagery in *Prester John* has its objective correlative in the landscape:

After that the country changed again. The wood was now getting like that which clothed the sides of the Berg. There were tall timber-trees . . . and the ground was carpeted with thick grass and ferns. The sight gave me my first earnest of safety. I was approaching my own country. Behind me was heathendom and the black fever flats. In front were the cool mountains and bright streams, and the guns of my own folk. (1956: 130)

And again, a little later in the novel after his final escape from Laputa, Crawfurd states:

I had thought that my entry into the cave, my time in it, and my escape had taken many hours, whereas at the most they had occupied two. It was little more than dawn, such a dawn as walks only on the hilltops. Before me was the shallow vale with its bracken and sweet grass, and farther on the shining links of the stream, and the loch still grey in the shadow of the beleaguering hills. Here was a fresh, clean land, a land for homesteads and orchards and children. All of a sudden I realized that at last I had come out of savagery. (189)

The "monarch-of-all-I-survey" trope, beloved of early African explorers and of Haggard as well, has become hardened into a strategic plan for the white man's survival in South Africa: seize the high ground, turn it into "home" (the "vale," "bracken," "loch" of the above passage) and leave the savages to the "black fever flats" of the earlier quotation. Couzens points out that this is "no coincidence" as British administrative thinking was running along similar lines, culminating in the Native Land Act of 1913 whereby "the pattern of land ownership was beginning to freeze in South Africa" (Couzens 1979: 41). Linked to this idea of territorial containment is Buchan's ending the novel with the introduction of educational containment in the creation of a "native training college... no factory for making missionaries and black teachers, but an institution for giving the Kaffirs the kind of training which fits them to be good citizens of the state" (1956: 202). This is certainly "different to the conception of Rider Haggard of independent African communities free from white missionary influence" (Rich 1981: 18). Buchan's imperialism (and racism) is far more categoric than Haggard's earlier visions of Noble Savagery superimposed onto the Zulus. Buchan, like Crawfurd, is a firm believer in the "white man's duty;" in "the difference between white and black, the gift of responsibility, the power of being in a little way a king; and so long as we know this and practise it, we will rule not in Africa alone but wherever there are dark men who live only for the day and their own bellies" (1956: 198).

Prester John, written by "the last Victorian" as Himmelfarb describes Buchan (1968: 249), is a work which sounds the fading bugle notes of the imperialist adventure story. As Gray points out, whereas "in Haggard... we have a man who, like Quatermain, raided, but finally retreated; in Buchan the flag is there to stay" (1979: 128), for Couzens the end of the book "records the final victory of white light" (1979: 53). Where Haggard was part of an expansionist phase of nineteenth-century British imperialism in Africa, allowing him to imagine ever new prospects (and fantasised dangers), Buchan is at the turning point, past the initiatory "penetration" of Darkest Africa. Echoes of this still sound, however, not least in Janet Smith's biography of Buchan in which she describes him investing *Prester John* with "his own exhilaration about riding on the veldt, penetrating the Wood Bush, catching hints of old mysteries" (1979: 54). Generally, however, there is little of Haggard's sexualising of African landscape, which is perhaps not surprising given Buchan's extremely disciplined and rather cold temperament. Etherington suggests that the exciting adventures of his fiction provided Buchan with an "outlet for the anxieties and risky impulses he suppressed in every other part of his life" (1981: 3). The Wood Bush is Buchan's desired locus, but neither the map of the area with which *Prester John* begins (see map 2), nor descriptions of the area betray any subconscious sexual fantasies. In fact Gray draws an explicit contrast between Haggard and Buchan in this regard:

In *King Solomon's Mines* Haggard contrived to leave the treasure chest of all Africa buried under a mountain the size of Sheba's breasts [not, strictly speaking, correct given the novel's topography], which in turn left the reader with the promise of suckling on further romance. But in Buchan the body of romance is given its hysterectomy, as it were; Crawfurd dynamites into smithereens the cave that was his entry into manhood, and he has no compunction about hocking everything but the most sacred of the "fetiches" in which all of Africa's power is (supposedly) vested. (1979: 131)

What is still left intact, however, despite the obvious political clouds gathering on Buchan's African horizon, is the possibility that still remains of "Africa-as-paradise," as garden perched on high ground above the wilderness, a thread that carries over into South African literature.

SOL PLAATJE: *MHUDI* (1930)

The leap from Haggard, specifically in *Nada the Lily* (1892), to Sol Plaatje's *Mhudi*, (1930) which was hailed as the first novel written in English by a black African, is not as big as it may superficially seem to be. For a start, Plaatje, in a letter to Silas Molema dated August 1920, described *Mhudi* as "a novel—a love story after the manner of romances; but based on historical facts . . . with plenty of love, superstition, and imaginations worked in between . . . wars. Just like the style of Rider Haggard when he writes about Zulus" (quoted in Chennells 1997: 37).[4]

Chrisman further draws the two writers together by noting that they "mark either end of the imperial trajectory in black South Africa," since Haggard's Zulu romance was written during a time of full British control over Zululand and Plaatje's *Mhudi* came at the end of an era of British imperialism in South Africa. Both were sympathetic to a pro-imperial British position, but anti-Boer; both used the historical romance form for a novel set during the period of the Mfecane (1992: 144). Chennells, however, disagrees that Haggard and Plaatje can be drawn too closely together, primarily on account of what he calls "the conscious ahistoricism of Haggard's Africa, where time and geography are blurred, and Mhudi's sensitivity to the multiple historical consequences of the initial encounter between Boer and Tswana." He finds Haggard's romances "finely formed" but *Mhudi* "ill-made": "The well-made novel is in part the creation of an authoritative narrative voice on which the reader can depend for access to a morally stable world which in Haggard is a world where honourable men still prevail. There is no equivalent stability in *Mhudi* and it is in the tentativeness of both his political and moral vision that Plaatje least resembles Haggard" (1997: 37-38).

While I would agree that Haggard is deliberately vague in many of his African romances about a precise location within Africa for his setting, and at times conveniently glosses over time jumps, this is not generally true of *Nada the Lily*, which is, possibly after *Jess*, the most specifically located African romance in Haggard's *oeuvre* in terms of both time and place. I have also tried to demonstrate, by looking at the contradictions and anxieties that cause the fissures in his African topography, that Haggard's moral and political universe was not as stable as one might have expected from a man of his class. Where I do agree with Chennells is in his useful observation of movement in Haggard's African romances "from African littoral to interior which is simultaneously a movement from literal to metaphorical" where "the narrating voice leaves the reader in no doubt that it is in the metaphorical that wisdom is revealed" (Chennells 1997: 37). In some ways, Plaatje employs the same device—it is in the almost allegorical scenes of pre-lapsarian Barolong life at peace with the land that his "wisdom"/critique is most keenly felt. I will briefly look at this small, specific area of overlap between Haggard and Plaatje.

Mhudi, though published in 1930, was written closer to 1917 when Plaatje published his *Native Life in South Africa*, a scathing attack on the Natives' Land Act of 1913, a law which restricted blacks to being wage labourers, unable to own or rent their own land outside the Reserves. For Haggard, who once wrote in a letter to Lord Gladstone, "I think that the Zulus are in a most unhappy position. Some two thirds of their land are in the hands of white people: often they are rent paying squatters on the territory which their fathers occupied" (1914a: 196), this would surely have also seemed a cruel, exploitative step to take. Though I can find no evidence of this in his diaries, it is tempting to speculate whether he heard Plaatje speak in London, where he travelled in 1913 as part of the African National Congress deputation mandated to appeal to the British government against this Act, and again as part of a second delegation to plead for British support for their cause during the European peace negotiations.

Mhudi tells the story of the displacement in the 1830s of the pastoralist Barolong people by the forces of Mzilikazi, their later ill-advised joining of forces with the Boers who had trekked up from the Cape, and their subsequent victory over Mzilikazi, who was forced to retreat to present-day Zimbabwe where he founded the Matabele nation. The narrative is seen through the lovers Mhudi and Ra-Thaga, Barolong refugees who shelter in the wilderness where they have a child, after which they join up with others of their clan at Thaba Ncho, befriend the Boers, and fight Mzilikazi's army, finally trekking off into the sunset in a Boer wagon given to them to start afresh at Thaba Ncho. Plaatje said in his preface that he wanted "to interpret to the reading public one phase of 'the back of the Native mind'" (Plaatje 1975: 17)—as Haggard also wished in *Nada the Lily* to "think with the mind and speak with the voice of a Zulu of the old régime" (1949: x)—which Couzens interprets as meaning that Plaatje intended in *Mhudi* to launch "a defence of traditional custom as well as a corrective view on history, . . . [and] also an implicit attack on the injustice of land distribution in South Africa in 1917 . . . The novel, in other words, is a moral attack on the descendants of those who were welcomed to the land and helped by their hosts to drive off those who threatened it" (Couzens in Plaatje 1975: 13).

It is in the nostalgic depiction of traditional custom and interdependence of people and land that Plaatje most echoes Haggard, in my view. Plaatje evokes in *Mhudi* "a veritable green world of romantic pastoral" (Chrisman 1992: 159). In describing the centuries-old ways of the Bechuana tribes in the central Transvaal and Kalahari regions, Plaatje writes:

In this domain they led their patriarchal life under their several chiefs who owed no allegiance to any king or simple emperor. They raised their native corn which satisfied their wants, and, when not engaged in hunting or in pastoral duties, the peasants whiled away their days in tanning skins or sewing magnificent fur rugs. They also smelted iron and manufactured useful implements which today would be pronounced very crude by their semi-westernized descendants.

Cattle breeding was the rich man's calling, and hunting a national enterprise. Their cattle, which carried enormous horns, ran almost wild and multiplied as prolifically as the wild animals of the day. Work was of a perfunctory nature, for mother earth yielded her bounties and the maiden soil provided ample sustenance for man and beast. (Plaatje 1975: 21)

Similarly, Haggard evokes in the opening pages of *Nada the Lily* a pastoral idyll based on an agrarian society at peace, prior to its destruction by Chaka some years hence:

Before the Zulus were a people—for I will begin at the beginning—I was born of the Langeni tribe.... Our tribe lived in a beautiful open country; the Boers whom we call the Amaboona, are there now, they tell me. My father, Makedama, was chief of the tribe, and his kraal was built on the crest of a hill.... One evening, when I was still little, standing as high as a man's elbow only, I went out with my mother below the cattle kraal to see the cows driven in. My mother was very fond of these cows, and there was one with a white face that would follow her about. She carried my little sister Baleka riding on her hip; Baleka was a baby then. We walked till we met the lady driving in the cows. My mother called the white-faced cow and gave it mealie leaves which she had brought with her. Then the boys went on with the cattle, but the white-faced cow stopped by my mother.... My mother sat down on the grass and nursed her baby, while I played round her, and the cow grazed. (1949: 23)

Both the passages from *Mhudi* and *Nada the Lily* sound the same elegiac note. Both societies described would shortly be crushed: the Langeni by Chaka, the Barolong by Mzilikazi who broke away from Chaka; in both books the spaces thus vacated by the defeated peoples would be overrun by the Boers. In both books too, the "wilderness" in its nurturing guise, offers the chief protagonists succour and shelter. Mhudi and Ra-Thaga find a hiding place in "an untenanted wilderness" (Plaatje 1975: 63) in which Ra-Ṭhaga is able to imagine himself as reigning supreme in his own kingdom with the wild animals as his subjects. In the "monarch-of-all-I-survey" convention, he is able to climb a tree next to the hut they have built and survey the land between his home and the horizon from a position of height. Unusually for the convention, Mhudi, who is shown as extremely wise and brave, is also given a bird's-eye view scene:

One day, I decided to walk along the stony slope to the summit of a koppie at the far end of the ridge. My limbs being much better in spite of the abiding stiffness, I could pick my way much more easily over the rocks. I couldn't tell what part of the world that was, but when I reached the summit, a wide stretch of country was exposed to view and the sight of the outer world fascinated me immensely.... I enjoyed the refreshing view for a time, although haunted by fear and loneliness; then I retraced my steps and wandered back towards the ravine where there was food and water. (37)

The vistas afforded to both Ra-Thaga and Mhudi are more circumscribed than those typical of Haggard's texts: Ra-Thaga cannot see the world lying before him like a map as can Quatermain in *King Solomon's Mines*, but his circumscribed view is at least clear; Mhudi enjoys the perfection of her "refreshing view" from the hilltop, though she remains "haunted by fear and loneliness," sentiments usually absent from the more confident, masculinist position of earlier imperialist texts. This is not surprising, given the imminent break-up of the pastoral edenic world they had once inhabited. What Plaatje conveys is a sense of historical forces closing in, leaving a latent desire for the untrammelled, "Africa-as-paradise" whose occupants live in harmony with the land. It is a "vision of a paradise destroyed by a combination of warring white tribes and Zulus, [which] bears some remarkable similarities to parts of the imperialist vision of paradise lost" (Hutchings 1981: 10). However, despite the gathering storm clouds, Plaatje manages to end *Mhudi* on a more regenerative note than does Haggard in *Nada the Lily*, which ends in a "genocidal closure" (Chrisman 1992: 166). In this way, Chrisman suggests that Plaatje follows the romance pattern more faithfully than Haggard, for the ending in *Mhudi*, in which Mhudi and Ra-Thaga leave the Boers to begin a new life and Mzilikazi and Umnandi are reunited in the birth of an heir, marks a new cycle of life. It is a new cycle tempered, however, by caution, aware as Plaatje was of the difficulties the black man in South Africa was to face from "such cruel people" (1975: 102) as the Boers, whom Haggard had similarly described.

THE POTBOILER LEGACY: STUART CLOETE AND WILBUR SMITH

A rather critical analysis of *Mhudi* states that "the novel shows only that Plaatje was capable of writing a potboiler in order to raise money for a more important set of projects [to collect and print Sechuana folktales], and that his really serious effort had gone into *Native Life in South Africa*" (Christie, Hutchings, Maclennan 1980: 81). Despite any imperfections *Mhudi* might have,[5] it is certainly not a potboiler. For Haggard's legacy in that vein of South African literature, we must turn to the novels of Stuart Cloete and Wilbur Smith. Cloete, who quite candidly described himself as "by my own definition a first-class second-class writer—neither highbrow nor lowbrow" (1973: 166), was born in England in 1897, the year of Queen Victoria's Diamond Jubilee. He was acutely aware of the changing world he occupied:

This was the world into which I was born. The very zenith of British glory. I have lived to see its nadir. I fought for an empire[6] and find myself in a Coloured Commonwealth with an England that has broken every promise she ever made. I have gone from a world that thought with Tennyson and Kipling to one in which the predominant influence is the London School of Economics. (Cloete 1972: 14)

Born into an upper middle-class family of South African origin, Cloete's formative years were spent in England and France, where his childhood reading included Kipling, Captain Marryat, Sir Gilbert Parker and Haggard, whose works "were the literary milk of my boyhood from which I have never been weaned" (quoted in Cohen 1965: 231). Given these literary influences, it was perhaps inevitable that, as Rabkin remarks on discussing South African literature, "Cloete's own works can be described as seeds of that same, now extinct, imperial flower, still flourishing in this last of all colonial gardens" (1978: 39). Pensioned out of the army because of war injuries, Cloete went farming, about which he seems to have felt much the same as his childhood author, Haggard, although he adopts here an unwittingly Marxist line: "[Farmers] have the immense satisfaction of knowing what they are doing. . . . How many men today make anything? Make the whole of it? What satisfaction to man's creative urges does 8 hours 5 days a week on an assembly line give him?" (Cloete 1972: 135). Perhaps it was this dissatisfaction with an increasingly changing, industrialised Europe that led Cloete to seek for new opportunities in South Africa; his interpretation of the move harks to a nostalgia for the wide open spaces of his forebears:

South Africa was in my blood. I had been brought up on stories of hunting lion and elephant, of Kaffir wars. . . . The vast horizon made me want to get on a horse and ride towards it. I wanted to hunt, to camp under the stars, to sink myself into it. Much of this was, of course, due to the way I had been brought up with stories of Africa, to what I had read—Rider Haggard, Livingstone's Travels, Du Chaillu, Selous and the works of other explorers. But I think it went deeper than that. It was in my blood as well as my brain. My family, father and son, had been here almost 300 years. . . . We were not newcomers nor had we taken land from other people as the American settlers had taken it from the Indians. (1973: 41, 72)

He managed a ranch in a very isolated part of the Transvaal bushveld (now Gauteng Province), eventually buying his own farm, Constantia, near Irene. Of Constantia, which in its name nostalgically and fruitlessly recalls its gracious, grander Cape namesake quite removed from the aridity of the Transvaal scrub, Cloete wrote: "It was, though I did not know it then, the place where I saw the Africa about which, later, I was to spend my life writing" (Cloete 1973: 107). It was here that his writing career got its start after he showed a few of his short stories to a visiting friend, Arnot Robertson (*Four Frightened People*), who in turn showed them to Sarah Gertrude Millin among others, all of whom said he had some talent. Cloete sold up and returned to England to devote himself to writing. His breakthrough came with *Turning Wheels* (1937). He acknowledges that the task of ending the book defeated him "so I killed the lot" (1973: 179). Nevertheless, it was chosen in the United States as a "Book of the Month," ensuring its success and his future career as a writer.

The Africa that Cloete nostalgically describes is still the "Africa-as-paradise" familiar to readers, but it is an Eden won at great cost, drenched in blood, and burdened with growing fears of the black man, resulting in a pervasive racism. *Turning Wheels* carries the weighty bitterness of an author who has just missed the imperial boat and feels cheated of his birthright. It is the story of Hendrik van den Berg and his followers, who leave the Cape Colony in 1836 on the Great Trek northwards to search, literally, for Hendrik's vision of paradise, which they find at Nylstrom (nowadays spelt Nylstroom) in the Transvaal. Unlike Haggard, who generally disliked the Boers, Cloete depicts them as "the white Noble Savage, the suitable inhabitants of Africa's spacious paradises.... Love of liberty, as Cloete points out, mingles in their search for the earthly paradise and lifts it above the mere greed for crops and herds" (Howe 1971: 125). Though Cloete invests the Zulus with some degree of noble savagery—"They were elephants that trampled those who opposed them. They were lions who ripped up and destroyed. They were Zulus: their glory was undenied" (1967: 372)—they are generally seen *en masse* as a barbaric and animal-like menace to the individualised, heroic Boers. After a Zulu attack on Nylstrom, Cloete writes: "The lands, too, were devastated. Here was wanton anger let loose. Here was the result of taking land from the natives and thinking that those who came down from their mountain fastness to stare and trade, or even to work, were tame" (1967: 343).

The phrase "taking land from the natives" seems, incidentally, to contradict Cloete's proud assertion that his forebears had not "taken land from other people" (previously quoted). Cloete's frequently disparaging and generally downright racist attitude to blacks in this novel and others leads Tucker to assert that Cloete "is the descendant of Rider Haggard, with this important distinction: he denigrates the black warrior, whereas Haggard idealized him" (1967: 203). Symbolically, this reduction in status of the black warrior in Cloete can perhaps be read into a change Cloete made to one of the black characters in this book. He remarked of a friend's editing efforts: "She destroyed a character I had who resembled Ryder [*sic*] Haggard's Umslopogaas, the big Zulu. I changed him into Rinkhals, a small wizened witch doctor" (1973: 179).

Despite the slip recorded above, in which he acknowledges the "natives" prior ownership of land, South Africa is generally seen by Cloete as empty and Africa in general as "a dark continent" (Cloete n.d.: 9)—"by and large this was a new and empty country washed clean of life by the spears of the Zulu impis" (20). *Rags of Glory* (1963), a "big novel... painted on the immense canvas of the South African veld" as the blurb tells the reader, and set at the time of the Anglo-Boer wars, confirms the "empty land" possibility.

Pretoria was where civilization ended in Africa. In one direction, to the south, were roads, railroads, towns—Cape Town, the ocean, and Europe. In the other, scattered farms like their own Groenplaas, and then nothing. It was true that the President had built a railroad to Delagoa Bay so that the republic would have an access to the sea that was not English. But it was an empty land the track ran through, a wilderness of low veld, and many had died of fever in its construction. (1974: 21)

The imperialist's enthusiasm for new, wide open spaces is tempered by the knowledge of how hard won the small settlements established in the vastness are and—with the hindsight of Empire's decline—there is a recognition of how ephemeral these enclaves were. Cloete carries the strain of imperialist and Boer aspirations in South Africa, and while he could reluctantly accept the decline of British imperialism in Africa, in *Turning Wheels* he pins his hopes on white Boer survival in South Africa. Hendrik van den Berg already starts "improving" paradise in his mind's eye once the promised land has been reached. His phrasing and imagery both recall Biblical passages:

On the third day he rode up a mountain and, crossing its flat top, saw, instead of another range, a wide expanse of country spread out beneath him. There, three thousand feet below, lay the promised land. There was the vlei, there were the trees, the herds of game, the rivers.... Already he saw the furrows cut along the hillsides, the fruit trees and the crops. Where there was new game he saw cattle, where there were now no people he saw many. (1967: 122-123)

This dream is defeated by a combination of Zulu might and "the slow wearing down of disease and from the outside pressure of the wilds . . . forcing them always into a smaller circle" (1967: 314). Even the bird's-eye view passages in Cloete combine the promise of power with the danger of defeat—Boers retreating from British onslaughts stop in *Rags of Glory* at a cliff edge overlooking Mozambique:

Below them the cliff fell in a granite curtain, the bush looking like a mossy carpet stretched to an infinite horizon, the green fading to the blue distance.... This was the wilds—as yet untamed, unknown except to a few hunters. A land held inviolate by its dangers. This was a country where death came quickly.... Death and beauty walked here hand in hand. There was no waste, no blood spilled in vain, the dead [*sic*] of one thing giving life to another, so the balance of life. (1974: 434-435)

As Cloete takes Haggard's African topography and demonises it with portents of blood, death and savagery, so too, does he transform in much of his writing a sexualised landscape into a swamp of truly terrifying black fecundity: "This was the womb of the world, her dark, moist womb. This was a breeding place, a spawning place, lush, dark, hot, fetid—a place where tremendous mushrooms grew in a night; where flights of locusts blackened the sky . . . where everything was strangled by its own fecundity" (Cloete quoted in Hammond and Jablow 1970: 149).

In a crude version of the England/Africa and male/female dichotomies of the nineteenth-century imperial project, Cloete generalises on the subject of African women: "One could see why white men took them as housekeepers. They were all woman.... They said with their dark eyes: We are women. You are a man. We know what you want" (Cloete 1957: 70-71). Overtaken as Cloete's dreams of Africa were by the harsh realities of history, his African novels keep alight the nostalgic latent lamp of desire for a vast, empty, fertile Africa, but he has lost Haggard's idealism and his contradictory, complex position on Africa. Instead, using crude tools, Cloete overlays Haggard's more subtle maps with garish, prurient nightmare.

Wilbur Smith is the current, reigning "modern Rider Haggard" (Johnson in Smith 1995a) and the first of the linked Haggard legatees to be born in Africa. He was born in 1933 in Northern Rhodesia, now Zambia, of British parents from Brighton who bought a maize farm on the Kafue River, near Mazabuka. His British roots, however, hold firm. Despite an African childhood, Smith maintains: "All my tradition is British, and if there ever had to be a choice for me, I would have to go with my British antecedents" (Smith 1995a). Some of these British roots include an education at Michaelhouse, an exclusive, British-style private boys' school in the KwaZulu Natal Midlands, and a reading diet of Rider Haggard together with other boys' adventure classics (Smith n.d.: 4). In his school holidays, however, he was able to live out the dreams of the classics he read:

It was a large farm... one small area was under maize and the rest was wild bush. There were bushbuck, duiker and all sorts of birds so I used to spend most of my school holidays wandering around, you know, with a little black guy as my companion.... There were always guns on the rack at home, fishing rods behind the door and pointer dogs lying on the hearth.

Every year we'd go on a big safari. We'd load up two or three trucks with all the farm personnel and everything we needed—beds, the whole lot, and head off down the Zambezi valley or out Solwezi way. You cut your own roads into the bush in those days. My dad had a light aircraft, a Tigermoth, and long before the safari he'd be out doing recces of the area to see where the game was concentrated. Then, six weeks or so before we were due to leave, he'd send some of our staff out with bicycles and bags full of matches to burn the bush. The first rains would come, and the new grass, and the game would congregate in droves in what was virtually a paradise. The safari was always this huge operation, building bridges across some of the small rivers, and we'd get into completely untouched country. Some of my happiest memories were out there with the old man. (Smith 1997b: 71-72)

It is worth quoting this passage at some length, for it is the twentieth-century version of the nineteenth-century dream—a masculine world, vast "untouched" open spaces, huge herds of game, dominant whites and subservient, biddable black "staff;" in short, "Africa-as-paradise." The tell-tale "in those days" (probably the 1940s, when Smith was a teenager) has already set the scene in amber, it is already awash with nostalgia, for history has made this vision no longer possible—various independence struggles had ruined the pliability of black "staff," land development had opened up previously unexplored areas, and the "old man" was dead.

Starting off his working career as a tax inspector for the Inland Revenue department in Salisbury, Southern Rhodesia, Smith wrote *When the Lion Feeds* (1964), which, though rejected by seventeen publishers, finally saw the light of day and changed its author's career path entirely. This novel begins the saga, set in the last quarter of the nineteenth century, of the Courtney family in South Africa. Like his other novels, which were to follow with disciplined regularity, it uses "the 'Haggard' recipe larded with adult sex [which] provides Wilbur Smith with his international best-seller fare: endless safaris and seductions, big game, game women, an Africa where the approved politics are thoroughly conservative" (Chapman 1996: 131). Always adamant that he writes to entertain rather than instruct—on *Rage* (1988) Smith commented "'It's not a political thriller and I'm no message writer. . . . The thought of being labelled one gives me goosepimples'" (1988: 10-11)—Smith has, however, consistently raised the ire of leftist academics (mainly historians) by his wilful manipulation of history to suit his novels' political ends. What Smith sees as creating an imaginative story "on a historically correct or factual background, and in the process tell[ing] a rollicking, rip-roaring story" (Smith 1995b: 97) such that "when people finish my books, they've learned something and have been given something to think about" (Smith 1992: 14)—which somewhat contradicts his earlier "no message" statement—Couzens sees differently: "His technique is to take actual or recounted historical incidents or myths and to embellish them with his own prejudices. By the introduction of historical events he gives his ideas a pseudo-authenticity which easily entraps the reader who has little knowledge with which to compare it. Wilbur Smith *uses* history: he does not feel any duty or responsibility to it" (1982-83: 6).

In a similar vein, Harries, reviewing *Rage*, remarks that "Smith still sees Africa through the eyes of Rider Haggard, and his African characters speak in pseudo-biblical tones borrowed from *King Solomon's Mines*. More dangerously, their pronouncements sometimes intertwine innocently with those of other non-fictional black leaders. Fact and fiction enter into complicity" (1989: 4).

Rage is particularly apposite as an example of fact and fiction intermingling. Set in the politically volatile context of the 1950s and 1960s in South Africa, it includes known historical figures such as Nelson Mandela, Verwoerd, Malan and Sobukwe; together with a thinly disguised Joe Slovo (Joe Cicero) and Winnie Mandela (Vicky Gama). It covers the documented events of the Defiance Campaign, Sharpeville and the formation of Umkonto we Sizwe and Poqo. There is nothing intrinsically sinister in this—many adventure tales are set against a verifiable historical backdrop—but what needles critics about Smith is his manipulation of historical events, his occasional alteration of historical sequence and characters to suit his own conservative political agenda. In the "Author's Note" placed unobtrusively after the last page of this long novel, Smith disingenuously writes: "Once again I have taken some small liberties with the timetable of history, in particular the dates on which *Umkhonto we Sizwe* and *Poqo* movements began. . . . I hope that you, the reader, will forgive me for the sake of the narrative" (1987). He is seen as an apologist for apartheid South Africa in his novels written during that time and, given the immense popularity of his books (as previously mentioned, sales of one hundred million to date, in countless editions and translations), it seems very probable that "in the English-speaking world outside Africa Wilbur Smith is having, via his fiction, a greater formative influence on the popular conception of Africa in general, and of South African society, history and politics in particular, than any other single individual" (Maughan-Brown 1990: 134-135).

Similarly, Stoneman reviewing *A Time to Die* (1989) finds that it "is remarkable only for giving a dangerously false impression about Zimbabwe and Mozambique. . . . Reactionary propaganda in the politico-racial field is matched by similarly atavistic sexual attitudes, crudely interwoven with anti-liberal propaganda" (1989: 6, 7). Unlike Haggard, who generally sets his novels in an imprecise period where history is not foregrounded, Smith seems to seek out the manifest level of discourse. Perhaps this is because in reality political struggles in the second half of the twentieth century in South Africa have been brought to the foreground so publicly as to make them hard to ignore.

On the flip-side of this coin, however, a nostalgic latent discourse provides an ever-present *leitmotif* and finds its keenest expression in the African landscape, as it did for Haggard. Asked what he felt about African land, Smith gave an answer that could have come from Haggard, Buchan or Cloete, though their political positioning varied quite considerably: "The dust and sun. The miles and miles of bloody Africa. The quality of light. The smell of the dust. . . . The smell of the people. Africans have a different smell to us. The smell of woodsmoke. All those very different things" (Smith 1995b: 98). There is the use of the tell-tale "us," which sets whites up in a position of binary opposition to blacks, which Haggard, believing in a common savagery, did not subscribe to in the same way; but besides that, the word-picture Smith draws recalls Baines's paintings of Africa of a century and more ago. Smith, in fact, revives Baines in his romance *A Falcon Flies* (1980) through the character Tom Harkness who, like Baines, is sacked from an expedition for supposedly stealing stores and who lives in the Cape creating brilliantly coloured paintings of African scenes. It is Baines's/ Harkness' map of Central Africa that leads Robyn and Zouga Ballantyne to the kingdom of Monomotapa, "the Ophir of the Bible, where Sheba mined her gold" (1980a: 73), in search of their father, Fuller Ballantyne:

It was a map of Central Africa, east to west coast, south to the Limpopo, north to the lakes, drawn in India ink and the borders were illuminated by Harkness' characteristic figures and animals. . . . The map was huge—at least five feet square—hand-drawn on the finest-quality linen-backed paper. It was unique, the detail enormous; the notations were profuse but succinct, the observations first hand, the details precise, written in a tiny elegant script that needed a reading glass to be deciphered with ease. . . . Harkness ran his hand southwards down the parchment to cover another vast void in the web of mountains and rivers. "Here," he said softly. "The forbidden kingdom of the Monomotapas." (1980a: 71-72)

The Ballantyne siblings' journey to this fabled land is reminiscent of "a well-researched Victorian adventure story" (M.G.S. in Smith 1980b: 3)—certainly *King Solomon's Mines* springs to mind—with its account of encounters with sickness, wild animals and dangerous natives. Their arrival at their destination is marked by a bird's-eye view description that encapsulates a number of features of latent Africanist discourse: "Africa-as-paradise," the "empty land" and "monarch-of-all-I-survey" possibilities:

> Low foothills fell away from beneath their feet, regular as the swells of the ocean, covered with stately trees whose trunks were tall and grey as the oaks of Windsor Park, and then beyond the hills the undulating lightly forested grasslands, golden as fields of ripe wheat, spread to a tall blue horizon.
> "It's beautiful," Robyn murmured, still holding Zouga's hand. "The kingdom of Monomotapa," Zouga answered her, his own voice husky with emotion.
> "No," Robyn answered softly. "There is no sign of man here, this is the new Eden."
> "A new land, there for the taking!" he said, still holding Robyn's hand. They were as close, in that moment, as they had ever been or would ever be again, and the land awaited them, wide, limitless, empty and beautiful. (Smith 1980a: 277-278)

It is a secure, almost domesticated scene ("the oaks of Windsor Park"), which could thrill the 1980s reader with its promise of potential white domination over unclaimed territory as much as could Haggard's description of Kukuanaland in 1885 in *King Solomon's Mines*: "It was like Paradise" (Haggard 1992: 109). Mindful, however, of late twentieth-century black claims to land, especially in the liberation war of Rhodesia coterminous with the writing of *A Falcon Flies*, Smith gets Zouga Ballantyne to forego the ancient name of Monomotapa for this region since to use it is tacitly to acknowledge prior claim to the land. Ballantyne opts instead for "Zambezia," "the land below the Zambezi river"(Smith 1980a: 293), a name and thus an area to which he lays claim—in typical European fashion—by writing it down in his private papers. Chennells points out how history overtakes Smith in this novel, the first in a trilogy set in Rhodesia/Zimbabwe (the other two being *Men of Men* (1981) and *The Angels Weep* (1982)). From the time of *A Falcon Flies*, in which the nineteenth-century Ballantyne family can represent dominant white settler interests, to *The Angels Weep*, in which Fuller Ballantyne's descendants leave the land because they have lost control over it, Smith has to accommodate a bitter historical change in the land of his young adulthood. Chennells remarks:

> There is sometimes an anger in these novels and it is an anger that grows out of nostalgia for a land which once demanded no more complex response than a simple heroism. Commercialism and politics have replaced heroism . . . . Commercialism is one of the reasons why the land is no longer an appropriate setting for romance—a way of looking at life and his art which Smith shares with Haggard. (1984: 43-44)

Rhodesia, post-liberation, was no longer for Smith the "safe and secret" place that Haggard maintained was required by the romance form.

The work, however, that most recalls Haggard and draws on the lost white civilisation theme most strongly is Smith's earlier novel *The Sunbird* (1972) "derived from the work of H. Rider Haggard" (Stotesbury 1996: 229). The story concerns the discovery of the Lost City of the Kalahari somewhere in

Botswana by archaeologist Ben Kazin and his sponsor Louren Sturvesant. This Carthaginian empire was based on gold mining over 2,000 years ago. Now all that is left are traces of the ruins, hidden treasure and the legend of "a race of fair-skinned golden-haired warriors from across the sea, who mined the gold, enslaved the indigenous tribes, built walled cities and flourished for hundreds of years before vanishing almost without trace" (Smith 1974: 21). The twist to this story's tale is that both Kazin and Sturvesant are reincarnations of two of the original residents of the Lost City: Kazin is the poet-priest, Sturvesant the king—in an echo of *She*, which is surely the inspiration for *The Sunbird*, Kazin, a hunchback, is similar to the simian Holly, while Sturvesant and Vincey are tall, golden men—and their fates are nearly repeated, though in his later incarnation Kazin narrowly escapes death. Couzens remarks on the similarities between *She* and *The Sunbird*:

> The whole plot of *The Sunbird*, like *She*, is based on the idea of reincarnation, of the great civilisation of the past, in Haggard's case Greek [actually not, rather Egyptian; Kallikrates is called "the Greek" to show his outsider status, Ayesha is more closely Egyptian in descent, as is Kôr], in Smith's Carthaginian, gradually destroyed with only the ruins left, tended by a degenerate mass of blacks. . . . Thus *The Sunbird* is a reincarnation itself—it is a reincarnation of Rider Haggard's writing nearly 100 years before. (1982: 47)

There is no Ayesha in *The Sunbird*, but there is a similar attempt in both books to imagine an ancient white civilisation in the heart of Africa. There is evidence that both before and after writing *The Sunbird*, Smith was preoccupied with this question. In a review of the novel, Smith is quoted as saying: "It is fashionable now to believe that Zimbabwe was built by Africans without outside influence—it is becoming a political/ archaeological matter but I don't set out to prove or disprove their theory—I leave the question open" (Smith 1972a: 17).

This is a little disingenuous as he goes on both in this article and in another to discuss archaeological ruins at Delphi in Greece, which he felt confirmed his "white built" theory in *The Sunbird*: "It was a tremendous thing—finding definite links and a building system in Greece echoed in Zimbabwe, thus reinforcing my ideas and making them more credible" (Smith 1972b: 28).[7] Tangri points out that far from remaining outside the political debate in archaeological circles current in Rhodesia during the 1960s and 1970s, Smith in *The Sunbird* launches "a general accusation running through the book that archaeologists are biased scoundrels siding with Black Nationalism, too blinkered to accept the truth of ancient Mediterranean colonists" (1990: 298). The Rhodesia Front of course sided with this opinion of Great Zimbabwe's origins, as it was in their interest to portray Rhodesia's most famous ruins as white in origin, thus justifying their own political existence. In 1976, Smith and his wife actually went on safari to look for the Lost City of the Kalahari and, according to an article he published in *The Reader's Digest*, they found it in Botswana. It was an expedition worthy of the Victorian explorers as they braved the difficult terrain, lions, a huge black mamba, and intense heat to discover their goal. "We spent two nights around our campfire outside the walls. We talked late, imagining the men who had come here from so far away, as our ancestors had done; and thinking about that race of foreigners—some say the Phoenicians—who built these cities, enslaved the local tribes, mined the gold and then disappeared mysteriously in the third century" (Smith 1978: 152).

Smith seems to sound a prophetic note in this account, which is echoed in *The Sunbird*: "Africa will not tolerate those who come only to take her gold and enslave her people" (1978: 152). Kazin's assistant, Sally Benator, commenting on the poor Punic art she discovers, says "'we white Africans are like the old Carthaginians . . . when there's gold in them thar hills who gives a hoot about painting pictures'" (1974: 198), while Kazin catalogues the wealth of the Carthaginian empire, which was eventually to be overrun by black hordes:

Gold from Zimbao and Punt, ivory from the southern plains of grass or from the forests along the great river, hides and dried meat, salted fish from the lakes, wine and oil from the terraced gardens of Zeng, copper from the hills of Tuya, and salt from pans along the west shores of the lakes, tin from the juncture of the two rivers, corn from the middle kingdom in baskets of woven cane, sun stones from the southern river of the crocodile, iron bars from the mines of Sala—and slaves, thousands upon thousands of human beings treated as domestic animals. (1974: 198)

It is one of these slaves who escapes across the Zambezi, organises black tribes there, and brings about the Lost City's downfall. In the twentieth-century incarnation the slave is now Tim Mageba, who betrays Kazin and becomes a terrorist leader of a guerilla band in Zimbabwe, which is ultimately foiled— but the warning is sounded by Smith. However, Couzens is correct when he observes that, unlike Haggard who "represents expanding British Imperialism" and its contradictions, "Smith contains the tensions of South African imperialism" (1982: 49). The Lost City does not threaten to overwhelm the Smiths as Kôr does Holly and Vincey, it is a set of (as yet unnamed by Smith) compass points on the map, and though its ancient origins and demise can coax a *frisson* in modern day readers, it has little of Kôr and its mistress Ayesha's mythical power. As Africa on a manifest level is made more and more known and knowable, so does the quest for a lost white civilisation in Africa become harder to sustain (though not less desirable on a latent level). In the 1990s, the Haggard legacy on this score is reduced to the glitzy theme park of the Lost City and its Palace, located in what was the apartheid homeland state of Boputhatswana.

THE POPULAR CULTURE LEGACY; THE LOST CITY AND INDIANA JONES

If ever one had to look for an example of a postmodern geographical and architectural site in South Africa, then The Lost City, located within the physical space known as Sun City, would be a good one to call upon—in true postmodern fashion, it is self-reflexive, self-ironising and intertexual. As Soja declares in *Postmodern Geographies* (1989): "Today ... it may be space more than time that hides consequences from us, the 'making of geography' more than the 'making of history' that provides the most revealing tactical and theoretical world. This is the insistent promise and premise of postmodern geographies" (1).

It is indeed true that The Lost City, opened in 1992, is a "made geography," created in the form of "a postmodern architectural dream" (Hall 1995: 179). It is a $300 million hotel complex set amidst fake sculptured rocks, hills, human-planted rain forests, a created dam, an artificial seaside complete with surfable waves and beach sand, a bridge that has a simulated earthquake every evening at dusk so that it trembles and smokes, and a synthetic chlorinated river through which an electrically generated tidal current flows. The brainchild of Sol Kerzner, known as the "Sun King" given his status at the time as chairman of Sun International Resorts, The Lost City in an ersatz manner draws on the discourse of Africanism which this book has outlined, together with that discourse's historical antecedents and successors—the narratives of early explorers to Africa, the adventure stories of the late nineteenth century (especially those of Haggard), the spectacular World Fairs and Exhibitions of Haggard's day, the blood-soaked, dangerous Africa of Cloete's potboilers, the novels of Wilbur Smith, the evergreen if worn myth of "Africa-as-paradise," and simultaneously as a heart of darkness. Each hotel room in each of Sun City's four hotels, of which The Palace of The Lost City is one, has an information file on the resort that includes the narrativising myth of The Lost City. It is a generic synopsis of any number of Haggard's novels that, it is tempting to surmise, could be seen as the inspiration for this constructed history of The Lost City pleasure resort. The "legend," as the narrativising myth is called, begins "A long time ago," which recalls the "Once upon a time" entry into the world of fairytale, and then proceeds to outline a formulaic, conservative European bed-time story of Africa, with a happy ending.

In essence, it describes the story of "the Ancient Ones" who were "a nomadic tribe from Northern Africa" (thus smarter and whiter than their southern, darker brethren, it implies, as such narratives always do) who settled in the Valley of the Sun "attracted by the fertility of the land and the perfection of the climate." This was for centuries a Haggardian "safe and secret" place, as the exotic city with its Palace was sited in a "secluded valley which was shaped by an ancient volcanic crater." However, one day a strong volcanic eruption destroyed this settlement, and the benevolent dictator-king and his family escaped "borne to safety on the backs of the alert kudus." Though the royal family returned, the Palace decayed and was finally deserted, but its fame lived on, however, in "the imaginations of explorers," one of whom apparently is Sol Kerzner:

Almost three hundred years after the great earthquake, in the last decade of the 20th century, an expedition came upon this sacred locale and its ruins. The leader of the expedition saw the crumbled towers, the heaps of stone and pieces of carvings, in the still majestic palace and the remains of the surrounding village, a legacy of untold value, silvered with age. He dedicated himself to restoring The Lost City to it's [sic] original splendour. (information sheet, The Lost City at Sun City)

The authors of this late twentieth-century version of the fairytale, "Africa as lost white civilisation in deepest, darkest Africa," are Kimberley, Allison, Goo and Wong, international resort designers based in California, whose "brief was to create a fantasy Africa" (Murray, S-A. 1996: 156), in much the same way as they had created a fantasy America in EuroDisney. The legend they created in The Lost City is deliberately derivative, referring to similar older romantic narratives; thus the legend can be exotic yet familiar to its visitors. It should give its consumers a sense of *déjà vu* and yet an equal sense of wonder at how well *afresh* the old Africa myth has been, literally, constructed. From the harsh realities of poverty-stricken former Boputhatswana, once ruled by the apartheid puppet Lucas Mangope, Kerzner lets rise like a phoenix the promise of treasure, a new Africa, an ancient (constructed) cultural heritage, all in keeping with the new South Africa freshly emerging from its dark political past with Mandela at its head. As Haggard created for his jaded, urban audience the promise of a new start elsewhere in Africa, so does Kerzner provide a new African theme-park in the political and natural wilderness. Murray makes a similar point: "In some ways, the actual and psychic landscapes associated with The Lost City—barrenness rendered paradisal, constructed wilderness, legend . . . ; monumentalism, the promise of wealth, and fantastic adventure might well be taken from the fiction of Haggard" (Murray, S-A. 1996: 158).[8]

It could even be said that some of the tensions of the imperialist age that found their expression in Haggard's fictional African topography can also be seen in The Lost City, but they have lost their subtlety and become banal and self-conscious. The golf course clubhouse constructed *à la* Great Zimbabwe has no mystery about its origins—the builders are black labourers hired temporarily by white-owned multinational conglomerates, the building plans drawn up in America, the empire-builder no jingoist imperialist like Rhodes but a late-capitalist entrepreneur who has "dedicated himself" to making money in a spectacular fashion. The range of possible interpretations and manifestations of latent discourse about Africa has been even further diminished: "The world has one role for Africa—as a destiny for other people's expeditions, and as the home of 'dark forces'. Rider Haggard, Wilbur Smith and Sol Kerzner have all seen this point—and have become wealthy" (Hall 1995: 198). While I would argue that Haggard had a far more complex vision of Africa than either Smith or Kerzner, I would agree that it is this monofocal view of Africa that pertains in the popular imagination. On this score Hall says:

The Legend of the Lost City is a component of that grantite [sic] Orientalism documented by Edward Said; a comprehensive system of belief which defines its own points of reference, and which "shares with magic and mythology the self-containing, self-reinforcing character of a closed system, in which objects are what they are, for once, for all time, for ontological reasons, that no empirical material can either dislodge or alter." (1995: 198)

Sol Kerzner has literally cashed in on this fixed romantic mythology surrounding Africa and has been, appropriately enough, pictured by the media "through character-formulae already popularized by the genre of adventure-romance, such as capitalist and cultural visionary, working-class boy makes good, and sexually and financially driven male hero" (Murray, S-A. 1996: 159). Both Hall and Murray find links between the media images of Kerzner as a metaphorical "Sun King" who "discovers" The Lost City at Sun City, and Louren Sturvesant in Wilbur Smith's *The Sunbird* who discovers the Lost City of the Kalahari, a man who is "building a chain of luxury vacation hotels across the islands of the Indian Ocean. Comores, Seychelles, Madagascar, ten of them" (Smith 1974: 205), and who with his "golden curly head, his sun-bronzed features" (24) appears as a literal sun king. Nuttall draws a link between the trope of lost, ancient civilisations so dear to the strand of adventure narrative and popular culture under discussion, and a wider market of cultural commodity consumption in Africa generally: "Kerzner's creations draw, as their master narrative, on the lost worlds of the Queen of Sheba and Prester John, mythologized in Haggard's *King Solomon's Mines* and Buchan's *Prester John*, Stephen [sic] Spielberg's *Indiana Jones* and Wilbur Smith's *Sunbird*, and which continue to structure the cultural politics of Africa" (Darian-Smith, Gunner, Nuttall 1996: 226).

As the above quotation shows, Kerzner has also been compared to the maverick adventurer Indiana Jones of the popular adventure films, and it is film as a medium for translating Haggard into a modern idiom that I will briefly consider before concluding this chapter on Haggard's legacy. The Indiana Jones film character who combines intelligence with commonsense and humour in his daring exploits in exotic locations, including Africa, has been seen as a latter day derivation of Haggard's Quatermain. Couzens, in a review of Pocock's biography of Haggard, remarks "Allan Quatermain lives on in Indiana Jones and perhaps even in bits of Crocodile Dundee" (1994: 7), and Stott similarly observes: "The adventuring spirit of Haggard lingers in twentieth-century film versions of heroism, as popular in the 1980s as Haggard was in the 1880s. The stories of Indiana Jones, himself a descendant of Haggard's Allan Quatermain, for instance, contain many underground passages and journeys into foreign territory, underground passages which threaten to consume the explorer as he travels deeper into otherness" (1989: 88).

The 1985 Hollywood version of *King Solomon's Mines,* starring Richard Chamberlain and Sharon Stone and filmed in Zimbabwe, was described as "an Indiana Jones type adventure yarn with loads of fun and action" (quoted in Murray, S-A. 1996: 161). Murray makes the useful point that for many contemporary film goers, the original Haggard romance of the film's title would be unknown except as hearsay or a long-ago childhood tale; hence the need for intertextual, comparative referencing to "explain" the film in more up-to-date fashion "in terms of a broader contemporary cinematic adventure genre which could be said to include Steven Spielberg's *Indiana Jones* epics, and *Romancing the Stone* and *The Jewel of the Nile*" (1996: 161).

An interesting idea to emerge from this is that remakes of classic nineteenth-century texts have the opportunity or licence to adapt the narrative as they like, since the original is no longer always current.[9] In the case of *King Solomon's Mines*, however, which has never been out of print and has had five film versions made of it thus far, the story (or idea behind it) has lingered on, albeit with some alterations. Film, however, is a visual and not a text-based medium, and it is potentially more far-reaching than the text; thus perhaps its real force in portraying romances based in Africa is its re-making and re-creating, through technological wizardry if need be, of an image of Africa, its lands and peoples. Davis, author of *In Darkest Hollywood*, subtitled "Exploring the jungles of cinema's South Africa," believes that "the invention of the movie camera began a second conquest of Africa, not merely in the acquisition of images, but in the way these images were presented.... Films gave the illusion of reality. Just like freebooting imperialists in their quest for plunder, motion picture photographers scurried all over the globe, frenetically gathering images—exotic, arcane, bizarre, sensational, revelatory—which became the 'reality' about the world for millions of people" (Davis 1996: 2).

Discussing various categories of film that have had southern Africa as their setting, Davis shows how black characters, as in the age of imperialism, generally appear as backdrop, like the landscape, and bemoans the "devastating impact of a generic 'Hollywood'" (1996: 4) in films that show blacks in a demeaning light, yet which are still more popular in Africa than African-made films. It is akin to a second wave of colonisation—the reactions of some film crews and actors show a repetition of the reactions of the nineteenth-century explorers. In an article entitled "Hollywood on Safari," Bull (1996) discusses the behind-scenes reactions on the film set of the 1950 version of *King Solomon's Mines*, shot in Kenya and starring Stewart Granger as Quatermain and Deborah Kerr, who replaces the character of Curtis with that of a lady looking for her husband. This, incidentally, has been one of the most telling alterations to Haggard's original tale. Haggard could imagine a love/sexual relationship between black and white, though he suppresses it eventually, but almost one hundred years later Hollywood apparently couldn't. The Good/Foulata relationship in *King Solomon's Mines* was replaced in the 1936 Gaumont British production and the 1950 and 1985 Hollywood productions by a white-white love interest, which makes for interesting speculation on the progress of race relations in the West and on what boosts box office sales in the twentieth century. Davis comments on these changes in relation to the 1936 version that stars Paul Robeson as Umbopa, who is therefore made to sing as well, that "it is unsettling to see what has become of it [the book, *King Solomon's Mines*]" for not only has the racial composition of the love interest been altered, but there is also a "shift in emphasis from a quest for a missing brother in the novel to the itch for diamonds in the film" (Davis 1996: 147). Bull recounts how the trip to Africa by actors and crew for the 1950 film version was headlined by *Life* magazine, "British Grit Overcomes Horrors of Savage Africa" (referring to Kerr's stamina) and how the trip recalled earlier imperialist expeditions: "Travelling 22, 000 kilometres around Africa in five months, moving by safari car, steamboat, plane and foot, with a party of 53 film-makers and some 130 Africans, including 82 servants, it was the largest safari since Theodore Roosevelt's" (Bull 1996: 118).

The chief cameraman deplored the climatic extremes of rains, snows, extreme heat, and also the ravages of malaria and typhoid fever that affected the crew, the dangerous animals and the group of 500 "Watussi [*sic*]" from Ruanda-Burundi who lacked "theatrical discipline." Out of a budget of R13.3 million, the African extras were paid 30 cents a day, "their salary held down by agreement with the colonial government which did not wish to disturb the native economy" (118). All in all, this sounds disturbingly familiar—despite some of the changes to the manifest discourse (the mode of transport is faster, the technology to capture Africa more advanced, the budget bigger), the latent discourse of desire juxtaposed with fear is relatively unchanged. Africa is still a place where one can be tested to the limit, experience adventure, capture treasure (now in the form of money-generating celluloid images) and be titillated by half-naked savages, intriguing and dangerous like the landscape used as backdrop. In the 1986 South African film of *Shaka Zulu* directed by William Faure, there is a deliberate flaunting of Henry Cele's body in the lead role together with the usual massed displays of maidens dancing semi-clad, yet Faure describes his aim in the film in sentiments that echo Haggard's in *Nada the Lily*, or even Plaatje's in *Mhudi*: "I felt that there was a big gap in the market in terms of interpreting black history both in our history books but definitely on the screen.... And I felt that it was time to give black history an entirely new perspective, give it the dignity and the respect that it deserved in terms of cinematic interpretation" (quoted in Davis 1996: 173). However, instead of the promised fresh look at black history, Faure draws on the tried and tested latent discourse of Africanism, which sees Zulus as muscular warriors dancing to their bloody deaths, as did the rest of South Africa and the movie world at the film's subsequent screenings.

What this chapter has tried to show is that Haggard's legacy has been far-reaching in this century and continues to be displayed, even in quite divergent forms derived from the original texts.[10] What this speaks of primarily is the enduring power of latent discourse on Africanism that Haggard tapped into, with its fixed dreams and fears of Africa articulated frequently through the use of landscape, which in the more popular cultural manifestations blurs people and landscape into one equation. The appeal of adventure, particularly Haggard's romance recipe, in a geographical world where there are few secrets left is seen in cultural forms as diverse as Wilbur Smith's novels and the nonfictional books and films of the National Geographic Society. In a recent advertisement promoting a book of the Society's history, the potential reader was told s/he could "rediscover 110 years of death-defying adventure . . . endless quests to challenge the elements . . . glorious journeys to faraway places" (1997: advertisement for the National Geographic Society's revised edition of *100 Years of Adventure and Discovery*), which repeats the familiar adventure story refrain. Thus the romance/adventure story, although formulaic, is capable of altering the pattern of the standard ingredients, so that Haggard's successors, like fairy tale tellers, strike their consumers both as telling tales that are familiar and also as refashioning them to suit the day. Phillips defines this feature of the adventure story as follows:

The transformative capacity of the adventure story is rooted in its ambivalent mixture of conservatism and radicalism, its ability to map and remap—naturalising and fixing geographies and identities in realistic space—but also to unmap—subverting and destabilising received constructions of geography and identity. Adventure, although popular literature and therefore highly conventional . . . is never a static or totally confining narrative. (1997: 165)

In its late twentieth-century manifestations as theme park site or the set for a slapstick movie-star adventurer, the Haggard legacy has been diminished and degraded to the level of watered-down commercial pap. It has lost touch with the complexities and occasional subtleties of the original Haggard topography, which, though it in turn built on the images of Africa that earlier explorers had brought back to Europe, achieved a fresh power that captured the imagination of his age. However, what has remained undiluted and in fact strengthened in the contemporary "green" nostalgia of the late twentieth, and early twenty-first, centuries is a romanticising of the landscape typical of Haggard, and it is to this phenomenon that I shall briefly turn in conclusion.

NOTES

1. This same paragraph, with slight alterations, appears in Christie, Hutchings and Maclennan (1980: 21).

2. For a fuller discussion of Haggard's influence on, and cross-fertilisation between, contemporary writers and those of the twentieth century, see Etherington (1984: 107-119). I have chosen writers who follow each other in a specific sequence, united by the common thread of Haggard. One writer I do not consider in the chapter as he falls somewhat outside the sequence established, but whom I shall briefly mention here, is Laurens van der Post. Hammond and Jablow single him out as one "who has given the most vivid portrayals of Africa and the Africans since Haggard. He has recaptured the wonder of the Africa of the early explorers" (1970: 146). Etherington (1984) sees Van der Post as further illustrating Haggard's influence on literature of the twentieth century. Van der Post, born in South Africa, was a Jungian novelist whose closest link with Haggard was a similar belief in Africa as representing a primitive and vital phase of the European psyche with which the European had to come to terms in order to progress. His work *Venture to the Interior* (1952) dramatises this encounter between European and African in central Africa, becoming in the course of the narrative "an

unavoidable mythic and personal quest where the protagonist searches for meaningful responsibility in the confused post-war world" (Christie, Hutchings, Maclennan 1980: 19).

Daphne Rooke is another writer who may be fruitful to explore in relation to Haggard in that both feature the same landscape and narrative devices in some of their novels. Rooke, also a popular writer in her time though not an adventure romance writer in the Haggard mould, features Ghost Mountain and Zululand in her best work. I am grateful to Professor Green of the University of Natal (Durban) for pointing out that Rooke in *Wizard's Country* (1957), very much like Haggard in *Nada the Lily*, attempts to tell of the end of the Zulu nation through a black narrator and from an entirely "Zulu" perspective. Their respective handling of the same geographical space would make for an interesting comparative study.

3. Chapter 5 of *She* is entitled "The Head of the Ethiopian," which refers to the huge, menacing sculpted rock head that guards the eastern African coastline. There is no doubt as to its malevolence—the head has "a most fiendish and terrifying expression" on "its devilish face;" it is a "warning and defiance to any enemies who approached the harbour" (1991: 42-43). See Couzens and Hughes (n.d.) for a discussion of Ethiopianism and its application in *Bayete!*, a South African novel. *Bayete!*, written in 1915 but only published in 1923, also describes a black revolt against whites led by another religious leader, Nelson, who is American-educated and charismatic, thus resembling Laputa in *Prester John*. Ethiopianism is seen as a real threat in *Prester John*, with the schoolmaster Wardlaw admitting he is "black afraid" for he "had been reading a lot about Ethiopianism, which educated American Negroes had been trying to preach in South Africa. He did not see why a kind of bastard Christianity should not be the motive of a rising" (Buchan 1956: 56). See Couzens, T. (1979) for a further discussion of Ethiopianism and *Prester John*.

4. Also quoted in Chrisman 1992: 144. Both Chennells and Chrisman give their source as Willan, B. 1984. *Sol Plaatje: South African Nationalist, 1876-1932*. Berkeley and Los Angeles: University of California Press: 254. On the subject of early black South African writers and Haggard's possible influence on their writing, Sir Henry Newbolt writes in the introduction to Thomas Mofolo's work *Chaka: an Historical Romance* (1931) that "[Mofolo] had read all the religious and historical Sesuto books then published, some English historical books on South Africa, and some novels by writers like Rider Haggard and Marie Corelli" (1931: ix).

Dr Gisela Feurle has kindly pointed out to me that Peter Sulzer's translation into German of Mofolo's *Chaka* also cites Haggard as a literary influence. She translates from his preface:

The picture of Shaka in the present historical research neither corresponds to the oral tradition nor to the published material available to Mofolo. C.F. Swanepoel has tried to give evidence which written sources Mofolo used when writing *Chaka*. The most important publications were: W.C. Holden, "Past and future of the Kaffir races" (1866), J.Y. Gibson, "The story of the Zulus" (1903), A.T. Bryant, "A Zulu-English dictionary" (1905), T. Arbousset, "Relation d'un voyage d'exploration au nord-est de la Colonie du Cap de Bonne Espérance" (1842), H. Rider Haggard, "Nada the Lily" (1933). . . . Certain things that from the present state of research seem to be literary deviation from reality are based on material the author found in these written sources. For example the murdering of the mother corresponds to the statements of Bryant, Holden and Rider Haggard. (Sulzer, P. *Thomas Mofolo: Chaka Zulu*. Zurich 1988: 33)

5. Couzens calls some readers' criticisms of Plaatje's style as "imitative or derivative," "a very superficial judgement" (Couzens in Plaatje 1975: 10). He discusses

the difficulties a black writer of the time would have had in placing a work with a publisher aware of a reading public "who could see no value in things black and who demanded ... slavish imitation of the whites" (11). Furthermore, Couzens points out that Plaatje as linguist would have been sensitive to nuances of language, as witnessed in the humour which "lies just below the surface of Plaatje's style" (11).

6. Cloete fought as part of the British Army in World War I, including the Battle of the Somme. Buchan, though unfit for active service, was sent to the front to cover War proceedings as a *Times* correspondent during the same war.

7. I am extremely grateful to Professor Richard Peck of Lewis and Clark College, Oregon for making available to me his extensive collection of newspaper cuttings from South African newspapers on Wilbur Smith; also for sharing with me his draft paper entitled "Beware the Gaboon Adder: Fascist Popular Literature and Politics in South Africa," which discusses the novels of Wilbur Smith, for discussion and comment. This paper finds fuller expression in his book, *A Morbid Fascination: White Prose and Politics in Apartheid South Africa* (Westport, CT: Greenwood Press, 1997).

8. Not only does The Lost City recall Haggard in its offer to rejuvenate the urban dweller in its constructed "natural" surrounds, but also in the resort's deliberate (in Haggard, unconscious) links with sexuality. Sun City, the umbrella name for the whole complex, has long been associated with risqué topless shows, soft porn "adult" movies and with the staging of the Miss World Pageant, an advertisement for which surely recalls *She*: "Africa unveils her latest goddess of eternal beauty" (quoted in Murray, S-A. 1996: 168-169).

9. Haggard, in an unpublished letter to his wife, lamented the filmmaker's licence to alter the original novel's narrative even when the novel *was* still relatively recent in the public (and author's) mind. Writing about the film production of his novel *Moon of Israel* (1918), Haggard said in a letter to Louie: "It is a marvellous production (in one scene there are 4,000 characters) but, as usual, aggravating to the author, because of the crudities and deficiencies—All the fine touches—or most of them gone!" (21 October 1924).

10. Haggard's influence can even be discerned in the work of a contemporary painter, Gary James, born and raised in Kenya but educated and currently living in England. He recently held an exhibition entitled "A Voyage into the Interior" at the Everard Read Gallery, Johannesburg. One of the gallery's owners described the paintings as "a celebration of an Africa sanctified by memory and myth, but with the precise, technically detailed view of an engineer and botanist ... an alluring world reminiscent of *Boys' Own Paper* and Rider Haggard, of rituals observed, of Western technology providing its users with a detached view of the exotic, the 'other'" (*The Sunday Independent* 20 July 1997: 14).

The South African television series *Hidden City*, shot in Knysna's forests in 1995 and screened in 1997, relies heavily on the idea of a lost civilisation à la Haggard. In an echo of Haggard's device of a framing "Editor," the credits list Dr. Tom Huffman as the "archaeology adviser" for the series, lending thereby a note of authenticity.

CHAPTER 6: CONCLUSION

"What remains? To wish well to South Africans. Well, I do that with all my heart, but perhaps, as an old Natalian I may be allowed to wish the best of all things to this dear and lovely land of yours—to this fair Natal. She has beauty, great beauty, if ever country had it; she has fertility to a marvellous degree; she has history, much history for so short a career. May she also have peace, prosperity and progress from generation to generation and from age to age."

"Advance Natal, God Bless Natal, white and black together and bless her gates of mountain and of sea!"

—Rider Haggard, *The Natal Witness*, 28 March 1914[1]

Bunn remarks in an article on Thomas Pringle's African landscapes of the 1820s:

For an increasingly jaded urban audience, colonial landscapes, and the South African landscape in particular, came to be perceived as repositories of romantic subject-matter. Clearly this revaluation is linked to the degradation of experience in metropolitan centers, the expansion of capitalism toward accumulation on a world scale, and the consequent displacement of the country-city dichotomy onto world geography.... By the end of the century, for instance, many who were weary of England's sprawling slums were ready to accompany Rider Haggard's Allan Quatermain back into the arms of "Nature" now displaced onto the colonies. (Mitchell 1994:128-129)

This desired exodus from city to "Nature" is as strongly felt in the late twentieth century as it was at the time of Pringle and Haggard, if the current interest in conservation, "green" issues and ecotourism is anything to go by. The great change, of course, is that "Nature" is a much scarcer commodity than it was at the time of Empire, with its seemingly limitless wild and empty spaces awaiting the traveller in the colonies; thus the tendency to romanticise the land has increased. Surviving wilderness areas in South Africa are now protected by fences and government proclamation; they are carefully and expensively administered, so as to appear as natural and untouched as possible, by people dressed in unobtrusive khaki clothing designed to blend in with the surroundings. Wild landscape has become a nostalgic commodity to be sold to those wishing to restore their spirits in a Haggardian manner away from the stresses of late capitalist urban living. Mitchell discusses this phenomenon:

> Landscape is now more precious than ever—an endangered species that has to be protected from and by civilization, kept safe in museums, parks, and shrinking "wilderness areas." Like imperialism itself, landscape is an object of nostalgia in a postcolonial and postmodern era, reflecting a time when metropolitan cultures could imagine their destiny in an unbounded "prospect" of endless appropriation and conquest. (1994:20)

How often has one not seen, in advertising brochures for game reserves and wilderness areas, photographs of visitors to the park gazing out over the wild, empty landscape from a high vantage point in an unconscious echo of the "monarch-of-all-I-survey" perspective so beloved of Haggard and other nineteenth-century writers (to whom Mitchell's above quotation refers)? The romanticisation of landscape and of humankind's potentially heroic position within the landscape still retains its appeal undiluted.

Haggard, as I have earlier shown, spoke frequently on the importance of maintaining a close association between people and the land. As Manthorpe observes, he was "[n]o traditionalist, he was well ahead of his time in his withdrawal from blood sports, while his appreciation of the importance of maintaining the spiritual equilibrium between man and nature is in line with the whole environmental movement of the later twentieth century" (1996:217).[2] The following extract from a speech Haggard gave to the Canadian Club in Ottawa in 1905 while he was a Commissioner appointed by the Colonial Office to look into the feasibility of the Salvation Army settlements, reiterates his fervent belief in maintaining a close connection with the land:

> The strength of a people, gentlemen, is not to be found in their Wall Streets, it is to be found in the farms and fields and villages. I will only add just this one word—that I do hope that what I have so humbly, so inadequately tried to say before you may perhaps go deep into the minds of some of you and set you thinking. For myself, I can only say that I have tried to carry out this task—not the task of speaking, but the bigger one—with a single heart, because I believe in its necessity, because I believe that no man can serve his generation better than by trying to point out these things and try to make the people think. (1926 vol. 2: 271-272)

Written in typical self-deprecating style, Haggard spoke from the heart. The drift of agricultural workers from the land to the cities was a subject about which he thought very seriously. Its imaginative corollary was the romantic African topography he so successfully created in his romances which, however, he rated less highly than his "serious" studies on land reform. In his romances he provided a "safe and secret" locus of desire, a romanticised and sexualised landscape whose twentieth-century equivalent can be seen in the national game reserves that maintain the safety and secrecy of the wilderness areas.

An ironic consequence of protected wilderness areas, where the illusion of unspoiled, "empty," untamed land, (almost) untouched by human hand depends on their being populated only by wild animals, is that any indigenous inhabitants of such lands must be displaced. In fact, as Pugh points out, game reserves are "areas of play that shut off nature from those who had traditionally derived immediate sustenance from it" (1988:12). The irony arises from Haggard's concern with preserving as far as possible the bond of South Africa's indigenous inhabitants, particularly the Zulus, with their land and traditional ways of life. In Haggard's African romances, even one such as *Nada the Lily*, which narrativises the fall of the Zulu nation, there is space in the wilderness for the Zulu kraals frozen in ethnographic portraits, but as the wilderness has steadily been cleared and settled by rapidly increasing towns, peri-urban settlements and farming ventures, the space for such traditional symbiotic living is eroded. Ironically, even some of these "traditional" living spaces have been commodified and marketed like the game reserves—the film-set village of Shaka's (Chaka's) kraal in the film *Shaka Zulu* (1986) directed by William Faure, is now a tourist destination called "Shakaland." Tourists visiting this place can sample traditional Zulu food in beehive huts, occupied by locals hired to wear traditional Zulu dress. This is a far cry from what Haggard envisaged in the prefatory dedication to James Stewart, ex-Assistant Secretary for Native Affairs in Natal, in *Child of Storm*: "From those [Zulus] who continually must face the last great issues of life or death, meanness and vulgarity are far removed. These qualities belong to the safe[3] and crowded haunts of civilised men, not to the kraals of Bantu savages where, at any rate of old, they might be sought in vain" (1952:vi).

Bunn, in a paper entitled "Comparative Barbarism: Game Reserves, Sugar Plantations and the Modernization of South African Landscape," examines how "Wac" Campbell, the sugar baron founder of the exclusive Mala Mala game reserve, strove to create a "traditional" hunting way of life, including songs and rituals for the black staff he employed within the reserve to add to the overall picture of ethnic wildness. Bunn compares "Wac" Campbell with Haggard's Sir Henry Curtis (the Curtis of the end of *Allan Quatermain* who vows to protect the Zu-Vendis way of life rather than the Curtis of *King Solomon's Mines*, though a closer comparison might have been with Haggard himself):

Like Rider Haggard's Sir Henry Curtis, Campbell believed absolutely in his ability to study, master, and conserve the Zulu past. People like him feared that the pageantry of the Zulu past (which they imagined, essentially, in terms of regimental warfare) was in danger of being undermined by proletarianization, and saw themselves as crucial custodians of a dying heroic tradition. (Bunn 1996:45)

This is clear in Haggard's despair by 1912 at what he perceived as a Europeanisation of the Zulus of a negative kind once they had been conquered by the British. An extract from the dedication to Stewart (referred to earlier) bears this out. In it, Haggard bemoans the changes conquest has brought to a traditional Zulu way of life, for it tarnishes the romantic image of the Zulu as noble savage, which he had so diligently cultivated in his romances:

> Still we may wonder what are the thoughts that pass through the mind of some ancient warrior of Chaka's or Dingaan's time, as he . . . watches men and women of the Zulu blood passing homeward from the cities or the mines, bemused, some of them, with the white man's smuggled liquor, grotesque with the white man's cast-off garments, hiding, perhaps, in their blankets examples of the white man's doubtful photographs—and then shuts his sunken eyes and remembers the plumed and kilted regiments making that same ground shake as, with a thunder of salute, they rushed out to battle. (1952:vi)

For both Haggard and the late twentieth-century readers of his texts, it is the latent discourse of Zulu as noble warrior that remains the desirable one, despite changes to the manifest discourse that informs the public of black unemployment statistics, the breakdown of family structure and tradition over the years of black migrant labour, even the more positive black rise to political power. It is Umbopa from *King Solomon's Mines* and Umslopogaas from *Allan Quatermain* and other romances who contain the powerful myth of brave, loyal, noble savage that carries over into the black game rangers who salute visitors who enter at the game reserve gates, the skin-clad "warriors" who greet dignitaries at airports or tourists at five star hotels. This romanticisation of the Zulu, seen as an integral human part of Haggard's African topography, has become ultimately patronising, although (as shown earlier) Haggard's position on the Zulus in Natal was one of great concern and respect despite the inevitable patronal relationship between Briton and Zulu of Shepstone's day.

The efforts to preserve "Nature" as wilderness, enclosed and contained for future generations, is one of the most positive spinoffs from Haggard's romanticisation of the African landscape he so loved, despite some of the ironic implications noted. From Pliny's famous dictum on Africa's novelty (with which this study began); to the explorers who built up an extensive discourse of Africa; to Haggard—who capitalised on existing discourses and his own South African experience to produce popular romances set in a topography that encapsulated his own and his readers' dreams and fears; to a strand of South African literature that drew on Haggard directly at first and then by hearsay; the power of African landscape as an arena for the imagination has been constant. Schama, in his work *Landscape and Memory*, summarises his book's thesis: "Landscapes are culture before they are nature, constructs of the imagination projected onto wood and water and rock. . . . But it should also be acknowledged that once a certain idea of landscape, a myth, a vision establishes itself in an actual place, it has a peculiar way of muddling categories, of making metaphors more real than their referents; of becoming, in fact, part of the scenery" (1995:61).

This is, in a sense, what happens when the latent strand of discourse takes precedence over the manifest. Generations—first of Europeans and more recently of settler South Africans—looking at Africa have drawn on the same relatively static tropes as Haggard's African topography: Africa as vast Eden, as wilderness, as dream underworld, as sexualised bodyscape, as home to ancient white civilisations. It was Haggard, however, who managed, almost despite himself, to draw these tropes together at a particular historical moment and in a particular historical context in an enormously powerful manner. It is difficult not to feel, even seventy-five years after Haggard's death, when standing on a high vantage point overlooking wide plains of (seemingly) uncultivated land in KwaZulu Natal in South Africa, that this kind of space presented to the gaze is "Haggard's Africa," or, as Schama proposes, that the metaphors have overtaken their referents.

NOTES

1. This extract is taken from a speech make by Haggard to The African Club members in Pietermaritzburg on 27 March 1914 during his stop there as part of the Dominions Royal Commission. His speech was quoted and paraphrased at length in *The Natal Witness* (Haggard 1914c: 1) and was featured on the front page together with a photograph of the Dominions Royal Commission members. Haggard's speech was entitled "Echoes of the Past," and in it he recalled his time in Natal as part of Shepstone's staff, his African romances and nonfictional works, and various anecdotes from the Anglo-Boer and Anglo-Zulu Wars. Judging from the number of cheers and "hear, hears" recorded, Haggard's speech was enthusiastically received. The reference to Natal's guarding "gates of mountain and of sea" recalls Haggard's enduring desire to find a "safe and secret" place in which his romances could flower—in this regard Natal and Zululand were his preferred locations, recalling his days of young manhood and early marital happiness.

2. Unlike Haggard, Wilbur Smith has not withdrawn from bloodsports but, however, does follow "the laws of ethical hunting" as he maintained in an interview: "I've shot most things in my life. Even elephant, though I wouldn't do it again. It was like shooting a sad old man. But though I love elephant, their numbers need to be kept down" (Smith 1997b:71).

In keeping with the eco-friendly mood of the nineties, Smith cultivates an image of being a "powerful propagandist for conservation" (*The Daily News* 14 January 1992) discussing issues of water scarcity and overpopulation in a newspaper interview. In another newspaper article, Smith's ranch outside Cape Town is described. In a proactive, environmentally progressive move, he has cleared out the cattle and installed twenty types of antelope, which he sporadically shoots to feed the servants (*The Sunday Times* 9 April 1995).

3. Haggard's use of "safe" in relation to "the crowded haunts of civilised men" refers to their despised tameness in comparison with the dangers attached to "the kraals of Bantu savages." This ironic use of "safe" carries none of the desire attached to Haggard's longing for a "safe and secret" place in which to situate his romances, which he found in Africa.

BIBLIOGRAPHY

Adewumi, M. *Racial Attitudes in the European Literature of Africa from H. Rider Haggard to Joyce Cary.* Ph.D. thesis, Arizona State University, 1977.

Appleton, J. *The Symbolism of Habitat: An Interpretation of Landscape in the Arts.* Seattle: University of Washington Press, 1990.

Arbousset, T. *Narrative of an Exploratory Tour to the North-East of the Colony of the Cape of Good Hope.* Translated by J. Crombie Brown. London, 1852.

Ashcroft, B., G. Griffiths and H. Tiffin. *The Empire Writes Back: Theory and Practice in Post-Colonial Literatures.* London: Routledge, 1989.

—— (eds.) *The Post-Colonial Studies Reader.* London and New York: Routledge, 1995.

Barrell, J. *The Idea of Landscape and the Sense of Place 1730-1840.* London: Cambridge University Press, 1972.

Beer, G. *The Romance.* London: Methuen, 1970.

Bhabha, Homi K. *The Location of Culture.* London and New York: Routledge, 1994.

Bivona, D. *Desire and Contradiction: Imperial Visions and Domestic Debates in Victorian Literature.* Manchester: Manchester University Press, 1990.

Bloom, H. (ed.) *Romanticism and Consciousness: Essays in Criticism.* New York: Norton, 1970.

Blunt, A. *Travel, Gender, and Imperialism: Mary Kingsley and West Africa.* New York: The Guildford Press, 1994.

Blunt, A. and G. Rose (eds.) *Writing Women and Space: Postcolonial Geographies.* New York and London: The Guildford Press, 1994.

Boehmer, E. *Colonial and Post-Colonial Literature.* Oxford and New York: Oxford University Press, 1995.

Boonzaaier, E. and J. Sharp (eds.) *South African Keywords.* Cape Town and Johannesburg: David Philip, 1988.

Bowle, J. *The Imperial Achievement.* London: Secker and Warburg, 1974.

Brantlinger, P. "Romances, Novels, and Psychoanalysis." *Criticism* 17 1975: 15-40.

────── *Rule of Darkness: British Literature and Imperialism 1830-1914.* Ithaca: Cornell University Press, 1988.

Bristow, J. *Empire Boys.* London: Harper Collins, 1991.

Buchan, J. *The African Colony.* London: William Blackwood and Sons, 1903.

────── *Memory Hold-the-Door.* London: Hodder and Stoughton, 1941.

────── *Prester John.* Harmondsworth: Penguin, 1956 (1910).

Bull, B. "Hollywood on Safari." *Out There* April 1996: 118-125.

Bunn, D. "Embodying Africa: Woman and Romance in Colonial Fiction." *English in Africa* 15(1) 1988: 1-28.

────── "Relocations: Landscape Theory, South African Landscape Practice, and the Transmission of Political Value." *Pretexts* 4(2) Summer 1993: 44-67.

────── "Comparative Barbarism: Games Reserves, Sugar Plantations, and the Modernization of South African Landscape." In: Darian-Smith, K., L. Gunner and S. Nuttall (eds.) *Text, Theory, Space.* London and New York: Routledge, 1996.

Bursey, W. *Rider Haggard: A Study in Popular Fiction.* D.Phil. thesis, Memorial University of Newfoundland, 1972.

Carrington, C. *Rudyard Kipling: His Life and Work.* London: Macmillan, 1955.

Carruthers, J. and M. Arnold. *The Life and Work of Thomas Baines.* Vlaeberg, SA: Fernwood Press, 1995.

Carter, E., J. Donald and J. Squires (eds.) *Space and Place: Theories of Identity and Location.* London: Lawrence and Wishart, 1993.

Carter, P. *The Road to Botany Bay: An Essay in Spatial History.* London: Faber and Faber, 1987.

────── "Turning the Tables—or, Grounding Post-Colonialism." In: Darian-Smith, K, L. Gunner and S. Nuttall (eds.) *Text, Theory, Space.* London and New York: Routledge, 1996.

Chapman, M. *Southern African Literatures.* London: Longman, 1996.

Chennells, A.J. *Settler Myths and the Southern Rhodesian Novel.* D. Phil. thesis, University of Zimbabwe, 1982.

────── "Just a Story: Wilbur Smith's Ballantyne Trilogy and the Problems of a Rhodesian Historical Romance." *Social Dynamics* 10(1) 1984: 38-45.

────── "Plotting South African History: Narrative in Sol Plaatje's *Mhudi*." *English in Africa* 24(1) 1997: 37-58.

Chilvers, H.A. *The Seven Wonders of Southern Africa.* Johannesburg: Authority of the Administration of the South African Railway and Harbours, 1929.

Chrisman, L. "The Imperial Unconscious? Representations of Imperial Discourse." *Critical Quarterly* 32(3) 1990: 38-58.

────── *Empire and Opposition: Literature of South Africa 1830-1920.* D. Phil thesis, Oxford University, 1992.

────── "Colonialism and Feminism in Olive Schreiner's 1890s Fiction." *English in Africa* 20(1) 1993: 25-38.

―――― Review of McClintock, A. *Imperial Leather: Race, Gender and Sexuality in the Colonial Context*. London and New York: Routledge. In: *Southern African Review of Books* September/October and November/December 1995: 41-43.

Christie, S., G. Hutchings and D. Maclennan. *Some Perspectives on South African Fiction*. Johannesburg: Ad. Donker, 1980.

Cloete, S. *South Africa: The Land, Its People and Achievements*. Johannesburg: Da Gama Publishers, n.d.

―――― *Storm Over Africa*. Cape Town: Culemburg Publishers, 1956.

―――― *The African Giant*. London: Collins, 1957.

―――― *Talking Points: A Series of 11 Radio Talks*. South African Broadcasting Corporation, 1964.

―――― *Turning Wheels*. London: Collins, 1967 (1937).

―――― *South Africa: Key to a Continent*. Johannesburg: Da Gama Publishers, 1967 (1937).

―――― *A Victorian Son: An Autobiography 1897-1922 Vol 1*. London: Collins, 1972.

―――― *The Gambler: An Autobiography Vol 2*. London: Collins, 1973.

―――― *Rags of Glory*. London: Fontana, 1974 (1963).

Coan, S. "'When I Was Concerned with Great Men and Great Events': Sir Rider Haggard in Natal." *Natalia* 26 (1997): 17-58.

Coetzee, C. *Writing the South African Landscape*. D.Phil. thesis, University of Cape Town, 1993.

Coetzee, J.M. *White Writing: On the Culture of Letters in South Africa*. New Haven and London: Yale University Press, 1988.

Cohen, M. *Rider Haggard: His Life and Works*. London: Hutchinson, 1960.

―――― (ed.) *Rudyard Kipling to Rider Haggard: The Record of a Friendship*. London: Hutchinson, 1965.

Cosgrove, D. *Social Formation and Symbolic Landscape*. London and Sydney: Croom Helm, 1984.

Cosgrove, D. and S. Daniels (eds.) *The Iconography of Landscape*. Cambridge: Cambridge University Press, 1988.

Couzens, T.J. "Literature and Ideology: the Patterson Embassy to Lobengula, 1878, and *King Solomon's Mines*." Institute of Commonwealth Studies Collected Seminar papers. vol 5. University of London, 1974.

―――― "'The Old Africa of a Boy's Dream': Towards Interpreting *Prester John*." *Africa Perspective* 13 Spring 1979: 34-57.

―――― "The Return of the Heart of Darkness." *English Academy Review* 1982: 36-52.

―――― Introduction to *Journal of Southern African Studies* 9 1982-1983: 1-7.

―――― "A Sense of Place." Book review of Pocock, T. *Rider Haggard and the Lost Empire*. In: *Southern African Review of Books* November/December 1994: 7.

Couzens, T. and H. Hughes. "'A Warning to White South Africa': G. H. Nicholls and his novel *Bayete!*" Unpublished paper, n.d.

Cross, C. *The British Empire*. London: Hamlyn, 1972.

Curtin, P. *The Image of Africa: British Ideas and Action, 1780-1856*. 2 vols. Madison:

University of Wisconsin Press, 1973 (1964).

Darian-Smith, K., L. Gunner and S. Nuttall (eds.) *Text, Theory, Space: Land, Literature and History in South Africa and Australia.* London and New York: Routledge, 1996.

Davis, P. *In Darkest Hollywood: Exploring the Jungles of Cinema's South Africa.* Athens: Ohio University Press/Randburg: Ravan Press, 1996.

Dawson, G. *Soldier Heroes: British Adventure, Empire and the Imagining of Masculinities.* New York: Routledge, 1994.

de Certeau, M. *The Practice of Everyday Life.* Berkeley and Los Angeles: University of California Press, 1984.

Deleuze, G. and F. Guattari. *Anti-Oedipus: Capitalism and Schizophrenia.* London: The Athlone Press, 1984.

Dixon, R. *Writing the Colonial Adventure.* Cambridge: Cambridge University Press, 1995.

Dobrée, B. *Rudyard Kipling: Realist and Fabulist.* London: Oxford University Press, 1967.

Duncan, J. *The City as Text: The Politics of Landscape Interpretation in the Kandyian Kingdom.* Cambridge: Cambridge University Press, 1990.

Eagleton, T., F. Jameson and E. Said. *Nationalism, Colonialism and Literature.* Minneapolis: University of Minneapolis Press, 1990.

Ellis, P.B. *H. Rider Haggard: A Voice from the Infinite.* London: Routledge and Kegan Paul, 1978.

Elwin, M. *Old Gods Falling.* London: Collins, 1939.

Etherington, N. "Rider Haggard's Imperial Romances." *Meanjin Quarterly* 36 July 1977a: 189-199.

―――― "South African Origins of Rider Haggard's Early African Romances." *Notes and Queries* October 1977b: 436-438.

―――― "Rider Haggard, Imperialism, and the Layered Personality." *Victorian Studies* 22 Autumn 1978: 71-88.

―――― "Imperialism in Literature: The Case of John Buchan." University of London: Institute of Commonwealth Studies, Collected Seminar Papers No. 27, 1981.

―――― *Rider Haggard.* Boston: Twayne Publishers, 1984.

Fairchild, H.N. *The Noble Savage: A Study in Romantic Naturalism.* New York: Russell and Russell, 1961.

Fisher, M. *The Bright Face of Danger: An Exploration of the Adventure Story.* London: Hodder and Stoughton, 1986.

Fitter, C. *Poetry, Space, Landscape: Towards a New Theory.* Cambridge: Cambridge University Press, 1996.

Forbes, V.S. *Pioneer Travellers of South Africa: A Geographical Commentary Upon Routes, Records, Observations and Opinions of Travellers at the Cape 1750-1800.* Cape Town: A.A. Balkema, 1965.

Foucault, M. "Questions of Geography." In: Gordan, C. (ed.) *Power/ Knowledge: Selected Interviews and Other Writings 1972-1979.* Brighton, Sussex: The Harvester Press, 1980.

────── "Of Other Spaces." *Diacritics* 16(1) Spring 1986: 22-27.

Fraser, N. *Unruly Practices: Power, Discourse and Gender in Contemporary Social Theory*. Minnesota: University of Minnesota Press, 1989.

Freud, S. *The Interpretation of Dreams*. Translated by James Strachey. The Pelican Freud Library Vol. 4. Harmondsworth: Penguin, 1983 (1953).

Frye, N. *Anatomy of Criticism: Four Essays*. Princeton: Princeton University Press, 1957.

────── *The Secular Scripture: A Study of the Structure of Romance*. Cambridge, Mass. and London: Harvard University Press, 1976.

Gallagher, J., R. Robinson and A. Denney. *Africa and the Victorians: The Climax of Imperialism in the Dark Continent*. London: Macmillan, 1961.

Gates, H.L. Jr. "Editor's Introduction: Writing 'Race' and the Difference It Makes." *Critical Inquiry* 12 Autumn 1985: 1-19.

George, R.M. *The Politics of Home: Postcolonial Relocations and Twentieth-Century Fiction*. Cambridge: Cambridge University Press, 1996.

Gilbert, E.L. *The Good Kipling*. Manchester: Manchester University Press, 1972.

Gilbert, S.M. "Rider Haggard's Heart of Darkness." *Partisan Review* 1 1983: 444-453.

Gilbert, S.M. and S. Gubar. "Heart of Darkness: The Agon of the Female Fatale." In: *No Man's Land Vol 2: Sexchanges*. New Haven and London: Yale University Press, 1989.

Gilman, S.L. "Black Bodies, White Bodies: Towards an Iconography of Female Sexuality in Late Nineteenth-Century Art, Medicine, and Literature." *Critical Inquiry* 12 Autumn 1985: 166-222.

Gordon, R. "Marginalia on 'Grensliteratuur': Or How/Why is Terror Culturally Constructed in Northern Namibia?" *Critical Arts* 5(3) 1991: 79-93.

Gray, S. "King's Solomon's Adventure Hero." *Communique* UNIN Language Bureau 4(2) June 1978: 23-30.

────── *Southern African Literature: An Introduction*. Cape Town: David Philip, 1979.

Green, G.V. *Aspects of the Colonial Novel*. MA thesis, Rand Afrikaans University, 1982.

Green, M. *Dreams of Adventure, Deeds of Empire*. New York: Basic Books, 1979.

Greene, G. *Collected Essays*. London: The Bodley Head, 1969.

Gregory, D. *Geographical Imaginations*. Cambridge, Mass. and Oxford: Blackwell, 1994.

Haggard, H.R. Letter to Olive Schreiner. Harry Ransom Humanities Research Center, The University of Texas at Austin, October 21, 1884.

────── Letter to brother Jack. MS67f: Brenthurst Archives, February 17, 1885.

────── "About Fiction." *Contemporary Review* LI 1887: 172-180.

────── *Cetywayo and His White Neighbours*. London: Trübner and Co, 1888 (1882).

────── *The Witch's Head*. London: Spencer Blackett, 1890.

────── "Illustrated Interviews No. VII—Mr. H. Rider Haggard." *Strand Magazine* 3 1892: 2-17.

——— "'Elephant Smashing' and Lion Shooting." *The African Review.* June 9, 1894: 762-763.

——— *The Wizard.* Bristol: Arrowsmith, 1896.

——— *Swallow: A Tale of the Great Trek.* London: Longmans, Green and Co, 1899a.

——— *A Farmer's Year Being His Commonplace Book for 1898.* London: Longmans, Green and Co, 1899b.

——— *Jess.* London: Smith, Elder and Co, 1900a (1887).

——— *The Last Boer War.* London: Kegan Paul, Trench, Trübner and Co. Ltd, 1900b.

——— "An Incident of African History." *The Windsor Magazine* 1900c: 112-119.

——— *Rural England.* 2 vols. London: Longmans, Green and Co, 1902.

——— *Black Heart and White Heart and Other Stories.* London: Longmans, Green and Co, 1903a (1900).

——— "Lost on the Veld." *The Windsor Magazine* 1903b: 185-194.

——— *A Gardener's Year.* London: Longmans, Green and Co, 1905a.

——— *The Poor and the Land.* London: Longmans, Green and Co, 1905b.

——— *The Ghost Kings.* London: Cassell and Co, 1908a.

——— "The Zulus: The Finest Savage Race in the World." *Pall Mall Magazine* 1908b: 764-770.

——— *Diary of an African Journey 11 February 1914—3 June 1914.* Manuscript in Norfolk Record Office, 1914a. S. Coan (ed.) *Diary of an African Journey: The Return of Rider Haggard.* Pietermaritzburg: University of Natal Press, 2000.

——— "Old Scenes—Sir Rider Haggard's Return to Natal." *The Natal Witness* March 26, 1914b: 1.

——— "Echoes of the Past: Famous Novelist's Reminiscences. Sir Rider Haggard and Natal." *The Natal Witness* March 28, 1914c: 1.

——— "Saved His Master's Life: Novelist and His Faithful Servant." *The Natal Witness* March 20, 1914d: 1.

——— "Sir Rider Haggard—Talks of Old Durban." *The Natal Mercury,* April 18, 1914e.

——— *The Holy Flower.* London and Melbourne: Ward, Lock and Co. Ltd, 1915.

——— "A Journey through Zululand." *Windsor Magazine* 45 1916a: 85-90.

——— *The After War Settlement and Employment of Ex-Servicemen.* London: Royal Colonial Institute, 1916b.

——— Letter to his wife, Louie. Norfolk Record Office, MC 32/39 (MS 21598), 1916c.

——— *Elissa: The Doom of Zimbabwe.* London: Hodder and Stoughton, 1917 (1900).

——— *Wisdom's Daughter.* London: Hutchinson and Co, 1923.

——— Letter to his wife, Louie. Norfolk Record Office, MC 32 (MS 21598), 1924.

——— *The Days of My Life.* 2 vols. London: Longmans, Green and Co. Ltd, 1926.

——— *Nada the Lily.* London: MacDonald, 1949 (1892).

——— *Allan's Wife with "Hunter Quatermain's Story", "A Tale of Three Lions" and "Long Odds."* London: MacDonald, 1951 (1889).

—— *Child of Storm*. London: MacDonald, 1952 (1913).

—— *Marie*. London: MacDonald, 1959 (1912).

—— *Finished*. London: MacDonald, 1962 (1917).

—— *Maiwa's Revenge*. London: MacDonald, 1965 (1888).

—— *Heu-Heu or The Monster*. London: Hutchinson Library Services, 1972 (1923).

—— *The Ivory Child*. London: MacDonald, 1973a (1916).

—— *The People of the Mist*. New York: Ballantine Books, 1973b (1894).

—— *The Private Diaries of Sir Henry Rider Haggard 1914-1925*. Edited by D.S. Higgins. London: Cassell, 1980.

—— *Benita*. Poole: New Orchard Editions Ltd, 1986a (1906).

—— *Ayesha: The Return of She*. Poole: New Orchard Editions Ltd, 1986b (1905).

—— *She*. A Critical Edition of H. Rider Haggard's Victorian Romance with Introduction and Notes by Norman Etherington. Bloomington and Indianapolis: Indiana University Press, 1991 (1886).

—— *King Solomon's Mines*. Oxford: Oxford University Press, 1992 (1885).

—— *Allan Quatermain*. Oxford and New York: Oxford University Press, 1995 (1887).

Haggard, L.R. *The Cloak That I Left*. London: Hodder and Stoughton, 1951.

Hall, M. "The Legend of the Lost City; Or, the Man with Golden Balls." *Journal of Southern African Studies* 21(2) 1995: 179-199.

Hamilton, C. *Terrific Majesty*. Cape Town and Johannesburg: David Philip, 1998.

Hammond, D. and A. Jablow. *The Africa That Never Was: Four Centuries of British Writing about Africa*. New York: Twayne Publishers, 1970.

Harley, J.B. "Maps, Knowledge and Power." In: Cosgrove D. and Daniels S. (eds.) *The Iconography of Landscape*. Cambridge: Cambridge University Press, 1988.

Harries, A. "Pandora's Box." Review essay on Wilbur Smith's *Rage*. In: *Southern African Review of Books* April/May 1989: 3-4.

Harrison, D. *The White Tribe of Africa: South Africa in Perspective*. Braamfontein: Macmillan, 1981.

Head, B. "Africa was Never 'The Dark Continent' to African People." In: *Serowe: Village of the Rain-Wind*. Cape Town: David Philip, 1981.

Hibbert, C. *Africa Explored: Europeans in the Dark Continent 1769-1889*. Harmondsworth: Penguin, 1984.

Higgins, D.S. (ed.) *The Private Diaries of Sir Henry Rider Haggard 1914-1925*. London: Cassell, 1980.

—— *Rider Haggard: The Great Storyteller*. London: Cassell, 1981.

Hillis Miller, J. *Topographies*. Stanford, California: Stanford University Press, 1995.

Himmelfarb, G. *Victorian Minds*. London: Weidenfeld and Nicolson, 1968 (1952).

Hinz, E.J. "Rider Haggard's *She*: An Archetypal 'History' of Adventure." *Studies in the Novel* 4 1972: 416-431.

Hofmeyr, C.I. *Mining, Social Change and Literature: An Analysis of South African Literature with Particular Reference to the Mining Novel 1870-1920*. Unpublished MA thesis, University of the Witwatersrand, 1980.

Hooper, M. "Cultural Translation and Cross-Border Readers: Ethnography and the Postcolonial Paradigm." *Current Writing* 6(1) 1994: 13-27.

Howe, S. *Novels of Empire*. New York: Columbia University Press, 1971 (1949).

Hutchings, G. "The Landscapes of Paradise." Paper given at Conference on Literature and Society in Southern Africa, University of York, 1981.

Hyam, R. *Empire and Sexuality*. Manchester: Manchester University Press, 1992.

Jacobs, J.M. *Edge of Empire: Postcolonialism and the City*. London and New York: Routledge, 1996.

James, G. "African Voyage." *The Sunday Independent* July 20, 1997: 14.

Jameson, F. "Narratives: Romance as Genre." *New Literary History* 7(1) 1975: 135-163.

JanMohamed, A.R. *Manichean Aesthetics: The Politics of Literature in Colonial Africa*. Amherst: University of Massachusetts Press, 1983.

—— "The Economy of Manichean Allegory: The Function of Racial Difference in Colonialist Literature." *Critical Inquiry* 12 Autumn 1985: 59-87.

Johnson, P. Review of *Rider Haggard and the Lost Empire: A Biography* by Tom Pocock. *Cape Times*, January 8, 1994: 4.

Katz, W. *Rider Haggard and the Fiction of Empire*. Cambridge: Cambridge University Press, 1987.

Kiernan, V.G. *Imperialism and its Contradictions*. London: Routledge, 1995.

Killam, G.D. *Africa in English Fiction 1874-1939*. Ibadan: Ibadan University Press, 1968.

Kliem, S. "Framing the Framer: The Embodied Gaze of the Stereoscope in Nineteenth Century Ethnography." *Inter Action IV* 1996: 83-92.

Lanning, G. and M. Mueller. *Africa Undermined: A History of the Mining Companies and the Underdevelopment of Africa*. Harmondsworth, UK: Penguin, 1979.

Lefebvre, H. *The Production of Space*. Oxford: Blackwell, 1991.

Lewis, C.S. *Of This and Other Worlds*. London: Fount Paperbacks, 1984.

Lewis, R. *Gendering Orientalism: Race, Femininity and Representation*. London and New York: Routledge, 1996.

Linnaeus, C. *Caroli Linnaei Systema Naturae (The System of Nature)*. Facsimile edition published by the British Museum, London, 1956 (1758).

Linnemann, R. *The British Literary Image of Africa in the Nineteenth and Twentieth Centuries*. 3 vols. D. Phil. thesis, University of Michigan, 1972.

Low, Ching-Liang G. "His Stories? Narratives and Images of Imperialism." In: Carter E., J. Donald and J. Squires (eds.) *Space and Place: Theories of Identity and Location*. London: Lawrence and Wishart, 1993.

—— *White Skins/Black Masks: Representation and Colonialism*. London and New York: Routledge, 1996.

Lowe, L. *Critical Terrains*. Ithaca and London: Cornell University Press, 1991.

MacDonnell, D. *Theories of Discourse: An Introduction*. Oxford: Basil Blackwell, 1986.

Mackenzie, J. (ed.) *Imperialism and Popular Culture*. Manchester: Manchester University Press, 1986.

Maclennan, D. and S. Christie. *Dream Life and Real Life: An Examination of the Modes and Mandates of White Writing in Southern Africa 1883-1973*. Unpublished document, National English Literary Museum Archives, 1973.

Manthorpe, V. *Children of the Empire: The Victorian Haggards*. London: Victor Gollancz, 1996.

Marinelli, P.V. *The Pastoral*. London: Methuen, 1971.

Maughan-Brown, D. "Myths on the March: The Kenyan and Zimbabwean Liberation Struggles in Colonial Fiction." *Journal of Southern African Studies* 9(1) 1982: 93-138.

——— "Images of War—Popular Fiction in English and the War on South Africa's Borders." *English Academy Review* 4 1987: 53-66.

——— "Raising Goose Pimples: Wilbur Smith and the Politics of *Rage*." In: Trump, M. (ed.) *Rendering Things Visible*. Johannesburg: Ravan Press, 1990.

Mazlish, B. "A Triptych: Freud's *The Interpretation of Dreams*, Rider Haggard's *She* and Bulwer Lytton's *The Coming Race*." *Comparative Studies in Society and History* 35(4) 1993: 726-745.

McClintock, A. *Double Jeopardy: Race and Gender in Victorian and South African Culture*. PhD thesis, Columbia University, 1989.

——— "Maidens, Maps and Mines: *King Solomon's Mines* and the Reinvention of Patriarchy in Colonial South Africa." In: Walker, C. (ed.) *Women and Gender in Southern Africa to 1945*. Cape Town: David Philip, 1990.

——— *Imperial Leather: Race, Gender and Sexuality in the Colonial Context*. New York and London: Routledge, 1995.

McClure, J. *Late Imperial Romance*. London: Verso, 1994.

Merrington, P. "Cape to Cairo: Tracing an Imperial Imaginary." *Inter Action IV* (1996): 93-97.

Mersham, G. "Mass Media Discourse and the Semiotics of Zulu Nationalism." *Critical Arts* 7 (1&2) 1993: 78-119.

Miller, H. *The Books In My Life*. London: P. Owens, 1952.

Millman, L. *Rider Haggard and the Male Novel. What is Pericles? Beckett Gags*. D. Phil. thesis, Rutgers University, 1974.

Mills, S. *Discourses of Difference: An Analysis of Women's Travel Writing and Colonialism*. New York and London: Routledge, 1993.

Mitchell, W.J.T. "The World as Exhibition." *Comparative Studies in Society and History* 31 1989: 217-236.

——— (ed.) *Landscape and Power*. Chicago and London: University of Chicago Press, 1994.

Mitford, B. *Through the Zulu Country: Its Battlefields and Its People*. London: Kegan Paul, Trench and Co, 1883.

Mofolo, T. *Chaka: An Historical Romance*. London: Humphrey Milford, 1931.

Morris, J. *Pax Brittanica: The Climax of Empire*. London: Faber, 1968.

Mphahlele, E. *The African Image*. London: Faber and Faber, 1962.

Murray, S-A. "Tropes and Trophies: The Lost City 'Discovered'." *Ariel* 27(1) 1996: 149-176.

Murray, T. "Archaeology and the Threat of the Past: Sir Henry Rider Haggard and the Acquisition of Time." *World Archaeology* 25(2) 1993: 175-185.

Noyes, J.K. *Colonial Space*. Amsterdam: Harwood Academic Publishers, 1992.

——— "The Representation of Spatial History." *Pretexts* 4(2) Summer 1993: 120-127.

Oboe, A. *Fiction, History and Nation in South Africa*. Venice: Supernova, 1994.

Parker, K. (ed.) *The South African Novel in English*. London: Macmillan, 1978.

——— "Telling Tales: Early Modern English Voyagers and the Cape of Good Hope." *The Seventeenth Century* X(1) Spring 1995: 121-149.

——— "Fertile Land, Romantic Spaces, Uncivilized Peoples: English Travel-Writing about the Cape of Good Hope, 1800-50." In: Schwartz, B. (ed.) *The Expansion of England: Race, Ethnicity and Cultural History*. London and New York: Routledge, 1996.

Parry, B. "The Content and Discontent of Kipling's Imperialism." In: Carter E., J. Donald and J. Squires (eds.) *Space and Place: Theories of Identity and Location*. London: Lawrence and Wishart, 1993.

Patteson, R.F. "*King Solomon's Mines*: Imperialism and Narrative Structure." *Journal of Narrative Technique* 8 1978: 112-123.

Peck, R. *A Morbid Fascination: White Prose and Politics in Apartheid South Africa*. Westport, CT: Greenwood Press, 1997.

Penn, N. "Mapping the Cape: John Barrow and the First British Occupation of the Colony, 1795-1803." *Pretexts* 4(2) Summer 1993: 20-43.

Penrose, E.F. (ed.) *European Imperialism and the Partition of Africa*. London: Frank Cass and Co. Ltd, 1975.

Phillips, R. *Mapping Men and Empire: A Geography of Adventure*. London and New York: Routledge, 1997.

Pierce, P.F. *Rider Haggard*. Unpublished B. Litt. thesis, Oxford University, 1975.

Pieterse, J.N. *White on Black: Images of Africa and Blacks in Western Popular Culture*. New Haven and New York: Yale University Press, 1992.

Pittock, M. "Rider Haggard and *Heart of Darkness*." *Conradiana* 19(3) 1987: 206-208.

Plaatje, S.T. *Mhudi*. Broadway: Quagga Press, 1975 (1930).

Pocock, D.C.D. *Humanistic Geography and Literature*. London: Croom Helm, 1981.

Pocock, T. *Rider Haggard and the Lost Empire: A Biography*. London: Weidenfeld and Nicolson, 1993.

Porter, D. *Haunted Journeys: Desire and Transgression in European Travel Writing*. Princeton, New Jersey: Princeton University Press, 1991.

Pratt, M.L. "Conventions of Representation: Where Discourse and Ideology Meet." In: Byrnes, H. (ed.) *Contemporary Perceptions of Language: Interdisciplinary Dimensions*. Georgetown: Georgetown University Press, 1982.

——— "Scratches on the Face of the Country; or What Mr Barrow Saw in the Land of the Bushmen." *Critical Inquiry* 12 Autumn 1985: 119-143.

―――― *Imperial Eyes: Travel Writing and Transculturation*. London: Routledge, 1992.

Pugh, S. *Garden―Nature―Language*. Manchester: Manchester University Press, 1988.

―――― (ed.) *Reading Landscape: Country―City―Capital*. Manchester and New York: Manchester University Press, 1990.

Rabkin, D. "Ways of Looking: Origins of the Novel in South Africa." *The Journal of Commonwealth Literature* 13(1) August 1978: 27-43.

Raby, P. *Bright Paradise: Victorian Scientific Travellers*. London: Pimlico, 1997.

Ranger, T. "Landscape Gendering in Zimbabwe." *Southern African Review of Books* 6(2) 1994: 7-8.

Reckwitz, E. "'I am not myself anymore': Problems of Identity in Writing by White South Africans." *English in Africa* 20(1) 1993: 1-23.

Rice, M. "Fictional Strategies and the Transvaal Landscape." History Workshop Paper, University of the Witwatersrand, 1981.

Rich, P. "Milnerism and a Ripping Yarn: Transvaal Land Settlement and John Buchan's Novel *Prester John*, 1901-1910." History workshop paper, University of the Witwatersrand, 1981.

―――― "Tradition and Revolt in South African Fiction: the Novels of Andre Brink, Nadine Gordimer and J.M. Coetzee." *Journal of Southern African Studies* 9 1982-1983: 54-73.

―――― "Romance and the Development of the South African Novel." In: White, L. and T. Couzens (eds.) *Literature and Society in South Africa*. Cape Town: Longman, 1984.

Richards, T. *The Imperial Archive: Knowledge and the Fantasy of Empire*. London and New York: Verso, 1993.

Ridley, H. *Images of Imperial Rule*. Beckenham: Croom Helm, 1983.

Robertson, G., M. Mash, L. Tickner, et al. (eds.) *Travellers Tales: Narratives of Home and Displacement*. London: Routledge, 1994.

Robinson, R., J. Gallagher and A. Denny. *Africa and the Victorians: The Official Mind of Imperialism*. London: Macmillan, 1961.

Rodgers, T. "Empire of the Imagination: Rider Haggard, Popular Fiction and Africa." In: Msiska, M-H. and P. Hyland (eds.) *Writing and Africa*. New York: Addison Wesley Longman, 1997.

Said, E.W. "Orientalism Reconsidered." In: Barker, F. et al. (eds.) *Europe and its Others Vol. I*. Proceedings of the Essex Conference on the Sociology of Literature, July. Colchester: University of Essex, 1985.

―――― "Representing the Colonized: Anthropology's Interlocutors." *Critical Inquiry* 15 1989: 205-225.

―――― "Narrative, Geography and Interpretation." *New Left Review* 180 1990: 81-97.

―――― *Culture and Imperialism*. London: Vintage, 1994 (1993).

―――― *Orientalism*. London: Penguin. Reprinted with new afterword, 1995 (1978).

Sandison, A. *The Wheel of Empire: A Study of the Imperial Idea in Some Late Nineteenth Century and Early Twentieth Century Fiction*. London: Macmillan,

1967.

Schaffer, K. *Women and the Bush: Forces of Desire in the Australian Cultural Tradition*. Cambridge: Cambridge University Press, 1990 (1988).

Schama, S. *Landscape and Memory*. London: Fontana Press, 1995.

Schreiner, O. *The Story of an African Farm*. Harmondsworth: Penguin, 1971 (1883).

Sévry, J. "Rider Haggard: A Literature for Children, or a Childish Africa." *Commonwealth Essays and Studies* 15(1) Autumn 1992: 1-11.

Shohat, E. "Imaging Terra Incognita: The Disciplinary Gaze of Empire." *Public Culture* 3(2) 1991: 41-70.

Showalter, E. *Sexual Anarchy*. London: Bloomsbury, 1991.

Sienaert, M. "French Writing in South Africa." *Alternation* 1(2) 1995: 71-82.

Sienaert, M. and L. Stiebel. "Writing on the Earth: Early European Travellers to Southern Africa." *Literator* 17(1) 1996: 91-101.

Smith, J.A. *John Buchan and his World*. London: Thames and Hudson, 1979.

Smith, R. "Allan Quatermain to Rosa Burger: Violence in South African Fiction." *World Literature Written in English* 22(2) 1983: 171-182.

Smith, W. (Interview with S. Cameron-Dow) "Meeting Mr Nice . . . Wilbur Smith." *Tomorrow* (n.d.): 4-6.

——— "Stoep Talk: Fact to Support Fiction." *The Star* September 28, 1972a: 17.

——— (Interview with E.A. Hart) "Cover to Cover." *The Argus* November 8, 1972b: 28.

——— *The Sunbird*. London: Pan, 1974 (1972).

——— "Search for a Lost City." *The Reader's Digest* October 1978: 149-152.

——— *A Falcon Flies*. London: Heinemann, 1980a.

——— (Reviewed by M.G.S.) "Review of *A Falcon Flies*." *The Natal Witness* September 26, 1980b: 3.

——— *Rage*. Heinemann: London, 1987.

——— (Interview with G. Bagnell) "Wilbur Smith." *Edgar's Club Newsletter* October 1988: 10-11.

——— (Reporter unnamed) "Wilbur Smith—True Son of Africa." *The Daily News* January 14, 1992: 14.

——— (Interview with B. Johnson) "The Lion Feeds and Moves On." *Sunday Times* April 9, 1995a.

——— (Interview with A. Donaldson) "Weird Sex with Beasts." *Style* August 1995b: 97-98.

——— (Interview with M. Macdonald) "King of the Blockbuster." *Sunday Times Inside* May 11, 1997a: 10-13.

——— (Article by J. Hull) "Profile: Wilbur Smith." *Out There* October 1997b: 70-80.

Snyman, J.P.L. *The South African Novel in English*. University of Potchefstroom for Christian Higher Education, SA, 1952.

Soja, E.W. *Postmodern Geographies*. London and New York: Verso, 1989.

Spiller, D. "Fiction, Fantasy and Form: Critical Perspectives and the Colonial Novel."

Association of University English Teachers of Southern Africa (AUETSA) paper, July, University of Natal, Durban, 1986.

Spurr, D. *The Rhetoric of Empire: Colonial Discourse in Journalism, Travel Writing and Imperial Administration.* Durham and London: Duke University Press, 1993.

Stiebel, L. "The Return of the Lost City: The Hybrid Legacy of Rider Haggard's African Romances." *Alternation* 4(2) 1997: 221-237; *Multiculturalism and Hybridity in African Literatures* Annual Selected Papers of the African Literature Association No. 7 (eds.) H. Wylie and B. Lindfors. Trenton, N.J. and Asmara, Eritrea: Africa World Press, 2000: 279-296.

——— "Imagining Empire's Margins: Land in Rider Haggard's African Romances." *Alternation* 5(2) 1998: 91-103; also in *Being/s in Transit ASNEL Papers 5* (ed.) Glage, L. Amsterdam: Rodopi, 2000: 125-140.

——— "'As Europe is to Africa, so is man to woman': Gendering Landscape in Haggard's *Nada the Lily*." *Current Writing* 12(1) 2000: 63-74.

Stoneman, C. "Killing People in Zimbabwe." *Southern African Review of Books* 3(2) 1989: 6-7.

Stotesbury, J.A. "The Intransigent Internal Colony: Narrative Strategies in Modern South African Popular Fiction." In: Giddings, R. (ed.) *Literature and Imperialism.* London: Macmillan, 1971.

——— "The Functions of Borders in the Popular Novel on South Africa." *English in Africa* 17(2) 1990: 71-89.

——— *Apartheid, Liberalism and Romance. A Critical Investigation of the Writing of Joy Packer.* Uppsala: Umea University Press, 1996.

Stott, R. "The Dark Continent: Africa as Female Body in Haggard's Adventure Fiction." *Feminist Review* 32 1989: 69-89.

Street, B. *The Savage in Literature.* London: Routledge and Kegan Paul, 1975.

Sulzer, P. *Thomas Mofolo: Chaka Zulu.* Zurich: Manesse Verlag, 1988.

Tangri, D. "Popular Fiction and the Zimbabwe Controversy." *History in Africa* 17 1990: 293-304.

Terblanche, J.D.V. *H. Rider Haggard: A Critical Study of His Prose Fiction.* MA thesis, Potchefstroom University for Christian Higher Education, SA, 1956.

Thornton, A.P. *The Imperial Idea and Its Enemies: A Study in British Power.* London: Macmillan, 1985.

Tiffin, C. and A. Lawson (eds.) *De-Scribing Empire: Post-Colonialism and Textuality.* New York and London: Routledge, 1994.

Trotter, D. "Colonial Subjects." *Critical Quarterly* 32(3) Autumn 1990: 3-20.

Tucker, M. *Africa in Modern Literature.* New York: Frederick Ungar, 1967.

Van der Watt, L. "Thomas Baines and the Colonisation of Space." *De Arte* 48 1993: 23-31.

Van Wyk Smith, M. *Grounds of Contest: A Survey of South African English Literature.* Kenwyn, SA: Juta, 1990.

——— "The Metadiscourses of Postcolonialism: 'Strong Othering' and European Images of Africa." *History and Anthropology* 9(2,3) 1996: 267-291.

Voss, A. "A Generic Approach to the South African Novel in English." *UCT Studies in English* 7 1977: 110-121.

——— "Travel Narratives." *Southern African Review of Books* 41 1995: 18-19.

Whatmore, D.E. *H. Rider Haggard: A Bibliography.* London: Mansell, 1987.

White, A. *Joseph Conrad and the Adventure Tradition.* Cambridge: Cambridge University Press, 1995.

Wilhelm, C. "H. Rider Haggard: *Allan Quatermain.*" *Crux* 9(2) May 1975: 48-52.

Willan, B. *Sol Plaatje: South African Nationalist, 1876-1932.* Berkeley and Los Angeles: University of California Press, 1984.

Wilmot, A. *Monomotapa (Rhodesia). Its Monuments, and Its History from the Most Ancient Times to the Present Century.* London: Fisher Unwin, 1896.

Young, R. *White Mythologies: Writing History and the West.* London and New York: Routledge, 1990.

——— *Colonial Desire: Hybridity in Theory, Culture and Race.* London and New York: Routledge, 1995.

Youngs, T. *Travellers in Africa: British Travelogues 1850-1900.* Manchester and New York: Manchester University Press, 1994.

ARCHIVAL WORK

Killie Campbell Africana Library, Durban

Don Africana Library, Durban

Brenthurst Library, Johannesburg

National English Literary Museum, Grahamstown

Norfolk Record Office, Norwich

Rhodes House Library, Oxford

Ditchingham House, Ditchingham, England

Rider Haggard Appreciation Society, England

Harry Ransom Humanities Research Center, The University of Texas at Austin

Royal Commonwealth Society Collections, Cambridge University

INDEX

Adventure, 61, 66, 76, 77, 127-128. *See also* Romance, as quest adventure

Africa: as dream underworld, 72-80; as Eden, 19, 57-64, 113, 114, 117, 120; as Eden in Cloete, 114; as Eden in Plaatje, 113; as Eden in Smith, 117, 120; eighteenth and nineteenth century perceptions of, 11-19; "Haggardesque", 53-55, 135; as home to ancient white civilisations, 91-98; image on film, 126; lost civilisation, 124; portrayal in Europe, 13, 14, 15, 16-19, 34-35 n.4, 53; as sexualised bodyscape, 20, 80-91; as wilderness, 16, 64-72. *See also* Land, "empty"

Africanism: discourse of, 6-7, 8, 9 n.1; discourse, latent, 15-19, 24, 25, 27, 30, 38, 47, 56, 63, 72, 105, 119-120, 124, 127; discourse, manifest, 13, 15, 19, 30, 47, 56, 63, 119-120

Allan Quatermain, 27, 55, 63, 64, 66, 70-71, 75, 133

Allan Quatermain (*character*), 12, 22-23, 45-46, 58, 64, 82-83

Allan's Wife, 55, 70, 76, 89

Allegory: manichean, 5-6

Ayesha, 29, 30, 77, 78-80, 85-88

Baines, Thomas, 15-16, 47, 119
Beatrice, 80
Benita, 64, 96
Bhabha, Homi K., 2, 4, 5, 72, 79
Blunt, Alison, 18-19
Bristow, David, 57, 78, 81, 82
Buchan, John, 105-110, Works: *Prester John*, xv, 105-110
Bunn, David, xii, 20, 51 n.1, 82, 83, 84, 91, 131, 133
Burton, Richard, 17

Caves as anxiety or nightmare, 46, 49, 75, 76-79
Chrisman, Laura, xii, 39, 98, 110, 111, 129 n.4
Civilisations: ancient white, 29-30, 78, 91, 94-98; rise and fall of, 63, 95-96; in Wilbur Smith, 121-122
Cloete, Stuart, 113-116; Works: *Turning Wheels*, 114-115
Cochrane, Arthur, 25, 38
Cohen, Morton, xii, 53, 100 n.12
Couzens, Tim, 106, 107, 108-109, 111, 118, 122, 125, 129 nn. 3, 4
Cultural relativity: in Haggard's novels, 15, 94-95. *See also* Race

152 Index

Desire and discourse, 5, 6, 47-48, 65; and landscape, 20, 48, 59-60, 80, 133. *See also* Landscape, sexualised; Sexuality in colonialist discourse
Dominions Royal Commission, 28, 32
Dreams, 40-41, 49-50, 72-74, 87. *See also* Nightmares

Elissa, 95
Ellis, Peter Berresford, xii
Empire Settlement Committee, 33
Enclosures. *See* Gardens
Etherington, Norman, xii, 16, 27, 50, 51 n.2, 57, 66, 81, 99 n.6, 100 n.10, 109
Ethiopianism, 129 n.3
Explorers in Africa, 16-20; masculinist tone of accounts of, 18; scientific mode of writing, 17-18; sentimental mode of writing, 17-18

A Falcon Flies (Wilbur Smith), 119-120
Ford, Ethel Rider, 24
Freud, Sigmund, 9, 20-21; Haggard as contemporary of, 49, 100 n.10
Frye, Northrop, 37-38, 41, 42-43, 44-45, 46, 50; point of epiphany, 47, 48-49, 70

Game reserves. *See* Landscape, wilderness
Gardens, in Haggard's novels, 68-72, 99 n.7. *See also* Landscape, wilderness
Gendered colonial subject, 5, 6, 18
The Ghost Kings, 59, 89, 90
Ghost Mountain, 48, 89, 90-91
Gilbert, Sandra M., xii, 74, 85, 87, 100 n.10
Great Zimbabwe, 28, 29, 30, 94-96
Gubar, Susan, xii, 74, 85, 87, 100 n.10
Gun, sexualising of, in *Marie,* 56-57

Haggard, Jock, 26, 27, 55
Haggard, Lilias, 25, 27,
Haggard, Louisa ("Louie"), 24-25, 27-28
Haggard, Rider: ambivalence, 8, 62, 63, 64, 90 93, 96; approach to naming, 12, 34 n.2; career, 7-8, 21-22, 23-24, 25-26, 27-28, 31-33; on fiction, 39-40; fiction, on morality in, 80-81; influence on South African writers, 110-122; and John Buchan, 106; marriage, 24-25, 27-28; as myth-maker, 29-30, 42; and necrophilia, 78-79; novels, popularity, 8, 9, 27,84-85, 103-104, 126; novels, sales, 27, 33, 54; and Olive Schreiner, 55, 98 n.1; personality, 21, 57; and Rudyard Kipling, 31, 35-36 n.10, 51 n.3; scholarship, xii; and Sigmund Freud, 49, 100 n.10; significance of land for, 7-8, 22-23, 43, 62, 100 n.9, 132. *See also* Land, "empty;" and Sol Plaatje, 110-113; and Wilbur Smith, 120-122; use of a framing "Editor," 30, 56-57, 96, 97; visits to South Africa, 21-26, 28-34; Zulu name, 32, 62; and Zulu people, 15, 23, 31, 93. *See also* Zulu people: represented in Haggard's novels; Works (fictional): *Allan Quatermain,* 27, 55, 63, 64, 66, 70-71, 75, 133; *Allan's Wife,* 55, 70, 76, 89; *Beatrice,* 80; *Benita,* 64, 96; *Elissa,* 95; *The Ghost Kings,* 59, 89, 90; *Heart of the World,* 49; *Heu Heu,* 76, 95; *The Holy Flower,* 96; *Jess,* 27, 55, 59-60, 69, 94; *King Solomon's Mines,* xiv, 14, 26, 27, 47, 48, 55, 58, 59, 63, 66, 77, 82, 126; *The Mahatma and the Hare,* 66; *Maiwa's Revenge,* 55; *Marie,* 93-94; *Nada the Lily,* 15, 27, 48, 55, 59, 88-91, 111, 112, 133; *People of the Mist,* 44, 64; *She,* 27, 28, 29, 42, 45, 49, 55, 59, 63, 66, 74, 84-88; *Wisdom's Daughter,* 87-88, *The Witch's Head,* 68; Works: (non-fictional), *The After War Settlement and Employment of Ex-Servicemen,* 72, 91; *Cetewayo and his White Neighbours,* 26; *A Farmer's Year,* 7, 91; *A Gardener's Year,* 7; *The Last Boer War,* 92; *The Poor and the Land,* 72, 92

Heart of the World, 49
Heu Heu, 76, 95

Higgins, D.S., xii, 24, 25, 35 n.7
Hilldrop, 25, 41, 51 n.1, 69
The Holy Flower, 96
Hunting, 9 n.1, 66, 132, 135 n.2

Imperialism: in the African romances of Rider Haggard, 22, 31, 58, 75; Haggard's views on, 22, 26, 31, 97-98; Mary Kingsley's position on, 19. *See also* Romance, imperial
Indiana Jones, 125-128

Jackson, Lilly, 24, 28
JanMohamed, A. R.: and the manichean allegory, 5-6
Jess, 27, 55, 59-60, 69, 94
Jess (*character*), 60
Jess' Cottage, 60, 68
Journey. *See* Adventure
Jung, Carl G., 9

Katz, Wendy, 43, 98 n.3
Kerzner, Sol, 125
Kingsley, Mary, 18-19
King Solomon's Mines, xiv, 14, 26, 27, 47, 48, 55, 58, 59, 63, 66, 77, 82, 126
King Solomon's Mines (film), 101 n.13, 125, 126-127
Kipling, Rudyard, 31, 35-36 n.10, 51 n.3
Kôr, 28, 74, 78, 96

Land: "empty," 14-15, 58, 63, 91-94,115, 120; "improvement," 58, 62, 92-93; and labour, 58, 62, 72, 92; settlement plan, 32, 35 n.9
Landscape: bird's eye view of, 16, 47, 61-62; bird's eye view of, to black and female characters, 63-64; bird's eye view of, in the media, 132; bird's eye view of, in Smith, 120; dreams and dreaming, 40-41, 49-50, 72-74; hierarchical, 46-47, 48-49, 71-72; "mental" linked with physical, 46-47, 48-49, 66-67; nightmare, 49, 74-76; painting, 15-16; paradisal, 41, 57-64; sexualised, 20, 69, 76, 80-91; sexualised, in *Alan Quatermain*, 81; sexualised, in *Allan's Wife*, 76; sexualised, in Cloete, 116; sexualised, in *Heu Heu*, 76-77; sexualised, in *Jess*, 41; sexualised, *in King Solomon's Mines*, 47, 48, 82-84; sexualised, in *Nada the Lily*, 48, 88-91; sexualised, in *She*, 84-87, 101 n.14; sexualised, in *Wisdom's Daughter*, 77, 87-88; as text, 50; "undeveloped," 43; wilderness, 64-72, 132. *See also* Land "empty"
Lang, Andrew, 14, 36, 37, 40, 55
Lewis, C.S., 42, 103
Linneaus, Carl: and classification, 13
Livingstone, David, 17
The Lost City, 122-125; narrativising myth of, 123-124

The Mahatma and the Hare, 66
Maiwa's Revenge, 55
Manthorpe, Victoria, 132
Map of the Gold Fields of South Eastern Africa (Thomas Baines), 16
Maps and mapping, xiv, xv, 13, 16; as bodyscape, 14, 63, 82-84; "empty" landscape, 14; in *A Falcon Flies*, 119; in *King Solomon's Mines*, xiv, 14, 63, 82-84, 99 n.5; political function of, 13-14
Marie, 93-94
Masculinity, 56, 57, 82
Masculinity of romantic hero, 45
Mazooku, 28
McClintock, Anne, 14, 20, 82, 88, 92, 96
Mhudi (Sol Plaatje), 110-113
Mofolo, Thomas, 129 n.4
Mooifontein, 41, 69
Moon of Israel (film), 130 n.9

Nada the Lily, 15, 27, 48, 55, 59, 88-91, 111, 112, 133
Nature. *See* Landscape, wilderness
"Nature's child" in Haggard's novels, 65-66
Nightmares, 49, 74-76. *See also* Caves as

anxiety or nightmare; Dreams
Nostalgia, 38, 104-105, 132; in Cloete, 114; function of, 58; and landscape, 54; in Plaatje, 111; in Smith, 117, 119. *See also* Romance, genre

Orient: as a construct, 3-4; and sex, 5
Orientalism, 3, 6; latent, 4, 8, 72; manifest, 4, 8, 72
Orientalist discourse. *See* Orientalism
Other and Otherness, 4, 8, 18, 20, 130 n.10

Painting. *See* Landscape, painting
"The Palatial," 60, 68, 69
Park, Mungo, 17, 18
People of the Mist, 44, 64
Phoenician civilisations in Africa. *See* Civilisations, ancient, white
Pierce, Peter F., xii, 28, 62, 63
Plaatje, Sol, 110-113
Place: naming, 11, 50; naming, Haggard's approach to, 12, 34 n.2,
Pocock, Tom, xii, 8-9, 25, 27, 125
Pratt, Mary Louise, 13, 17, 62, 93
Prester John (John Buchan), xv, 105-110

Race: and racial prejudice, 94, 95; theories of, 29, 102 n.17
Rice, Michael, xii, 60
Rich, Paul, xii, 59, 60, 70, 104, 107, 108
Romance: genre, 37-38, 39, 70; genre, Haggard's views on, 39-41, 42; genre, sales of novels, 27, 33, 54, 84; genre, as used by Plaatje, 113; genre, and sexuality, 5-6, 8; genre, writing of, 40-41, 42; imperial (adventure story), 39, 44-45, 104; imperial, importance of landscape in, 50; as quest adventure, 17, 43-44; as quest adventure by Buchan, 105, 106
Rooke, Daphne, 129 n.2
Roosevelt, Theodore, 33, 36 n.10
Royal Colonial Institute, 32, 33
Ruins: in Haggard's novels, 29, 30, 72, 78, 91, 94, 95; in Wilbur Smith's, 121

Said, Edward: on imperialism and the novel, 1; on land and imperialism, 2, 12, 50; and Orientalism, 3-4, 6, 8, 9 n.1, 72, 85, 104-105
Schama, Simon, 134-135
Schreiner, Olive, 55, 56, 98 n.1; Works: *Story of an African Farm,* 55-56, 87
Sexuality: in colonialist discourse, 5, 20; Haggard's, 100 n.12; in Haggard's romances, 8, 20, 41, 47-49, 76-77, 80-91, 101 n.14; 101 n.15; in Lost City, 130 n.8
Shaka Zulu (film), 133
She, 27, 28, 29, 42, 45, 49, 55, 59, 63, 66, 74, 84-88; film, 30, 33.
Shepstone, Theophilus ("Sompseu"), 21-22, 26, 54, 89
Smith, Wilbur, 113-122: popularity, 118, use of history, 118; Works: *A Falcon Flies,* 119-120; *Rage,* 118; *The Sunbird,* 121-122; *A Time to Die,* 119; *When the Lion Feeds,* 117
Space/place, 2, 8, 50
Speke, John, 17
Stevenson, Robert Louis, 26, 39, 51 n.3
Story of an African Farm (Olive Schreiner), 55-56, 87
Stott, Rebecca, xii, 18, 83
The Sunbird (Wilbur Smith), 121-122
Sun City. *See* The Lost City

Turning Wheels (Stuart Cloete), 114-115

Umslopogaas, 76, 90, 98 n.2

van der Post, Laurens, 89, 128 n.2

Wilderness. *See* Landscape, as wilderness
Wisdom's Daughter, 87-88
The Witch's Head, 68
Women, role of: in Cloete, 116; in Haggard's novels, 24, 64, 65, 79-80, 85. *See also* Landscape, sexualised;

Sexuality

Writers, twentieth-century, influenced by Haggard, 105-122

Zimbabwe Ruins. *See* Great Zimbabwe

Zulu people: as represented in Haggard's novels, 15, 88-89, 93, 102 n.17; in *Finished*, 31; *in Nada the Lily*, 93, 129 n.2, 133

About the Author

LINDY STIEBEL is Senior Lecturer in the School of Languages and Literature at the University of Durban-Westville, where she specializes in South African literature. She has published on South African popular fiction, nineteenth-century empire writing and mapping, and gender studies.